in-depth research and comparative studies on program design and evaluation; investigates specific issues and problems and prepares reports as directed; prepares systematic analyses of agency programs including budgetary aspects, relationships to other city, state or federal programs, and alternate proposals for program modification; may serve as principal assistant to a high level agency executive; conducts programs for the training and development of supervisory personnel in the proper application of new systems, methods, and procedures and management engineering techniques; may supervise one or more subordinate analysts and technicians or serve as a project manager.

TESTS

The multiple-choice test may involve questions concerning, and the ability to analyze problems in, the following areas: descriptive statistics; arithmetic reasoning; ability to collect and analyze data; ability to interpret written materials; written communication, including ability to review and edit correspondence, reports and other written documents; principles of supervision, including planning, organizing and monitoring work; staff training; job analysis, budget planning and analysis; management and methods; organization and structures; policy programming, planning, and evaluation; space utilization and other fields related to the duties included in this class of positions. It may also include questions on methods, tools, and techniques involved in all aspects of personnel administration included in the typical tasks for this title; all aspects of budgeting and fiscal control pertinent to the typical tasks; municipal labor relations; the preparation and conduct of management surveys, policy program analysis; administrative techniques; research techniques applicable to the fields indicated in the typical tasks including quantitative analysis techniques; computer utilization; report writing techniques; comprehension and interpretation of complex pertinent written materials including technical data; cost analysis and cost accounting; supervisory and administrative problems and techniques; public and employee relations, and other skills related to the duties of the position.

HOW TO TAKE A TEST

I. YOU MUST PASS AN EXAMINATION

A. WHAT EVERY CANDIDATE SHOULD KNOW

Examination applicants often ask us for help in preparing for the written test. What can I study in advance? What kinds of questions will be asked? How will the test be given? How will the papers be graded?

As an applicant for a civil service examination, you may be wondering about some of these things. Our purpose here is to suggest effective methods of advance study and to describe civil service examinations.

Your chances for success on this examination can be increased if you know how to prepare. Those "pre-examination jitters" can be reduced if you know what to expect. You can even experience an adventure in good citizenship if you know why civil service exams are given.

B. WHY ARE CIVIL SERVICE EXAMINATIONS GIVEN?

Civil service examinations are important to you in two ways. As a citizen, you want public jobs filled by employees who know how to do their work. As a job seeker, you want a fair chance to compete for that job on an equal footing with other candidates. The best-known means of accomplishing this two-fold goal is the competitive examination.

Exams are widely publicized throughout the nation. They may be administered for jobs in federal, state, city, municipal, town or village governments or agencies.

Any citizen may apply, with some limitations, such as the age or residence of applicants. Your experience and education may be reviewed to see whether you meet the requirements for the particular examination. When these requirements exist, they are reasonable and applied consistently to all applicants. Thus, a competitive examination may cause you some uneasiness now, but it is your privilege and safeguard.

C. HOW ARE CIVIL SERVICE EXAMS DEVELOPED?

Examinations are carefully written by trained technicians who are specialists in the field known as "psychological measurement," in consultation with recognized authorities in the field of work that the test will cover. These experts recommend the subject matter areas or skills to be tested; only those knowledges or skills important to your success on the job are included. The most reliable books and source materials available are used as references. Together, the experts and technicians judge the difficulty level of the questions.

Test technicians know how to phrase questions so that the problem is clearly stated. Their ethics do not permit "trick" or "catch" questions. Questions may have been tried out on sample groups, or subjected to statistical analysis, to determine their usefulness.

Written tests are often used in combination with performance tests, ratings of training and experience, and oral interviews. All of these measures combine to form the best-known means of finding the right person for the right job.

II. HOW TO PASS THE WRITTEN TEST

A. NATURE OF THE EXAMINATION

To prepare intelligently for civil service examinations, you should know how they differ from school examinations you have taken. In school you were assigned certain definite pages to read or subjects to cover. The examination questions were quite detailed and usually emphasized memory. Civil service exams, on the other hand, try to discover your present ability to perform the duties of a position, plus your potentiality to learn these duties. In other words, a civil service exam attempts to predict how successful you will be. Questions cover such a broad area that they cannot be as minute and detailed as school exam questions.

In the public service similar kinds of work, or positions, are grouped together in one "class." This process is known as *position-classification*. All the positions in a class are paid according to the salary range for that class. One class title covers all of these positions, and they are all tested by the same examination.

B. FOUR BASIC STEPS

1) Study the announcement

How, then, can you know what subjects to study? Our best answer is: "Learn as much as possible about the class of positions for which you've applied." The exam will test the knowledge, skills and abilities needed to do the work.

Your most valuable source of information about the position you want is the official exam announcement. This announcement lists the training and experience qualifications. Check these standards and apply only if you come reasonably close to meeting them.

The brief description of the position in the examination announcement offers some clues to the subjects which will be tested. Think about the job itself. Review the duties in your mind. Can you perform them, or are there some in which you are rusty? Fill in the blank spots in your preparation.

Many jurisdictions preview the written test in the exam announcement by including a section called "Knowledge and Abilities Required," "Scope of the Examination," or some similar heading. Here you will find out specifically what fields will be tested.

2) Review your own background

Once you learn in general what the position is all about, and what you need to know to do the work, ask yourself which subjects you already know fairly well and which need improvement. You may wonder whether to concentrate on improving your strong areas or on building some background in your fields of weakness. When the announcement has specified "some knowledge" or "considerable knowledge," or has used adjectives like "beginning principles of…" or "advanced … methods," you can get a clue as to the number and difficulty of questions to be asked in any given field. More questions, and hence broader coverage, would be included for those subjects which are more important in the work. Now weigh your strengths and weaknesses against the job requirements and prepare accordingly.

3) Determine the level of the position

Another way to tell how intensively you should prepare is to understand the level of the job for which you are applying. Is it the entering level? In other words, is this the position in which beginners in a field of work are hired? Or is it an intermediate or advanced level? Sometimes this is indicated by such words as "Junior" or "Senior" in the class title. Other jurisdictions use Roman numerals to designate the level – Clerk I, Clerk II, for example. The word "Supervisor" sometimes appears in the title. If the level is not indicated by the title, check the description of duties. Will you be working under very close supervision, or will you have responsibility for independent decisions in this work?

4) Choose appropriate study materials

Now that you know the subjects to be examined and the relative amount of each subject to be covered, you can choose suitable study materials. For beginning level jobs, or even advanced ones, if you have a pronounced weakness in some aspect of your training, read a modern, standard textbook in that field. Be sure it is up to date and has general coverage. Such books are normally available at your library, and the librarian will be glad to help you locate one. For entry-level positions, questions of appropriate difficulty are chosen – neither highly advanced questions, nor those too simple. Such questions require careful thought but not advanced training.

If the position for which you are applying is technical or advanced, you will read more advanced, specialized material. If you are already familiar with the basic principles of your field, elementary textbooks would waste your time. Concentrate on advanced textbooks and technical periodicals. Think through the concepts and review difficult problems in your field.

These are all general sources. You can get more ideas on your own initiative, following these leads. For example, training manuals and publications of the government agency which employs workers in your field can be useful, particularly for technical and professional positions. A letter or visit to the government department involved may result in more specific study suggestions, and certainly will provide you with a more definite idea of the exact nature of the position you are seeking.

III. KINDS OF TESTS

Tests are used for purposes other than measuring knowledge and ability to perform specified duties. For some positions, it is equally important to test ability to make adjustments to new situations or to profit from training. In others, basic mental abilities not dependent on information are essential. Questions which test these things may not appear as pertinent to the duties of the position as those which test for knowledge and information. Yet they are often highly important parts of a fair examination. For very general questions, it is almost impossible to help you direct your study efforts. What we can do is to point out some of the more common of these general abilities needed in public service positions and describe some typical questions.

1) General information

Broad, general information has been found useful for predicting job success in some kinds of work. This is tested in a variety of ways, from vocabulary lists to questions about current events. Basic background in some field of work, such as sociology or economics, may be sampled in a group of questions. Often these are principles which have become familiar to most persons through exposure rather than through formal training. It is difficult to advise you how to study for these questions; being alert to the world around you is our best suggestion.

2) Verbal ability

An example of an ability needed in many positions is verbal or language ability. Verbal ability is, in brief, the ability to use and understand words. Vocabulary and grammar tests are typical measures of this ability. Reading comprehension or paragraph interpretation questions are common in many kinds of civil service tests. You are given a paragraph of written material and asked to find its central meaning.

3) Numerical ability

Number skills can be tested by the familiar arithmetic problem, by checking paired lists of numbers to see which are alike and which are different, or by interpreting charts and graphs. In the latter test, a graph may be printed in the test booklet which you are asked to use as the basis for answering questions.

4) Observation

A popular test for law-enforcement positions is the observation test. A picture is shown to you for several minutes, then taken away. Questions about the picture test your ability to observe both details and larger elements.

5) Following directions

In many positions in the public service, the employee must be able to carry out written instructions dependably and accurately. You may be given a chart with several columns, each column listing a variety of information. The questions require you to carry out directions involving the information given in the chart.

6) Skills and aptitudes

Performance tests effectively measure some manual skills and aptitudes. When the skill is one in which you are trained, such as typing or shorthand, you can practice. These tests are often very much like those given in business school or high school courses. For many of the other skills and aptitudes, however, no short-time preparation can be made. Skills and abilities natural to you or that you have developed throughout your lifetime are being tested.

Many of the general questions just described provide all the data needed to answer the questions and ask you to use your reasoning ability to find the answers. Your best preparation for these tests, as well as for tests of facts and ideas, is to be at your physical and mental best. You, no doubt, have your own methods of getting into an exam-taking mood and keeping "in shape." The next section lists some ideas on this subject.

IV. KINDS OF QUESTIONS

Only rarely is the "essay" question, which you answer in narrative form, used in civil service tests. Civil service tests are usually of the short-answer type. Full instructions for answering these questions will be given to you at the examination. But in case this is your first experience with short-answer questions and separate answer sheets, here is what you need to know:

1) Multiple-choice Questions

Most popular of the short-answer questions is the "multiple choice" or "best answer" question. It can be used, for example, to test for factual knowledge, ability to solve problems or judgment in meeting situations found at work.

A multiple-choice question is normally one of three types—

- It can begin with an incomplete statement followed by several possible endings. You are to find the one ending which *best* completes the statement, although some of the others may not be entirely wrong.
- It can also be a complete statement in the form of a question which is answered by choosing one of the statements listed.
- It can be in the form of a problem – again you select the best answer.

Here is an example of a multiple-choice question with a discussion which should give you some clues as to the method for choosing the right answer:

When an employee has a complaint about his assignment, the action which will *best* help him overcome his difficulty is to
A. discuss his difficulty with his coworkers
B. take the problem to the head of the organization
C. take the problem to the person who gave him the assignment
D. say nothing to anyone about his complaint

In answering this question, you should study each of the choices to find which is best. Consider choice "A" – Certainly an employee may discuss his complaint with fellow employees, but no change or improvement can result, and the complaint remains unresolved. Choice "B" is a poor choice since the head of the organization probably does not know what assignment you have been given, and taking your problem to him is known as "going over the head" of the supervisor. The supervisor, or person who made the assignment, is the person who can clarify it or correct any injustice. Choice "C" is, therefore, correct. To say nothing, as in choice "D," is unwise. Supervisors have and interest in knowing the problems employees are facing, and the employee is seeking a solution to his problem.

2) True/False Questions

The "true/false" or "right/wrong" form of question is sometimes used. Here a complete statement is given. Your job is to decide whether the statement is right or wrong.

SAMPLE: A roaming cell-phone call to a nearby city costs less than a non-roaming call to a distant city.

This statement is wrong, or false, since roaming calls are more expensive.
This is not a complete list of all possible question forms, although most of the others are variations of these common types. You will always get complete directions for

answering questions. Be sure you understand *how* to mark your answers – ask questions until you do.

V. RECORDING YOUR ANSWERS

Computer terminals are used more and more today for many different kinds of exams.

For an examination with very few applicants, you may be told to record your answers in the test booklet itself. Separate answer sheets are much more common. If this separate answer sheet is to be scored by machine – and this is often the case – it is highly important that you mark your answers correctly in order to get credit.

An electronic scoring machine is often used in civil service offices because of the speed with which papers can be scored. Machine-scored answer sheets must be marked with a pencil, which will be given to you. This pencil has a high graphite content which responds to the electronic scoring machine. As a matter of fact, stray dots may register as answers, so do not let your pencil rest on the answer sheet while you are pondering the correct answer. Also, if your pencil lead breaks or is otherwise defective, ask for another.

Since the answer sheet will be dropped in a slot in the scoring machine, be careful not to bend the corners or get the paper crumpled.

The answer sheet normally has five vertical columns of numbers, with 30 numbers to a column. These numbers correspond to the question numbers in your test booklet. After each number, going across the page are four or five pairs of dotted lines. These short dotted lines have small letters or numbers above them. The first two pairs may also have a "T" or "F" above the letters. This indicates that the first two pairs only are to be used if the questions are of the true-false type. If the questions are multiple choice, disregard the "T" and "F" and pay attention only to the small letters or numbers.

Answer your questions in the manner of the sample that follows:

32. The largest city in the United States is
    A. Washington, D.C.
    B. New York City
    C. Chicago
    D. Detroit
    E. San Francisco

1) Choose the answer you think is best. (New York City is the largest, so "B" is correct.)
2) Find the row of dotted lines numbered the same as the question you are answering. (Find row number 32)
3) Find the pair of dotted lines corresponding to the answer. (Find the pair of lines under the mark "B.")
4) Make a solid black mark between the dotted lines.

VI. BEFORE THE TEST

Common sense will help you find procedures to follow to get ready for an examination. Too many of us, however, overlook these sensible measures. Indeed, nervousness and fatigue have been found to be the most serious reasons why applicants fail to do their best on civil service tests. Here is a list of reminders:

- Begin your preparation early – Don't wait until the last minute to go scurrying around for books and materials or to find out what the position is all about.
- Prepare continuously – An hour a night for a week is better than an all-night cram session. This has been definitely established. What is more, a night a week for a month will return better dividends than crowding your study into a shorter period of time.
- Locate the place of the exam – You have been sent a notice telling you when and where to report for the examination. If the location is in a different town or otherwise unfamiliar to you, it would be well to inquire the best route and learn something about the building.
- Relax the night before the test – Allow your mind to rest. Do not study at all that night. Plan some mild recreation or diversion; then go to bed early and get a good night's sleep.
- Get up early enough to make a leisurely trip to the place for the test – This way unforeseen events, traffic snarls, unfamiliar buildings, etc. will not upset you.
- Dress comfortably – A written test is not a fashion show. You will be known by number and not by name, so wear something comfortable.
- Leave excess paraphernalia at home – Shopping bags and odd bundles will get in your way. You need bring only the items mentioned in the official notice you received; usually everything you need is provided. Do not bring reference books to the exam. They will only confuse those last minutes and be taken away from you when in the test room.
- Arrive somewhat ahead of time – If because of transportation schedules you must get there very early, bring a newspaper or magazine to take your mind off yourself while waiting.
- Locate the examination room – When you have found the proper room, you will be directed to the seat or part of the room where you will sit. Sometimes you are given a sheet of instructions to read while you are waiting. Do not fill out any forms until you are told to do so; just read them and be prepared.
- Relax and prepare to listen to the instructions
- If you have any physical problem that may keep you from doing your best, be sure to tell the test administrator. If you are sick or in poor health, you really cannot do your best on the exam. You can come back and take the test some other time.

VII. AT THE TEST

The day of the test is here and you have the test booklet in your hand. The temptation to get going is very strong. Caution! There is more to success than knowing the right answers. You must know how to identify your papers and understand variations in the type of short-answer question used in this particular examination. Follow these suggestions for maximum results from your efforts:

1) Cooperate with the monitor

The test administrator has a duty to create a situation in which you can be as much at ease as possible. He will give instructions, tell you when to begin, check to see that you are marking your answer sheet correctly, and so on. He is not there to guard you, although he will see that your competitors do not take unfair advantage. He wants to help you do your best.

2) Listen to all instructions

Don't jump the gun! Wait until you understand all directions. In most civil service tests you get more time than you need to answer the questions. So don't be in a hurry. Read each word of instructions until you clearly understand the meaning. Study the examples, listen to all announcements and follow directions. Ask questions if you do not understand what to do.

3) Identify your papers

Civil service exams are usually identified by number only. You will be assigned a number; you must not put your name on your test papers. Be sure to copy your number correctly. Since more than one exam may be given, copy your exact examination title.

4) Plan your time

Unless you are told that a test is a "speed" or "rate of work" test, speed itself is usually not important. Time enough to answer all the questions will be provided, but this does not mean that you have all day. An overall time limit has been set. Divide the total time (in minutes) by the number of questions to determine the approximate time you have for each question.

5) Do not linger over difficult questions

If you come across a difficult question, mark it with a paper clip (useful to have along) and come back to it when you have been through the booklet. One caution if you do this – be sure to skip a number on your answer sheet as well. Check often to be sure that you have not lost your place and that you are marking in the row numbered the same as the question you are answering.

6) Read the questions

Be sure you know what the question asks! Many capable people are unsuccessful because they failed to *read* the questions correctly.

7) Answer all questions

Unless you have been instructed that a penalty will be deducted for incorrect answers, it is better to guess than to omit a question.

8) Speed tests

It is often better NOT to guess on speed tests. It has been found that on timed tests people are tempted to spend the last few seconds before time is called in marking answers at random – without even reading them – in the hope of picking up a few extra points. To discourage this practice, the instructions may warn you that your score will be "corrected" for guessing. That is, a penalty will be applied. The incorrect answers will be deducted from the correct ones, or some other penalty formula will be used.

9) Review your answers

If you finish before time is called, go back to the questions you guessed or omitted to give them further thought. Review other answers if you have time.

10) Return your test materials

If you are ready to leave before others have finished or time is called, take ALL your materials to the monitor and leave quietly. Never take any test material with you. The monitor can discover whose papers are not complete, and taking a test booklet may be grounds for disqualification.

VIII. EXAMINATION TECHNIQUES

1) Read the general instructions carefully. These are usually printed on the first page of the exam booklet. As a rule, these instructions refer to the timing of the examination; the fact that you should not start work until the signal and must stop work at a signal, etc. If there are any *special* instructions, such as a choice of questions to be answered, make sure that you note this instruction carefully.

2) When you are ready to start work on the examination, that is as soon as the signal has been given, read the instructions to each question booklet, underline any key words or phrases, such as *least, best, outline, describe* and the like. In this way you will tend to answer as requested rather than discover on reviewing your paper that you *listed without describing*, that you selected the *worst* choice rather than the *best* choice, etc.

3) If the examination is of the objective or multiple-choice type – that is, each question will also give a series of possible answers: A, B, C or D, and you are called upon to select the best answer and write the letter next to that answer on your answer paper – it is advisable to start answering each question in turn. There may be anywhere from 50 to 100 such questions in the three or four hours allotted and you can see how much time would be taken if you read through all the questions before beginning to answer any. Furthermore, if you come across a question or group of questions which you know would be difficult to answer, it would undoubtedly affect your handling of all the other questions.

4) If the examination is of the essay type and contains but a few questions, it is a moot point as to whether you should read all the questions before starting to answer any one. Of course, if you are given a choice – say five out of seven and the like – then it is essential to read all the questions so you can eliminate the two that are most difficult. If, however, you are asked to answer all the questions, there may be danger in trying to answer the easiest one first because you may find that you will spend too much time on it. The best technique is to answer the first question, then proceed to the second, etc.

5) Time your answers. Before the exam begins, write down the time it started, then add the time allowed for the examination and write down the time it must be completed, then divide the time available somewhat as follows:

- If 3-1/2 hours are allowed, that would be 210 minutes. If you have 80 objective-type questions, that would be an average of 2-1/2 minutes per question. Allow yourself no more than 2 minutes per question, or a total of 160 minutes, which will permit about 50 minutes to review.
- If for the time allotment of 210 minutes there are 7 essay questions to answer, that would average about 30 minutes a question. Give yourself only 25 minutes per question so that you have about 35 minutes to review.

6) The most important instruction is to *read each question* and make sure you know what is wanted. The second most important instruction is to *time yourself properly* so that you answer every question. The third most important instruction is to *answer every question*. Guess if you have to but include something for each question. Remember that you will receive no credit for a blank and will probably receive some credit if you write something in answer to an essay question. If you guess a letter – say "B" for a multiple-choice question – you may have guessed right. If you leave a blank as an answer to a multiple-choice question, the examiners may respect your feelings but it will not add a point to your score. Some exams may penalize you for wrong answers, so in such cases *only*, you may not want to guess unless you have some basis for your answer.

7) Suggestions
   a. Objective-type questions
      1. Examine the question booklet for proper sequence of pages and questions
      2. Read all instructions carefully
      3. Skip any question which seems too difficult; return to it after all other questions have been answered
      4. Apportion your time properly; do not spend too much time on any single question or group of questions
      5. Note and underline key words – *all, most, fewest, least, best, worst, same, opposite,* etc.
      6. Pay particular attention to negatives
      7. Note unusual option, e.g., unduly long, short, complex, different or similar in content to the body of the question
      8. Observe the use of "hedging" words – *probably, may, most likely,* etc.
      9. Make sure that your answer is put next to the same number as the question
      10. Do not second-guess unless you have good reason to believe the second answer is definitely more correct
      11. Cross out original answer if you decide another answer is more accurate; do not erase until you are ready to hand your paper in
      12. Answer all questions; guess unless instructed otherwise
      13. Leave time for review

   b. Essay questions
      1. Read each question carefully
      2. Determine exactly what is wanted. Underline key words or phrases.
      3. Decide on outline or paragraph answer

4. Include many different points and elements unless asked to develop any one or two points or elements
5. Show impartiality by giving pros and cons unless directed to select one side only
6. Make and write down any assumptions you find necessary to answer the questions
7. Watch your English, grammar, punctuation and choice of words
8. Time your answers; don't crowd material

8) Answering the essay question

Most essay questions can be answered by framing the specific response around several key words or ideas. Here are a few such key words or ideas:

M's: manpower, materials, methods, money, management
P's: purpose, program, policy, plan, procedure, practice, problems, pitfalls, personnel, public relations

  a. Six basic steps in handling problems:
     1. Preliminary plan and background development
     2. Collect information, data and facts
     3. Analyze and interpret information, data and facts
     4. Analyze and develop solutions as well as make recommendations
     5. Prepare report and sell recommendations
     6. Install recommendations and follow up effectiveness

  b. Pitfalls to avoid
     1. *Taking things for granted* – A statement of the situation does not necessarily imply that each of the elements is necessarily true; for example, a complaint may be invalid and biased so that all that can be taken for granted is that a complaint has been registered
     2. *Considering only one side of a situation* – Wherever possible, indicate several alternatives and then point out the reasons you selected the best one
     3. *Failing to indicate follow up* – Whenever your answer indicates action on your part, make certain that you will take proper follow-up action to see how successful your recommendations, procedures or actions turn out to be
     4. *Taking too long in answering any single question* – Remember to time your answers properly

IX. AFTER THE TEST

Scoring procedures differ in detail among civil service jurisdictions although the general principles are the same. Whether the papers are hand-scored or graded by machine we have described, they are nearly always graded by number. That is, the person who marks the paper knows only the number – never the name – of the applicant. Not until all the papers have been graded will they be matched with names. If other tests, such as training and experience or oral interview ratings have been given, scores will be combined. Different parts of the examination usually have different weights. For example, the written test might count 60 percent of the final grade, and a rating of training and experience 40 percent. In many jurisdictions, veterans will have a certain number of points added to their grades.

After the final grade has been determined, the names are placed in grade order and an eligible list is established. There are various methods for resolving ties between those who get the same final grade – probably the most common is to place first the name of the person whose application was received first. Job offers are made from the eligible list in the order the names appear on it. You will be notified of your grade and your rank as soon as all these computations have been made. This will be done as rapidly as possible.

People who are found to meet the requirements in the announcement are called "eligibles." Their names are put on a list of eligible candidates. An eligible's chances of getting a job depend on how high he stands on this list and how fast agencies are filling jobs from the list.

When a job is to be filled from a list of eligibles, the agency asks for the names of people on the list of eligibles for that job. When the civil service commission receives this request, it sends to the agency the names of the three people highest on this list. Or, if the job to be filled has specialized requirements, the office sends the agency the names of the top three persons who meet these requirements from the general list.

The appointing officer makes a choice from among the three people whose names were sent to him. If the selected person accepts the appointment, the names of the others are put back on the list to be considered for future openings.

That is the rule in hiring from all kinds of eligible lists, whether they are for typist, carpenter, chemist, or something else. For every vacancy, the appointing officer has his choice of any one of the top three eligibles on the list. This explains why the person whose name is on top of the list sometimes does not get an appointment when some of the persons lower on the list do. If the appointing officer chooses the second or third eligible, the No. 1 eligible does not get a job at once, but stays on the list until he is appointed or the list is terminated.

X. HOW TO PASS THE INTERVIEW TEST

The examination for which you applied requires an oral interview test. You have already taken the written test and you are now being called for the interview test – the final part of the formal examination.

You may think that it is not possible to prepare for an interview test and that there are no procedures to follow during an interview. Our purpose is to point out some things you can do in advance that will help you and some good rules to follow and pitfalls to avoid while you are being interviewed.

What is an interview supposed to test?
The written examination is designed to test the technical knowledge and competence of the candidate; the oral is designed to evaluate intangible qualities, not readily measured otherwise, and to establish a list showing the relative fitness of each candidate – as measured against his competitors – for the position sought. Scoring is not on the basis of "right" and "wrong," but on a sliding scale of values ranging from "not passable" to "outstanding." As a matter of fact, it is possible to achieve a relatively low score without a single "incorrect" answer because of evident weakness in the qualities being measured.

Occasionally, an examination may consist entirely of an oral test – either an individual or a group oral. In such cases, information is sought concerning the technical knowledges and abilities of the candidate, since there has been no written examination for this purpose. More commonly, however, an oral test is used to supplement a written examination.

Who conducts interviews?

The composition of oral boards varies among different jurisdictions. In nearly all, a representative of the personnel department serves as chairman. One of the members of the board may be a representative of the department in which the candidate would work. In some cases, "outside experts" are used, and, frequently, a businessman or some other representative of the general public is asked to serve. Labor and management or other special groups may be represented. The aim is to secure the services of experts in the appropriate field.

However the board is composed, it is a good idea (and not at all improper or unethical) to ascertain in advance of the interview who the members are and what groups they represent. When you are introduced to them, you will have some idea of their backgrounds and interests, and at least you will not stutter and stammer over their names.

What should be done before the interview?

While knowledge about the board members is useful and takes some of the surprise element out of the interview, there is other preparation which is more substantive. It *is* possible to prepare for an oral interview – in several ways:

1) Keep a copy of your application and review it carefully before the interview

This may be the only document before the oral board, and the starting point of the interview. Know what education and experience you have listed there, and the sequence and dates of all of it. Sometimes the board will ask you to review the highlights of your experience for them; you should not have to hem and haw doing it.

2) Study the class specification and the examination announcement

Usually, the oral board has one or both of these to guide them. The qualities, characteristics or knowledges required by the position sought are stated in these documents. They offer valuable clues as to the nature of the oral interview. For example, if the job involves supervisory responsibilities, the announcement will usually indicate that knowledge of modern supervisory methods and the qualifications of the candidate as a supervisor will be tested. If so, you can expect such questions, frequently in the form of a hypothetical situation which you are expected to solve. NEVER go into an oral without knowledge of the duties and responsibilities of the job you seek.

3) Think through each qualification required

Try to visualize the kind of questions you would ask if you were a board member. How well could you answer them? Try especially to appraise your own knowledge and background in each area, *measured against the job sought*, and identify any areas in which you are weak. Be critical and realistic – do not flatter yourself.

4) Do some general reading in areas in which you feel you may be weak

For example, if the job involves supervision and your past experience has NOT, some general reading in supervisory methods and practices, particularly in the field of human relations, might be useful. Do NOT study agency procedures or detailed manuals. The oral board will be testing your understanding and capacity, not your memory.

5) Get a good night's sleep and watch your general health and mental attitude

You will want a clear head at the interview. Take care of a cold or any other minor ailment, and of course, no hangovers.

What should be done on the day of the interview?

Now comes the day of the interview itself. Give yourself plenty of time to get there. Plan to arrive somewhat ahead of the scheduled time, particularly if your appointment is in the fore part of the day. If a previous candidate fails to appear, the board might be ready for you a bit early. By early afternoon an oral board is almost invariably behind schedule if there are many candidates, and you may have to wait. Take along a book or magazine to read, or your application to review, but leave any extraneous material in the waiting room when you go in for your interview. In any event, relax and compose yourself.

The matter of dress is important. The board is forming impressions about you – from your experience, your manners, your attitude, and your appearance. Give your personal appearance careful attention. Dress your best, but not your flashiest. Choose conservative, appropriate clothing, and be sure it is immaculate. This is a business interview, and your appearance should indicate that you regard it as such. Besides, being well groomed and properly dressed will help boost your confidence.

Sooner or later, someone will call your name and escort you into the interview room. *This is it.* From here on you are on your own. It is too late for any more preparation. But remember, you asked for this opportunity to prove your fitness, and you are here because your request was granted.

What happens when you go in?

The usual sequence of events will be as follows: The clerk (who is often the board stenographer) will introduce you to the chairman of the oral board, who will introduce you to the other members of the board. Acknowledge the introductions before you sit down. Do not be surprised if you find a microphone facing you or a stenotypist sitting by. Oral interviews are usually recorded in the event of an appeal or other review.

Usually the chairman of the board will open the interview by reviewing the highlights of your education and work experience from your application – primarily for the benefit of the other members of the board, as well as to get the material into the record. Do not interrupt or comment unless there is an error or significant misinterpretation; if that is the case, do not hesitate. But do not quibble about insignificant matters. Also, he will usually ask you some question about your education, experience or your present job – partly to get you to start talking and to establish the interviewing "rapport." He may start the actual questioning, or turn it over to one of the other members. Frequently, each member undertakes the questioning on a particular area, one in which he is perhaps most competent, so you can expect each member to participate in the examination. Because time is limited, you may also expect some rather abrupt switches in the direction the questioning takes, so do not be upset by it. Normally, a board member will not pursue a single line of questioning unless he discovers a particular strength or weakness.

After each member has participated, the chairman will usually ask whether any member has any further questions, then will ask you if you have anything you wish to add. Unless you are expecting this question, it may floor you. Worse, it may start you off on an extended, extemporaneous speech. The board is not usually seeking more information. The question is principally to offer you a last opportunity to present further qualifications or to indicate that you have nothing to add. So, if you feel that a significant qualification or characteristic has been overlooked, it is proper to point it out in a sentence or so. Do not compliment the board on the thoroughness of their examination – they have been sketchy, and you know it. If you wish, merely say, "No thank you, I have nothing further to add." This is a point where you can "talk yourself out" of a good impression or fail to present an important bit of information. Remember, *you close the interview yourself.*

The chairman will then say, "That is all, Mr. _____, thank you." Do not be startled; the interview is over, and quicker than you think. Thank him, gather your belongings and take your leave. Save your sigh of relief for the other side of the door.

How to put your best foot forward

Throughout this entire process, you may feel that the board individually and collectively is trying to pierce your defenses, seek out your hidden weaknesses and embarrass and confuse you. Actually, this is not true. They are obliged to make an appraisal of your qualifications for the job you are seeking, and they want to see you in your best light. Remember, they must interview all candidates and a non-cooperative candidate may become a failure in spite of their best efforts to bring out his qualifications. Here are 15 suggestions that will help you:

1) Be natural – Keep your attitude confident, not cocky

If you are not confident that you can do the job, do not expect the board to be. Do not apologize for your weaknesses, try to bring out your strong points. The board is interested in a positive, not negative, presentation. Cockiness will antagonize any board member and make him wonder if you are covering up a weakness by a false show of strength.

2) Get comfortable, but don't lounge or sprawl

Sit erectly but not stiffly. A careless posture may lead the board to conclude that you are careless in other things, or at least that you are not impressed by the importance of the occasion. Either conclusion is natural, even if incorrect. Do not fuss with your clothing, a pencil or an ashtray. Your hands may occasionally be useful to emphasize a point; do not let them become a point of distraction.

3) Do not wisecrack or make small talk

This is a serious situation, and your attitude should show that you consider it as such. Further, the time of the board is limited – they do not want to waste it, and neither should you.

4) Do not exaggerate your experience or abilities

In the first place, from information in the application or other interviews and sources, the board may know more about you than you think. Secondly, you probably will not get away with it. An experienced board is rather adept at spotting such a situation, so do not take the chance.

5) If you know a board member, do not make a point of it, yet do not hide it

Certainly you are not fooling him, and probably not the other members of the board. Do not try to take advantage of your acquaintanceship – it will probably do you little good.

6) Do not dominate the interview

Let the board do that. They will give you the clues – do not assume that you have to do all the talking. Realize that the board has a number of questions to ask you, and do not try to take up all the interview time by showing off your extensive knowledge of the answer to the first one.

7) Be attentive

You only have 20 minutes or so, and you should keep your attention at its sharpest throughout. When a member is addressing a problem or question to you, give him your undivided attention. Address your reply principally to him, but do not exclude the other board members.

8) Do not interrupt

A board member may be stating a problem for you to analyze. He will ask you a question when the time comes. Let him state the problem, and wait for the question.

9) Make sure you understand the question

Do not try to answer until you are sure what the question is. If it is not clear, restate it in your own words or ask the board member to clarify it for you. However, do not haggle about minor elements.

10) Reply promptly but not hastily

A common entry on oral board rating sheets is "candidate responded readily," or "candidate hesitated in replies." Respond as promptly and quickly as you can, but do not jump to a hasty, ill-considered answer.

11) Do not be peremptory in your answers

A brief answer is proper – but do not fire your answer back. That is a losing game from your point of view. The board member can probably ask questions much faster than you can answer them.

12) Do not try to create the answer you think the board member wants

He is interested in what kind of mind you have and how it works – not in playing games. Furthermore, he can usually spot this practice and will actually grade you down on it.

13) Do not switch sides in your reply merely to agree with a board member

Frequently, a member will take a contrary position merely to draw you out and to see if you are willing and able to defend your point of view. Do not start a debate, yet do not surrender a good position. If a position is worth taking, it is worth defending.

14) Do not be afraid to admit an error in judgment if you are shown to be wrong

The board knows that you are forced to reply without any opportunity for careful consideration. Your answer may be demonstrably wrong. If so, admit it and get on with the interview.

15) Do not dwell at length on your present job

The opening question may relate to your present assignment. Answer the question but do not go into an extended discussion. You are being examined for a *new* job, not your present one. As a matter of fact, try to phrase ALL your answers in terms of the job for which you are being examined.

Basis of Rating

Probably you will forget most of these "do's" and "don'ts" when you walk into the oral interview room. Even remembering them all will not ensure you a passing grade. Perhaps you did not have the qualifications in the first place. But remembering them will help you to put your best foot forward, without treading on the toes of the board members.

Rumor and popular opinion to the contrary notwithstanding, an oral board wants you to make the best appearance possible. They know you are under pressure – but they also want to see how you respond to it as a guide to what your reaction would be under the pressures of the job you seek. They will be influenced by the degree of poise you display, the personal traits you show and the manner in which you respond.

ABOUT THIS BOOK

This book contains tests divided into Examination Sections. Go through each test, answering every question in the margin. At the end of each test look at the answer key and check your answers. On the ones you got wrong, look at the right answer choice and learn. Do not fill in the answers first. Do not memorize the questions and answers, but understand the answer and principles involved. On your test, the questions will likely be different from the samples. Questions are changed and new ones added. If you understand these past questions you should have success with any changes that arise. Tests may consist of several types of questions. We have additional books on each subject should more study be advisable or necessary for you. Finally, the more you study, the better prepared you will be. This book is intended to be the last thing you study before you walk into the examination room. Prior study of relevant texts is also recommended. NLC publishes some of these in our Fundamental Series. Knowledge and good sense are important factors in passing your exam. Good luck also helps. So now study this Passbook, absorb the material contained within and take that knowledge into the examination. Then do your best to pass that exam.

————

EXAMINATION SECTION

EXAMINATION SECTION
TEST 1

DIRECTIONS: Each question or incomplete statement is followed by several suggested answers or completions. Select the one that BEST answers the question or completes the statement. *PRINT THE LETTER OF THE CORRECT ANSWER IN THE SPACE AT THE RIGHT.*

1. The number of subordinates that can be supervised directly by one person tends to   1._____
   A. *increase* as the level of supervision progresses from the first-line supervisory level to the management level
   B. *decrease* as the duties of the subordinates increase in difficulty and complexity
   C. *decrease* with an increase in the knowledge and experience of the subordinates
   D. *increase* as the physical distance between supervisor and subordinates, as well as between the individual subordinates, increases

2. A study of the supervision of employees in an agency reveals that the bureau chiefs are   2._____
   reluctant to delegate responsibility and authority to their assistants.
   This study is *most likely* to reveal, in addition, that
   A. the organizational structure of this agency should be centralized
   B. the bureau chiefs tend to spend too much of their time on minor aspects of their work
   C. the number of employees supervised by bureau chiefs is excessive
   D. significant deviations from planned performance are not called to the attention of the bureau chiefs

3. The delegation of responsibility and authority to subordinates by their superior generally   3._____
   does NOT
   A. facilitate a division of labor or the development of specialization
   B. permit the superior to carry out programs of work that exceed his immediate personal limits of physical energy and knowledge
   C. result in a downward transfer of work, both mental and manual
   D. involve a transfer of ultimate responsibility from superior to subordinate

4. Horizontal coordination is achieved when the various units of a bureau work with mutual   4._____
   harmony and assistance.
   The achievement of such coordination is generally made *more difficult* when the chief of a large bureau
   A. conducts periodic conferences with supervisors of his operating units
   B. delegates some of his coordinating tasks to a staff assistant
   C. increases the number of specialized units in his bureau and the degree of their specialization
   D. transfers, subordinates from one to another of his operating units to broaden their understanding of the bureau's work

5. Some subdivision of work is imperative in large-scale operation. However, in subdividing   5.____
work the superior should adopt the methods that have the greatest number of advantages and the fewest disadvantages.
The one of the following that is *most likely* to result from subdivision of work is

    A. measuring work performed by employees is made more difficult
    B. authority and responsibility for performance of particular operations are not clearly
        defined
    C. standardizing work processes is made more difficult
    D. work is delayed in passing between employees and between operating units

6. In developing a system for controlling the production of a bureau, the bureau chief should   6.____
give consideration to reducing the fluctuations in the bureau's work load.
Of the following, the technique that is generally LEAST helpful in reducing fluctuations
in work load is

    A. staffing the bureau so that it can handle peak loads
    B. maintaining a controlled backlog of work
    C. regulating the timing of work routed to the bureau
    D. changing the order of steps in work processes

7. The flow of work in an organization may be divided and channeled according to either a   7.____
serial method or a parallel method. Under the serial method, the work moves through a
single channel with each job progressing step by step through various work stations
where a worker at each station completes a particular step of the job. Under the parallel
method, the jobs are distributed among a number of workers, each worker completing all
the steps of a job. **The MOST accurate of the following statements regarding these**
two methods of dividing the flow of work is that

    A. the training or break-in time necessary for workers to acquire processing skills is
        generally shorter under the parallel method
    B. the serial method enables the workers to obtain a fuller understanding of the signif-
        icance of their work
    C. the parallel method tends to minimize the need for control devices to keep track of
        individual jobs in process
    D. flexibility in the use of available staff is generally increased under the serial method

8. The executive who has immediate responsibility for a group of functions should have the   8.____
right to decide what the structure of his organization shall be.
In making such decision, the executive should realize that

    A. the lower the competence of a staff, the more important it is to maintain a sound
        organizational structure
    B. the productivity of a competent staff will not be affected by an impairment in organi-
        zational structure
    C. the productivity of a staff whose level of competency is low cannot be improved by
        an improvement in organizational structure
    D. where there is a sound organizational structure there must of necessity be a sound
        organization

9. Of the following means that a bureau chief may utilize in training his understudy, the   9._____
    LEAST acceptable one is for him to

    A. give the understudy assignments which other employees find too difficult or
        unpleasant
    B. discuss with the understudy the important problems that confront the bureau chief
    C. rotate the assignments given the understudy
    D. give the understudy an opportunity to attend some of the meetings of bureau
        chiefs

10. Of the following practices and techniques that may be employed by the conference   10._____
    leader, the one that the conference leader should ordinarily AVOID is

    A. permitting certain participants to leave the conference to get back to their work
        when the discussion has reached the point where their special interests or qualifi-
        cations are no longer involved
    B. encouraging the participants to take full written notes for later comparison with the
        minutes of the meeting
    C. helping a participant extricate himself from an awkward position in which the par-
        ticipant has placed himself by an illadvised remark
    D. translating the technical remarks of a speaker for the benefit of some participants
        who would otherwise fail to grasp the meaning of the remarks

11. In assigning work to his subordinates, a supervisor is MOST likely to lose the respect   11._____
    of his subordinates if he

    A. reviews with a new employee the main points of an oral order issued to this
        employee
    B. issues written orders instead of oral orders when a subordinate has repeatedly
        failed to carry out oral orders
    C. gives oral orders regarding a task which the subordinate has performed satisfacto-
        rily in the past
    D. gives an oral order which he feels the subordinate will not carry out

12. Both Agency X and Agency Y have district offices in all areas of the city. In Agency X the   12._____
    activities of the various districts are administered under centralized control, whereas in
    Agency Y the activities of the various district offices are administered under decentral-
    ized control.
    The one of the following which is MORE characteristic of Agency X than of Agency Y is
    that in Agency X

    A. activities of the district offices can more readily be adapted to meet the problems of
        the district served
    B. there are greater opportunities for district administrators to develop resourceful-
        ness
    C. agency policies can be carried out with greater uniformity
    D. decisions are made by individuals closer to the points at which problems arise

13. Of the following training methods, the one that is generally MOST valuable in teaching   13._____
    employees new clerical skills is

    A. organized group discussion
    B. individual instruction on the job
    C. use of visual aids, such as charts and pictures
    D. supervised reading, research and inspection

14. Department X maintains offices in each district of the city. Data gathered by the district offices are submitted monthly to the main office on a standard set of forms which are somewhat complicated.
    Of the following methods of issuing detailed instructions for filing out the forms properly, the one generally considered MOST **acceptable is**

    A. incorporating the instructions in the department's procedure manual
    B. including an instructions sheet with each package of blank forms sent to a district office
    C. printing the instructions on the back of each form
    D. conducting periodic staff conferences devoted exclusively to discussions of the proper method of filling out the form

14.____

15. The one of the following which is usually LEAST affected by an increase in the personnel of an organization is the

    A. problems of employee relationships
    B. average amount of work performed by an employee
    C. importance of coordinating the work of organizational units
    D. number of first-line supervisors required

15.____

16. As part of his program to simplify clerical procedures, the chief of the records management division has decided to make an analysis of the forms used by his agency and to establish a system of forms control. He has assigned the assistant bureau chief to perform the bulk of the work in connection with this project. This assistant will receive part-time help from four subordinate employees.
    Of the following actions the bureau chief may take in planning the work on this project, the MOST appropriate one is for him to

    A. have the plans drawn up by the assistant and then submitted for final approval to the four part-time subordinates before work on the project is begun
    B. have the assistant work with him in drawing up the plans and then present the plans to the four part-time subordinates for their comments
    C. join with the five employees as a committee to formulate the plans for the project
    D. prepare the plans himself and then submit the plans for approval to all five employees who are to work on the project

16.____

17. Bureau X is composed of several clerical units, each supervised by a unit head accountable to the bureau chief. Assume that the bureau chief has a special task for an employee of one of the clerical units and wishes to issue instructions directly to the employee regarding this task.
    The LEAST appropriate of the following procedures for the bureau chief to follow is to

    A. issue the instructions to the employee without notifying the employee's unit head
    B. give the instructions to the employee in the presence of the unit head
    C. ask the unit head to send the employee to him for instructions on this special task
    D. tell the employee to inform his unit head of the bureau chief's instructions

17.____

18. A bureau chief has scheduled a conference with the unit heads in his bureau to obtain their views on a major problem confronting the bureau.
    The LEAST appropriate action for him to take in conducting this conference is to

18.____

A. present his own views on the solution of the problem before asking the unit heads for their opinions
B. call upon a participant in the conference for information which this participant should have as part of his job
C. weigh the opinions expressed at the conference in the light of the individual speaker's background and experience
D. summarize briefly at the conclusion of the conference, the important points covered and the conclusions reached

19. Of the following, the greatest stress in selecting employees for office supervisory positions should ordinarily be placed on   19._____

    A. intelligence and educational background
    B. knowledge of the work and capacity for leadership
    C. sincere interest in the activities and objectives of the agency
    D. skill in performing the type of work to be supervised

20. The MOST acceptable of the following guides in preparing the specifications for a form is that   20._____

    A. when forms are to be printed on colored paper, the dark shades of colored paper should be used
    B. *tumble* or *head-to-foot* should be used if forms printed on both sides of the sheet are to be placed in binders with side binding
    C. provision for ballot-type entries should be made if items requiring *yes* or *no* entries are to appear on the form
    D. all-rag ledger paper rather than all-wood pulp bond paper should be used for forms which will receive little handling and will be kept for a short time

21. Suppose you are the chief of a bureau which contains several operating units. On one occasion you observe one of your unit heads severely reprimand a subordinate for violating a staff regulation. This subordinate has a good record for observing staff regulations, and you believe the severe reprimand will seriously undermine the morale of the employee.   21._____
    Of the following, the BEST action for you to take in this situation is to

    A. call both the unit head and the subordinate into your office at the same time and have each present his views on the matter to you
    B. refrain from intervening in this matter because the unit head may resent any interference
    C. take the subordinate aside, inform him that the unit head had not intended to reprimand him severely, and suggest that the matter be forgotten
    D. discuss the matter with the unit head and suggest that he make some mitigating explanation to the subordinate

22. In addition to a report on its activities for the year, the one of the following items which it is MOST appropriate to include in an agency's annual report is   22._____

    A. praise for each of the accomplishments of the agency during the year
    B. pictures of agency personnel
    C. history of the agency
    D. descriptions of future activities and plans of the agency

23. Before transferring material from the active to the inactive files, the supervisor of the filing unit always consults the bureau heads directly concerned with the use of this material. This practice by the supervisor is

    A. *desirable* chiefly because material that is no longer current for some bureaus may still be current for others
    B. *undesirable* chiefly because it can only lead to disagreement among the bureau heads consulted
    C. *desirable* chiefly because it is more economical to store records in transfer files than to keep them in the active files
    D. *undesirable* chiefly because the filing supervisor is expected to make his own decision

23.____

24. The determination of essential factors in a specific kind of work and of qualifications of a worker necessary for its competent performance is MOST accurately defined as

    A. job analysis
    B. micro-motion study
    C. cost analysis
    D. production control

24.____

25. In the clinical approach to disciplinary problems, attention is focused on the basic causes of which the overt relations are merely symptomatic rather than on the specific violations which have brought the employee unfavorable notice.
The MOST accurate implication of this quotation is that the clinical approach

    A. places emphasis on the actual violation rather than on the cause of the violation
    B. attempts to promote greater insight into the underlying factors which have led to the infractions
    C. does not evaluate the justness and utility of applying a specific penalty in a given situation
    D. avoids the necessity for disciplinary action

25.____

26. The LEAST accurate of the following statements regarding the conduct of a conference is that

    A. when there is great disparity in the rank of the participants at a conference, the conference leader should ordinarily refrain from requesting an opinion point blank from a participant of relatively low rank
    B. when the aim of a conference is to obtain the opinion of a group of approxmately the same rank, the rank of the conference leader should ordinarily not be too much higher than that of the participants
    C. in general, the chances that a conference will be fruitful are greatly increased if the conference leader's direct superior is one of the participants
    D. a top administrator invited to present a brief talk sponsoring a series of conferences for line supervisors should generally arrange to leave the conference as soon as appropriate after he has made his speech

26.____

27. In preparing a report for release to the general public, the bureau chief should GENERALLY present at the beginning of the report

    A. a description of the methods used in preparing the report
    B. anticipated criticism of the report and the answer to this criticism
    C. his conclusions and recommendations
    D. a bibliography of the sources used in preparing the report

27.____

28. Staff or functional supervision in an organization   28.____

    A. is least justified at the operational level
    B. is contrary to the principle of Unity of Command
    C. is more effective than authoritative supervision
    D. normally does not give the right to take direct disciplinary action

29. Suppose that you are the supervisor of Clerical Unit A in a city agency. Work processed   29.____
in your unit is sent to Clerical Unit B for further processing. One of your subordinates
complains to you that the supervisor of Clerical Unit B has been offering him unwarranted criticism of the method in which his work is performed.
Of the following actions you may take, the MOST appropriate one for you to take
FIRST is to

    A. request the supervisor of Clerical Unit B to meet with you and your subordinate to
       discuss this matter
    B. report this matter to this unit supervisor's immediate superior and request that this
       unsolicited criticism be discontinued
    C. obtain the facts from the subordinate and then discuss the matter with this unit
       supervisor
    D. tell your subordinate to refer the unit supervisor to you the next time he offers any
       criticism

30. This chart presents graphically a comparison of what is done and what is to be done. It is   30.____
so ruled that each division of space represents both an amount of time and the quantity
of work to be done during the particular unit of time. Horizontal lines drawn through these
spaces show the relationship between the quantity of work actually done and that which
is scheduled.
The chart referred to is known generally as a _____ chart.

    A. progress or Gantt   B. job correlation
    C. process or flow of work   D. Simo work simplification

31. The personnel survey is a systematic and reasonably exhaustive analysis and statement   31.____
of the facts and forces in an organization which affect the relations between employees
and management, and between employees and their work, followed by recommendations as to ways of developing better personnel policies and procedures.
On the basis of this statement, it is LEAST accurate to state that one of the purposes
served by a personnel survey is to

    A. appraise operating efficiency through an objective study of methods of production
       and a statistical interpretation of the facts
    B. set forth items and causes of poor morale in an inclusive way and in their proper
       perspective
    C. secure the facts to determine whether there is need of a more progressive person-
       nel policy in an organization where personnel work is as yet undeveloped
    D. evaluate the effectiveness of a personnel policy where a progressive personnel
       policy is already in operation

32. It is generally recognized that there is a relationship between the size of an organization's staff, the number of supervisory levels and the span of control (number of workers
assigned to a supervisor).
The MOST accurate of the following statements regarding the relationship of these
three elements is that

    A. if the size of an organization's staff should remain unchanged and the span of con-
trol should increase, then the number of supervisory levels would tend to increase
    B. if the size of the staff should decrease and the number of levels of supervision
should increase, then the span of control would tend to decrease
    C. if the size of the staff should increase and the number of supervisory levels should
remain unchanged, then the span of control would tend to decrease
    D. if the size of the staff should increase and the span of control should decrease,
then the number of supervisory levels would tend to decrease

32.____

Questions 33-35.

DIRECTIONS: Questions 33 to 35 are to answered on the basis of the organization chart
shown below. This chart presents the organizational structure of a division in a
hypothetical agency. Each box designates a position in the organizational
structure of this division. The symbol in each box represents the name of the
individual occupying the position designated by the box. Thus, the name of the
head of this division is represented by the symbol 1A.

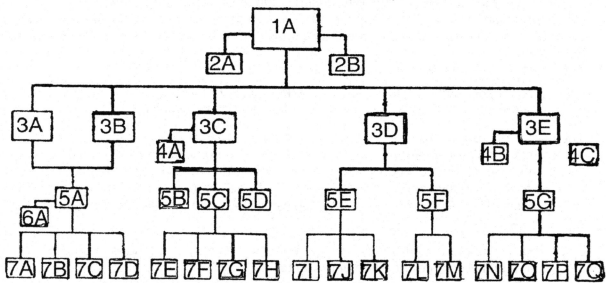

33. The one of the following who heads a subdivision which BEST illustrates in its organizational structure the characteristics of the pure line type of organization is

33.____

    A. 3B   B. 3C   C. 3D   D. 3E

34. The member of the organization who is MOST LIKELY to receive conflicting orders
because he is directly accountable to more than one superior is

34.____

    A. 5A   B. 4A   C. 5B   D. 4C

35. Assume that 7K and 7P wish to exchange positions. Approval of this exchange must be obtained from each superior in the line of authority extending upward from 7K and from each superior in the line of authority extending upward from 7P. The one of the following who is NOT in a line of authority extending upward from either 7K or 7P is

35._____

    A. 1A   B. 3E   C. 5F   D. 3D

KEY (CORRECT ANSWERS)

1.	B	11.	D	21.	D
2.	B	12.	C	22.	D
3.	D	13.	B	23.	A
4.	C	14.	A/C	24.	A
5.	D	15.	B	25.	B
6.	A	16.	B	26.	C
7.	C	17.	A	27.	C
8.	A	18.	A	28.	D
9.	A	19.	B	29.	C
10.	B	20.	C	30.	A
		31.	A		
		32.	B		
		33.	C		
		34.	A		
		35.	C		

TEST 2

1. Analysis and simplification of office procedures are functions that should be conducted in all offices and on a continuing basis. These functions may be performed by the line supervisor, by staff methods specialists, or by outside consultants on methods analysis. An appraisal of these three methods of assigning responsibility for improving office procedures reveals that the LEAST accurate of the following statements is that   1.____

    A. outside consultants employed to simplify office procedures frequently bring with them a vast amount of previous experience as well as a fresh viewpoint
    B. line supervisors usually lack the special training which effective procedure analysis work requires
    C. continuity of effort and staff cooperation can better be secured by periodically employed consultants than by a permanent staff of methods analysts
    D. the reason line supervisors fail to keep procedures up to date is that the supervisor is too often overburdened with operating responsibilities

2. A man cannot serve two masters.   2.____
    This statement emphasizes MOST the importance in an organization of

    A. span of control   B. specialization of work
    C. delegation of authority   D. unity of command

3. An important aid in good office management is knowledge on the part of subordinates of the significance of their work. The possession of such knowledge by an employee will probably LEAST affect his   3.____

    A. interest in his work
    B. understanding of the relationship between the work of his unit and that of other units
    C. willingness to cooperate with other employees
    D. ability to undertake assignments requiring special skills

4. For mediocre executives who do not have a flair for positive administration, the implantation in subordinates of anxiety about job retention is a safe, if somewhat unimaginative, method of insuring a modicum of efficiency in the working organization.   4.____
    Of the following, the MOST accurate statement according to this quotation is that

    A. implanting anxiety about job retention is a method usually employed by the mediocre executive to improve the efficiency of his organization
    B. an organization will operate with at least some efficiency if employees realize that unsatisfactory work performance may subject them to dismissal
    C. successful executives with a flair for positive administration relieve their subordinates of any concern for their job security
    D. the implantation of anxiety about job security in subordinates should not be used as a method of improving efficiency

5. Savings of 20 per cent or more in clerical operating costs can often be achieved by improvement of the physical conditions under which office work is performed.
In general, the MOST valid of the following statements regarding physical conditions is that

    A. conference rooms should have more light than small rooms
    B. the tops of desks should be glossy rather than dull
    C. noise is reflected more by hard-surfaced materials than by soft or porous materials
    D. yellow is a more desirable wall color for offices receiving an abundance of sunlight than for offices receiving little sunlight

5.____

6. To the executive who directs the complex and diverse operations of a large organizational unit, the conference is an important and, at times, indispensable tool of management. The inexperienced executive may, however, ploy the conference for a purpose for which it is ill fitted.
Of the following, the LEAST use of the conference by the executive is to

    A. reconcile conflicting views or interests
    B. develop an understanding by all concerned of a policy already adopted
    C. coordinate an activity involving several line supervisors
    D. perform technical research on a specific project

6.____

7. In planning the layout of office space, the office supervisor should bear in mind that one large room is a more efficient operating unit than the same number of square feet split up into smaller rooms.
Of the following, the LEAST valid basis for the preceding statement is that in the large room

    A. better light and ventilation are possible
    B. flow of work between employees is more direct
    C. supervision and control are more easily maintained
    D. time and motion studies are easier to conduct

7.____

8. The one of the following companies which is BEST known as a manufacturer of filing cabinets and office furniture is

    A. Pitney-Bowes, Inc.
    B. Dennison Manufacturing Co.
    C. Wilson-Jones Co.
    D. Shaw-Walker Co.

8.____

9. The program used to deliver audio-visual office presentations is known as

    A. PowerPoint   B. Excel   C. CGI   D. Dreamweaver

9.____

10. The principles of scientific office management are MOST FREQUENTLY applied by government office supervisors in

    A. maintaining flexibility in hiring and firing
    B. developing improved pay scales
    C. standardizing clerical practices and procedures
    D. revising organizational structure

10.____

11. The one of the following factors to which the bureau head should attach LEAST importance in deciding on the advisability of substituting machine for manual operations in a given area of office work is the
    11.____

    A. need for accuracy in the work
    B. relative importance of the work
    C. speed with which the work must be completed
    D. volume of work

12. The clerk displayed a *rudimentary* knowledge of the principles of supervision.
    The word *rudimentary* as used in this sentence means MOST NEARLY
    12.____

    A. thorough　　B. elementary　　C. surprising　　D. commendable

13. This is an *integral* part of our program.
    The word *integral* as used in this sentence means MOST NEARLY
    13.____

    A. minor　　B. unknown　　C. essential　　D. well-developed

14. A *contiguous* office is one that is
    14.____

    A. spacious　　　　　　　　　B. rectangular in shape
    C. adjoining　　　　　　　　　D. crowded

15. This program was *sanctioned* by the department head.
    The word *sanctioned* as used in this sentence means MOST NEARLY
    15.____

    A. devised　　B. approved　　C. modified　　D. rejected

16. The file clerk performed his work in a *perfunctory* manner.
    The word *perfunctory* as used in this sentence means MOST NEARLY
    16.____

    A. quiet　　B. orderly　　C. sullen　　D. indifferent

17. He did not *impugn* the reasons given for the change in policy.
    The word *impugn* as used in this sentence means MOST NEARLY
    17.____

    A. make insinuations against　　　B. verify in whole or part
    C. volunteer support for　　　　　　D. overlook or ignore

18. The supervisor was unable to learn the identity of the *culpable* employee.
    The word *culpable* as used in this sentence means MOST NEARLY
    18.____

    A. inaccurate　　B. careless　　C. guilty　　D. dishonest

19. The announcement was made at a *propitious* time.
    The word *propitious* as used in this sentence means MOST NEARLY
    19.____

    A. unexpected　　B. busy　　C. favorable　　D. significant

20. He showed no *compunction* in carrying out this order.
    The word *compunction* as used in this sentence means MOST NEARLY
    20.____

    A. feeling of remorse　　　　　B. hesitation or delay
    C. tact or discretion　　　　　　D. disposition to please

21. He acted in a *fiduciary* capacity.
The word *fiduciary* as used in this sentence means MOST NEARLY

    21._____

    A. administrative or executive in nature
    B. quasi-legal in nature
    C. involving confidence or trust
    D. requiring auditing or budgetary ability

22. To *temporize* means MOST NEARLY to

    22._____

    A. allay temporarily the fears of
    B. render a temporary service
    C. yield temporarily to prevailing opinion
    D. react temperamentally

23. The new supervisor was *sanguine* about the prospects of success.
The word *sanguine* as used in this sentence means MOST NEARLY

    23._____

    A. uncertain   B. confident   C. pessimistic   D. excited

24. The supervisor was asked to *implement* the new policy.
The word *implement* as used in this sentence means MOST NEARLY

    24._____

    A. explain   B. revise   C. delay the announcement of
    D. carry into effect

25. The word *intimation* means MOST NEARLY

    25._____

    A. friendliness   B. an attempt to frighten
    C. a difficult task   D. an indirect suggestion

26. Mr. Jones has a *penchant* for this type of work.
The word *penchant* as used in this sentence means MOST NEARLY

    26._____

    A. record of achievement   B. unexplainable dislike
    C. lack of aptitude   D. strong inclination

27. The speaker's comments were *desultory*.
The word *desultory* as used in this sentence means MOST NEARLY

    27._____

    A. inspiring   B. aimless   C. pertinent   D. rude

Questions 28-35.

DIRECTIONS: Questions 28 through 35 are to be answered SOLELY on the basis of the following chart which relates to the Investigation Division of Dept. X. This chart contains four curves which connect the points that show for each year the variations in percentage deviation from normal in the number of investigators, the number of clerical employees, the cost of personnel, and the number of cases processed for the period 2002-2012 inclusive. The year 2002 was designated as the normal year. The personnel of the Investigation Division consists of investigators and clerical employees only.

INVESTIGATION DIVISION, DEPARTMENT X

VARIATIONS IN NUMBER OF CASES PROCESSED, COST OF PERSONNEL.
NUMBER OF CLERICAL EMPLOYEES, AND NUMBER OF INVESTIGATORS
FOR EACH YEAR FROM 2002 to 2012 INCLUSIVE
(In percentages from normal)

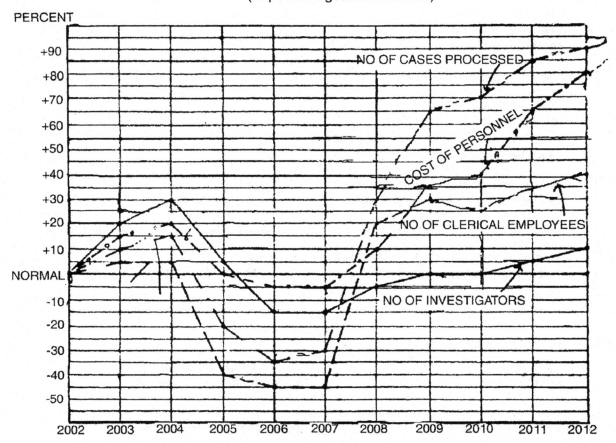

Example: If there were 80 clerical employees in the division in 1992, then the number
of clerical employees in the division in 1999 was 104.

28. If 1300 cases were processed by the division in 2006, then the number of cases pro-   28._____
cessed in 2002 was

    A. 2000   B. 1755   C. 2145   D. 1650

29. Of the following, the year in which there was no change in the size of the division's total   29._____
staff from that of the preceding year is

    A. 2005   B. 2006   C. 2009   D. 2011

30. Of the following, the year in which the size of the division's staff *decreased* MOST   30._____
sharply from that of the preceding year is

    A. 2005   B. 2006   C. 2007   D. 2008

31. An inspection of the chart discloses that the curve that fluctuates *least* as determined by   31._____
the average deviation from normal, is the curve for the

    A. number of cases processed   B. cost of personnel
    C. number of clerical employees   D. number of investigators

32. A comparison of 2006 with 2012 reveals an increase in 2006 in the

    A. cost of personnel for the division
    B. number of cases processed per investigator
    C. number of cases processed per clerical employee
    D. number of clerical employees per investigator

32._____

33. If the personnel cost per case processed in 2002 was $12.30, then the personnel cost per case processed in 2012 was MOST NEARLY

    A. $9.85   B. $10.95   C. $11.65   D. $13.85

33._____

34. Suppose that there was a total of 108 employees in the division in 2002 and a total of 125 employees in 2010.
On the basis of these figures, it is MOST accurate to state that the number of investigators employed in the division in 2010 was

    A. 40   B. 57   C. 68   D. 85

34._____

35. It is predicted that the number of cases processed in 2013 will exceed the number processed in 2002 by exactly the same quantity that the number processed in 2012 exceeded that processed in 2011. It is also predicted that the personnel cost in 2013 will exceed the personnel cost in 2012 by exactly the same amount that the 2012 personnel cost exceeded that for 2011. On the basis of these predictions, it is MOST accurate to state that the personnel cost per case in 2013 will be

    A. ten per cent less than the personnel cost per case in 2012
    B. exactly the same as the personnel cost per case in 2012
    C. twice as much as the personnel cost per case in 2002
    D. exactly the same as the personnel cost per case in 2002

35._____

KEY (CORRECT ANSWERS)

1. C	11. B	21. C	
2. D	12. B	22. C	
3. D	13. C	23. B	
4. B	14. C	24. D	
5. C	15. B	25. B	
6. D	16. D	26. D	
7. D	17. A	27. B	
8. D	18. C	28. A	
9. A	19. C	29. B	
10. C	20. A	30. A	
	31. D		
	32. C		
	33. C		
	34. A		
	35. D		

EXAMINATION SECTION
TEST 1

DIRECTIONS: Each question or incomplete statement is followed by several suggested answers or completions. Select the one that BEST answers the question or completes the statement. *PRINT THE LETTER OF THE CORRECT ANSWER IN THE SPACE AT THE RIGHT.*

1. In organizational theory, the optimum span of control, that is, the number of subordinates who can be effectively supervised by one man above the level of the first line supervisor, is GENERALLY set at between

    A. 3 and 6   B. 6 and 12   C. 12 and 18   D. 18 and 24

1._____

2. Which of the following is LEAST desirable as a basic guide to normal conventional office layout?

    A. Arrange desks so that work flows in a normal fashion.
    B. Place files nearest to the persons who will use them.
    C. Utilize a number of small areas to provide privacy.
    D. Utilize one single large area.

2._____

3. *A set of objects together with relationships between the objects and between their attributes* is the definition of

    A. a perceptual whole and its subcomponents
    B. a system in the terms of specific systems theory
    C. an organism
    D. forms control

3._____

4. A technique of time study in which each employee maintains a record of his own time is GENERALLY known as_____ study.

    A. estimated time   B. observed time
    C. time log   D. wristwatch

4._____

5. An employee has approached a supervisor with a request for a change involving his personal status or with a suggestion for making an improvement in the work. The supervisor knows that the suggestion cannot be granted.
Of the following, the BEST procedure would be for the supervisor to

    A. refer the matter to the personnel department
    B. refer the matter to his superior for action
    C. reject the proposal, explaining the defects or objections which cannot be overcome
    D. shelve the idea so that the employee will realize it cannot be acted upon

5._____

6. There are, in general, a number of common methods of drawing samples for statistical work.
The method in which a regularly ordered interval is maintained between the items chosen is BEST termed _____ sampling.

    A. random   B. stratified or selective
    C. systematic   D. work

6._____

7. The multi-column process chart can be put to all of the following general uses EXCEPT   7.___
to

   A. improve office layout   B. improve procedures
   C. standardize procedures   D. train personnel

8. If one wished to show the percentage of change over a period of time, the MOST appro-   8.___
priate type of graph or chart GENERALLY would be the ____ chart.

   A. bar
   B. line or curve
   C. logarithmic or semi-logarithmic
   D. pie

9. A chart designed for the explicit purpose of portraying graphically information relating to   9.___
the degree of responsibility of key individuals for the performance of various functions is
BEST described as a(n)_____ chart.

   A. linear responsibility   B. work distribution
   C. work process   D. staff

10. The technique of work measurement LEAST useful for setting up a program of office   10.___
incentive pay GENERALLY would be

   A. log sheets   B. stopwatch time study
   C. wristwatch time study   D. work sampling

11. There are a number of steps to be taken in making a work sampling study in order to set   11.___
production standards. Three of the steps listed below are peculiar only to work sampling,
in contrast with other work measurement techniques. The one EXCEPTION is:

   A. Define the breakdown of work into the proper elements of work and no-work or
      delay to be observed
   B. Determine the required number of observations needed for the specified degree of
      reliability
   C. Establish the observation intervals
   D. Make a preliminary estimate of work and no-work or delay element percentages for
      step A

12. A number of standardized flow process chart symbols have been generally accepted.   12.___
The symbol v̄ GENERALLY indicates a(n)

   A. delay   B. storage or file
   C. inspection   D. operation

13. A number of standardized flow process chart symbols have been generally accepted.   13.___
The symbol [____] GENERALLY indicates a(n)

   A. delay   B. storage or file
   C. inspection   D. operation

14. The type of work for which short interval scheduling generally would be LEAST applicable would be the work of a group of   14._____

    A. calculating clerks
    C. technically-oriented clerks
    B. order clerks
    D. typists

15. In writing a business report, the BEST expression to use, in general, of those listed below would NORMALLY be: 15._____

    A. Because
    C. In view of the fact that
    B. Inasmuch as
    D. With reference to

16. Of the following, the MAJOR advantage of a random access data processing system, as compared with a sequential-type system, is its   16._____

    A. ability to use more than one input system
    B. demand for more sophisticated systems and programming
    C. greater storage capacity and access speed
    D. potential for processing data on a *first-come, first-served* basis

17. A good rule to remember with regard to decision making is that decisions should be made   17._____

    A. at the highest level competent to make such a decision
    B. at the lowest level competent to make such a decision
    C. by the person responsible for carrying out the decision
    D. by the person responsible for the work of the unit

18. Which of the following potential systems would LEAST likely be improved by being on-line? A(n)_____ system.   18._____

    A. budgeting control
    C. employee payroll
    B. welfare eligibility
    D. inventory control

19. A management information and control system essentially should be designed to provide management personnel with up-to-date information which will enable them to improve control over their operations.
In designing such a system, the FIRST step to determine is: 19._____

    A. What information is needed to effectively control operations?
    B. What information is presently available?
    C. What organization changes are necessary to implement the system?
    D. Who is presently processing the information that might be used?

20. In designing control reports, which of the following guidelines is of MOST importance?   20._____

    A. Financial information should always be carried to the nearest penny.
    B. The report should be a simple and concise statement of only the pertinent facts
    C. The report should indicate the source of original data and how the computations were made.
    D. The report should have the broadest possible distribution at all levels of management.

21. A situation which enables a number of users at remote locations to have access to a SINGLE computer is called

    A. multiprocessing   B. multiprogramming
    C. process overlap   D. time sharing

21.____

22. The computer device which would offer the GREATEST speed in reading input is the

    A. CRT display   B. magnetic tape
    C. optical scanner   D. paper tape

22.____

23. Which of the following steps is LEAST desirable in designing an electronic data processing system?

    A. Design the EDP system first, then relate it to current operations.
    B. Develop a corollary chart for the corresponding flow of information
    C. Develop a flow chart for the functions affected by the system
    D. Obtain from available EDP equipment that which best fits current operations

23.____

24. Electronic data processing equipment can produce more information faster than can be generated by any other means. Because this is true, one wonders whether our ability to generate information has not far outstripped our ability to assimilate it.
In view of this, a PERSISTENT danger management faces is in

    A. determining the budget for management information systems
    B. determining what information is of real worth
    C. finding enough computer personnel
    D. keeping their computers fully occupied

24.____

25. The one of the following that is an ADVANTAGE of a visual display terminal over the typewriter-type terminal employed in an on-line system is:

    A. Information retrieval is somewhat faster
    B. Operators can be trained more easily
    C. There is no advantage
    D. They are less expensive to operate

25.____

KEY (CORRECT ANSWERS)

1. A
2. C
3. A
4. C
5. C

6. C
7. A
8. C
9. A
10. A

11. A
12. B
13. C
14. C
15. A

16. D
17. B
18. C
19. A
20. B

21. D
22. A
23. A
24. B
25. A

TEST 2

DIRECTIONS: Each question or incomplete statement is followed by several suggested answers or completions. Select the one that BEST answers the question or completes the statement. *PRINT THE LETTER OF THE CORRECT ANSWER IN THE SPACE AT THE RIGHT.*

1. In analyzing data for the acquisition of new equipment, an analyst gathers the facts, analyzes them, and develops new procedures which will be required when the new equipment arrives.
   In analyzing the factors involved, which one of the following is normally LEAST important in the evaluation of new equipment?

    A. Cost factors
    B. Layout and installation factors
    C. Production planning
    D. Operational experience of manufacturers of allied equipment

1.____

2. If an analyst is required to recommend the selection of a machine for an office operation, he can BEST judge the expected output of a particular machine by pursuing which of the following courses of action?
   Obtain

    A. an actual test run of the machine in his office
    B. data from the manufacturer of the machine
    C. information on the percentage of working time the machine will be used
    D. the experience of actual users of similar machines elsewhere

2.____

3. Of the following, the BEST definition of records management is

    A. storage of all types of records at minimum expense
    B. planned control of all types of records
    C. storage of records for maximum accessibility
    D. systematic filing of all types of records

3.____

4. The one of the following which is NOT a primary objective of a records retention and disposal system is to

    A. assure appropriate preservation of records having permanent value
    B. dispose of records not warranting further preservation
    C. establish retention standards for archives
    D. provide an opportunity to use miniaturization

4.____

5. Of the following functions of management, the one which should NORMALLY precede the others is

    A. coordinating   B. directing
    C. organizing   D. planning

5.____

6. One of the more famous studies of organizations is called the Hawthorne study.   6.____
   This work was one of the first to point out the importance of

   A. employee's benefit and retirement programs
   B. informal organization among employees
   C. job engineering
   D. styles of position classification

7. In organization theory, the type of position in which an individual is appointed to give   7.____
   technical aid to management on a particular problem area is generally BEST termed a(n)

   A. administrative assistant   B. assistant to
   C. staff assistant   D. staff specialist

8. In organizing, doing what *works* in the particular situation, with due regard to both short   8.____
   and long range objectives, is BEST termed

   A. ambivalence   B. authoritarianism
   C. decentralization   D. pragmatism

9. If an effort were made to reduce the number of private offices in a new layout, the LEAST   9.____
   effective substitute in offering privacy would be the use of

   A. an open area with lower movable partitions or railings separating each individual.
   B. conference rooms
   C. larger desks
   D. modular desk units

10. The term *administrative substation* NORMALLY refers to   10.____

    A. a work station handling a number of office services for an office organization
    B. a work station where middle level supervisors are located
    C. an office for handling management trainees
    D. the functions allocated to particular levels of administrative managers

11. An operations research technique which would be applied to determine the optimum   11.____
    number of window clerks or interviewers to have in an agency serving the public would
    MOST likely be the use of

    A. line of balance   B. queuing theory
    C. simulation   D. work sampling

12. A type of file which permits the operator to remain seated while the file can be moved   12.____
    backward and forward as required is BEST termed a _____ file.

    A. lateral   B. movable
    C. reciprocating   D. rotary

13. The technique of work measurement in which the analyst observes the work at random   13.____
    times of the day is BEST termed

    A. indirect observation   B. logging
    C. ratio delay   D. wristwatch

14. Examples of predetermined time systems generally should include all of the following   14.____
EXCEPT

    A. Master Clerical Data   B. Methods Time Measurement
    C. Short Interval Data   D. Work Factor

15. A technique by which the supervisor or an assistant distributes a predetermined batch of   15.____
work to the employees at periodic intervals of the day is generally BEST known as

    A. backlog control scheduling
    B. production control scheduling
    C. short interval scheduling
    D. workload balancing

16. E. Wright Bakke defined his *fusion process* as: The   16.____

    A. work environment to some degree remakes the organization and the organization
       to some degree remakes the work environment
    B. fusing of the interests of both management and labor unions
    C. community of interest between first line supervisors and top management
    D. organization to some degree remakes the individual and the individual to some
       degree remakes the organization

17. The title of a recent best-selling book by Robert Townsend is: 17.____

    A. MANAGEMENT ANALYSIS: WAVE OF THE FUTURE
    B. MANAGEMENT FOR RESULTS
    C. THE HUMAN SIDE OF ENTERPRISE
    D. UP THE ORGANIZATION

18. In planning office space for a newly established bureau, it would usually be LEAST desir-   18.____
able to

    A. concentrate, rather than disperse, the chief sources of office noises
    B. design an office environment with about the same brightness as the office desk
    C. designate as reception rooms, washrooms and other service areas those areas
       that will receive lesser amounts of illumination than those areas in which private
       office work will be performed
    D. eliminate natural light in cases where it is not the major light source

19. A private office should be used when its use is dictated by facts and unbiased judgment.   19.____
It should never be provided simply because requests and sometimes pressure have
been brought to bear.
Of the following reasons used to justify use of a private office, the one that requires the
MOST care in determining whether a private office is actually warranted is

    A. an office has always been provided for a particular job
    B. prestige considerations
    C. the confidential] nature of the work
    D. the work involves high concentration

20. Theoretically, an ideal organization structure can be set up for each enterprise. In actual   20._____
practice, the ideal organization structure is seldom, if ever, obtained.
Of the following, the one that normally is of LEAST influence in determining the organization structure is the

    A. existence of agreements and favors among members of the organization
    B. funds available
    C. opinions and beliefs of top executives
    D. tendency of management to discard established forms in favor of new forms

21. An IMPORTANT aspect to keep in mind during the decision-making process is that   21._____

    A. all possible alternatives for attaining goals should be sought out and considered
    B. considering various alternatives only leads to confusion
    C. once a decision has been made, it cannot be retracted
    D. there is only one correct method to reach any goal

22. Implementation of accountability requires   22._____

    A. a leader who will not hesitate to take punitive action
    B. an established system of communication from the bottom to the top
    C. explicit directives from leaders
    D. too much expense to justify it

23. Of the following, the MAJOR difference between systems and procedures analysis and   23._____
work simplification is:

    A. The former complicates organizational routine and the latter simplifies it
    B. The former is objective and the latter is subjective
    C. The former generally utilizes expert advice and the latter is a *do-it-yourself*
       improvement by supervisors and workers
    D. There is no difference other than in name

24. Systems development is concerned with providing   24._____

    A. a specific set of work procedures
    B. an overall framework to describe general relationships
    C. definitions of particular organizational functions
    D. organizational symbolism

25. Organizational systems and procedures should be   25._____

    A. developed as problems arise as no design can anticipate adequately the require-
       ments of an organization
    B. developed jointly by experts in systems and procedures and the people who are
       responsible for implementing them
    C. developed solely by experts in systems and procedures
    D. eliminated whenever possible to save unnecessary expense

———

KEY (CORRECT ANSWERS)

1.	D		11.	B
2.	A		12.	C
3.	B		13.	C
4.	D		14.	C
5.	D		15.	C
6.	B		16.	D
7.	D		17.	D
8.	D		18.	D
9.	C		19.	A
10.	A		20.	D

21.	A
22.	B
23.	C
24.	B
25.	B

TEST 3

DIRECTIONS: Each question or incomplete statement is followed by several suggested answers or completions. Select the one that BEST answers the question or completes the statement. *PRINT THE LETTER OF THE CORRECT ANSWER IN THE SPACE AT THE RIGHT.*

1. The CHIEF danger of a decentralized control system is that

   A. excessive reports and communications will be generated
   B. problem areas may not be detected readily
   C. the expense will become prohibitive
   D. this will result in too many *chiefs*

   1.____

2. Of the following, management guides and controls clerical work PRINCIPALLY through

   A. close supervision and constant checking of personnel
   B. spot checking of clerical procedures
   C. strong sanctions for clerical supervisors
   D. the use of printed forms

   2.____

3. Which of the following is MOST important before conducting fact-finding interviews?

   A. Becoming acquainted with all personnel to be interviewed
   B. Explaining the techniques you plan to use
   C. Explaining to the operating officials the purpose and scope of the study
   D. Orientation of the physical layout

   3.____

4. Of the following, the one that is NOT essential in carrying out a comprehensive work improvement program is

   A. standards of performance   B. supervisory training
   C. work count/task list   D. work distribution chart

   4.____

5. Which of the following control techniques is MOST useful on large complex systems projects?

   A. A general work plan   B. Cantt chart
   C. Monthly progress report   D. PERT chart

   5.____

6. The action which is MOST effective in gaining acceptance of a study by the agency which is being studied is

   A. a directive from the agency head to install a study based on recommendations included in a report
   B. a lecture-type presentation following approval of the procedures
   C. a written procedure in narrative form covering the proposed system with visual presentations and discussions
   D. procedural charts showing the *before* situation, forms, steps, etc. to the employees affected

   6.____

7. Which of the following is NOT an advantage in the use of oral instructions as compared with written instructions? Oral instruction(s)

    A. can easily be changed
    B. is superior in transmitting complex directives
    C. facilitate exchange of information between a superior and his subordinate
    D. with discussions make it easier to ascertain understanding

7._____

8. Which organization principle is MOST closely related to procedural analysis and improvement?

    A. Duplication, overlapping, and conflict should be eliminated.
    B. Managerial authority should be clearly defined.
    C. The objectives of the organization should be clearly defined.
    D. Top management should be freed of burdensome detail.

8._____

9. Which one of the following is the MAJOR objective of operational audits?

    A. Detecting fraud
    B. Determining organization problems
    C. Determining the number of personnel needed
    D. Recommending opportunities for improving operating and management practices

9._____

10. Of the following, the formalization of organization structure is BEST achieved by

    A. a narrative description of the plan of organization
    B. functional charts
    C. job descriptions together with organization charts
    D. multi-flow charts

10._____

11. Budget planning is MOST useful when it achieves

    A. cost control
    C. performance review
    B. forecast of receipts
    D. personnel reduction

11._____

12. The UNDERLYING principle of sound administration is to

    A. base administration on investigation of facts
    B. have plenty of resources available
    C. hire a strong administrator
    D. establish a broad policy

12._____

13. Although questionnaires are not the best survey tool the management analyst has to use, there are times when a good questionnaire can expedite the *fact-finding* phase of a management survey.
Which of the following should be AVOIDED in the design and distribution of the questionnaire?   13._____

    A. Questions should be framed so that answers can be classified and tabulated for analysis.
    B. Those receiving the questionnaire must be knowledgeable enough to accurately provide the information desired.
    C. The questionnaire should enable the respondent to answer in a narrative manner.
    D. The questionnaire should require a minimum amount of writing.

14. Of the following, the formula which is used to calculate the arithmetic mean from data grouped in a frequency distribution is: 14._____

$$A.\ M = \frac{N}{\Sigma f \chi} \qquad B.\ M = N(\Sigma f \chi) \qquad C.\ M = \frac{\Sigma f \chi}{N} \qquad D.\ M = \frac{\Sigma \chi}{f N}$$

15. Arranging large groups of numbers in frequency distributions   15._____

    A. gives a more composite picture of the total group than a random listing
    B. is misleading in most cases
    C. is unnecessary in most instances
    D. presents the data in a form whereby further manipulation of the group is eliminated

16. After a budget has been developed, it serves to   16._____

    A. assist the accounting department in posting expenditures
    B. measure the effectiveness of department managers
    C. provide a yardstick against which actual costs are measured
    D. provide the operating department with total expenditures to date

17. Of the following, which formula is used to determine staffing requirements?   17._____

    A. $\dfrac{\text{Hours per man–Day}}{\text{Volume x standard}} = \text{Employees Needed}$

    B. $\dfrac{\text{Hours per man–Day x Standard}}{\text{Volume}} = \text{Employees Needed}$

    C. $\dfrac{\text{Hours per man–Day x Volume}}{\text{Standard}} = \text{Employees Needed}$

    D. $\dfrac{\text{Volume x Standard}}{\text{Hours per man–Day}} = \text{Employees Needed}$

18. Of the following, which formula is used to determine the number of days required to process work?

    A. $\dfrac{Employees \times Daily\ Output}{Volume} = Days\ to\ Process\ Work$

    B. $\dfrac{Employees \times volume}{Daily\ output} = Days\ to\ Process\ Work$

    C. $\dfrac{Volume}{Employees \times Daily\ Output} = Days\ to\ Process\ Work$

    D. $\dfrac{Volume \times Daily\ Output}{Employees} = Days\ to\ Process\ Work$

18.____

19. Identify this symbol, as used in a Systems Flow Chart.

    A. Document   B. Decision   C. Preparation   D. Process

19.____

20. Of the following, the MAIN advantage of a form letter over a dictated letter is that a form letter

    A. is more expressive
    B. is neater
    C. may be mailed in a window envelope
    D. requires less secretarial time

20.____

21. The term that may be defined as *a systematic analysis of all factors affecting work being done or all factor's that will affect work to be done, in order to save effort, time, or money* is

    A. flow process charting   B. work flow analysis
    C. work measurement   D. work simplification

21.____

22. Generally, the LEAST important basic factor to be considered in developing office layout improvements is to locate

    A. office equipment, reference facilities, and files as close as practicable to those using them
    B. persons as close as practicable to the persons from whom they receive their work
    C. persons as close as practicable to windows and/or adequate ventilation
    D. persons who are friendly with each other close together to improve morale

22.____

23. Of the following, the one which is LEAST effective in reducing administrative costs is   23.____
    A. applying objective measurement techniques to determine the time required to per-form a given task
    B. establishing budgets on the basis of historical performance data
    C. motivating supervisors and managers in the importance of cost reduction
    D. selecting the best method -- manual, mechanical, or electronic -- to process the essential work

24. *Fire-fighting* is a common expression in management terminology.   24.____
    Of the following, which BEST describes *fire-fighting* as an analyst's approach to solv-ing paperwork problems?

    A. A complete review of all phases of the department's processing functions
    B. A studied determination of the proper equipment to process the work
    C. An analysis of each form that is being processed and the logical reasons for its processing
    D. The solution of problems as they arise, usually at the request of operating person-nel

25. Assume that an analyst with a proven record of accomplishment on many projects is   25.____
    having difficulties on his present assignment.
    Of the following, the BEST course of action for his superior to take is to

    A. assume there is a personality conflict involved and transfer the analyst to another project
    B. give the analyst some time off
    C. review the nature of the project to determine whether or not the analyst is equipped to handle the assignment
    D. suggest that the analyst seek counseling

KEY (CORRECT ANSWERS)

1.	B	11.	A
2.	D	12.	A
3.	C	13.	C
4.	B	14.	C
5.	D	15.	A
6.	C	16.	C
7.	B	17.	D
8.	A	18.	C
9.	D	19.	A
10.	C	20.	D

21.	D
22.	D
23.	B
24.	D
25.	C

———

EXAMINATION SECTION
TEST 1

DIRECTIONS: Each question or incomplete statement is followed by several suggested answers or completions. Select the one that BEST answers the question or completes the statement. *PRINT THE LETTER OF THE CORRECT ANSWER IN THE SPACE AT THE RIGHT.*

1. If an analyst recommends to the head of a newly established agency that the latter institute a line type of organization, he should also point out that this structure has the following MAJOR disadvantage:

    A. Delay will be encountered in reaching decisions
    B. Coordination will be difficult to secure
    C. Authority and responsibility will be diffused
    D. Discipline will be hard to maintain

1.____

2. Of the following statements which relate to the use of office space, the one that is LEAST valid is:

    A. A request for a conference room on the basis of privacy for meetings usually cannot be justified, for most private offices are suitable for meetings
    B. Private offices are objectionable because they tend to slow up the work by interfering with supervisory effectiveness
    C. The reception room should not handle ordinary and necessary traffic between different areas in the office
    D. The space utilization of private offices is about 35 to 50 percent of that of the open area arrangement

2.____

3. In preparing the layout for a small office, PARAMOUNT consideration should be given to a design that will

    A. accommodate the flows representing the largest volumes of work
    B. cause work to progress through its production cycle regardless of backtracking in a straight line or U
    C. increase the speed and movement of papers involved in the flow of work to the shortest compass feasible
    D. take into account vertical relationships of floor locations in the work flow

3.____

4. When centralization of office activities is instituted, which one of the following conditions will MOST likely occur?

    A. Confidentiality of office work will decrease.
    B. Equitable wage schedules will be undermined.
    C. Office machine maintenance costs will increase.
    D. Training of office employees will be delayed.

4.____

5. Descriptor is a term COMMONLY used in

    A. information retrieval   B. network analysis
    C. planning and forecasting   D. systems analysis

5.____

6. Of the following, the BEST way to secure effective management is *usually* to   6.___

    A. allow staff agencies to help solve the administrative problems of line management
    B. provide a good organization structure
    C. select capable managers and administrators
    D. set up conservative spans of control

7. The MOST effective way of graphically representing the division of total costs into com-   7.___
ponent costs as they vary over a period of time is by means of a

    A. band chart   B. pictograph
    C. pie diagram   D. histogram

8. During the past 50 years, the rate of increase in the number of office workers has been   8.___
much greater than that of our total working force.
The LEAST likely reason to cause this increase is the

    A. dispersal of clerical operations which accompanied the growth in manufacturing
    B. development of "service industries"
    C. use of more factual information by managers
    D. expansion in business legislation and governmental regulatory agencies

9. In attempting to discover flaws in an organization, an organization chart has been pre-   9.___
pared.
The condition that will be LEAST likely to be disclosed through use of the organization
chart will be

    A. executives who are burdened with details
    B. work schedules that are unmet
    C. promotional possibilities that are not being provided
    D. functions which are becoming secondary due to splitting among departmental
units

10. The PRIMARY function of systems analysis in the Planning Programming Budgetary   10.___
System is to

    A. cost out various alternatives
    B. develop a PERT chart for evaluating program content
    C. develop better alternatives than those which are in the currently approved program
    D. provide perspective in judging the validity of an expenditure

11. Systems analysis would be LEAST effective in solving which of these problems? The   11.___

    A. determination of need for a new pier
    B. problem of air pollution
    C. selection of a site for a police station
    D. selection of engineering personnel

12. In procedural analysis, when the purpose of a particular step has been shown to be justi-   12.___
fiable to the end purpose of the procedure, the NEXT necessary step is, usually, to

    A. determine the time limits for the step
    B. weigh the value of the step against the expense involved
    C. sell the idea to the supervisory staff
    D. make it a part of the procedure

13.   ▽ is a symbol used in records management flow diagrams to indicate   13._____

    A.   destruction of paper
    B.   filing and/or permanent storage
    C.   inspection
    D.   microfilming is necessary

14.   The concept that decisions should be made at the lowest level in an organization where   14._____
    all the (required) information and competence are available is MOST particularly a general rule in

    A.   communications theory
    B.   decentralization of authority
    C.   incremental decision-making
    D.   span of control

15.   An office quality control program may comprise several approaches.   15._____
    The one LEAST desirable of the following normally is to

    A.   follow a policy of spot or sample checking
    B.   follow a practice of 100% checking of all work to verify its correctness
    C.   inspect the work by means of a statistical quality control program
    D.   review and tally errors being detected from present checking operations to determine the amount of checking presently being followed and the results being obtained

16.   When a form is to be completed by an electronic data processing machine, which of the   16._____
    following is LEAST necessary?

    A.   Form number   B.   Form title
    C.   Lines   D.   Margins

17.   Under a PPBS system, the selection of the proper alternative program should be made   17._____
    by the

    A.   administrator responsible for the program, with the approval of the mayor and city legislative body
    B.   budget director, basing his decision according to the optimum alternative
    C.   budget examiner who reviews the administration budget
    D.   chief systems analyst who programmed the alternatives

18.   Which of the following is LEAST applicable in describing PPBS as a general concept? A   18._____

    A.   quantitative method of budgeting for the coming year
    B.   system of defining long-range alternative programs and planning the allocation of resources on the basis of the cost of the long-range program versus the benefit derived over the planning period
    C.   system of measuring budgeted performance against pre-established goals
    D.   system that establishes the importance of a program in terms of the expected cost of executing it

19. Under a PPBS system, substantive planning is NORMALLY defined as   19.____

    A. fiscal planning
    B. planning of future budgets
    C. planning of objectives-ultimate and intermediate
    D. planning of programs-ultimate and intermediate

20. The method of selection which would provide the TIGHTEST standard under the logging   20.____
method of work measurement would be

    A. one-third array
    B. modal average
    C. selected arithmetic average
    D. upper quartile

21. A concept for the evaluation of managers whereby goals are set and agreed upon for   21.____
each manager, and then his attainment of those goals is evaluated at a particular prearranged target date, is BEST termed

    A. management by objectives
    B. management evaluation planning
    C. managerial performance appraisal
    D. program evaluation

22. When work is organized so that the work is broken into a series of jobs, and each unit of   22.____
work (a customer order, invoice, etc.) moves progressively from position to position until
completion, we would NORMALLY refer to this as the

    A. parallel plan of work subdivision
    B. serial plan
    C. unit assembly plan
    D. unit process plan

23. The type of organization in which employees report to a nominal manager for administra-   23.____
tive purposes but are assigned to *ad hoc* supervisors as various assignments arise is
BEST termed the _____ type of organization.

    A. functional   B. process
    C. project or task force   D. unit assembly

24. The expression which BEST defines a generalized situation in which several programs   24.____
may be executed simultaneously or concurrently is

    A. multiprocessing
    B. multiprogramming
    C. on-line, real time programming
    D. process overlap

25. The sampling technique which consists of taking selections at constant intervals (every   25.____
nth unit) from a list of the universe is called_____ sampling.

    A. area   B. quota
    C. stratified random   D. systematic

26. A method of project scheduling and control which shows the MOST optimistic, MOST   26.____
pessimistic, and MOST probable estimate of time for how long each task in a project will
take is called

    A. CPM (Critical Path Method)
    B. Gantt charting
    C. Linear Responsibility Charting
    D. PERT

27. The idea that classic organizational structure tends to create work situations having   27.____
requirements counter to those for psychological success and self-esteem, sometimes
called the "organizational dilemma", is MOST closely associated with which one of the following persons?

    A. Chris Argyris   B. Frederick Taylor
    C. Luther Gulick   D. Max Weber

28. Charles J. Hitch is known PRIMARILY for his work in the area of   28.____

    A. administrative behavior   B. behavioral sciences
    C. organizational analysis   D. PPBS

Questions 29-30.

DIRECTIONS: Questions 29 and 30 relate to the paragraph below.

    *If one were to observe the information, in all its variant forms, that flows to a manager in
the typical American enterprise, he would have a word for it: chaos. Subordinates want to be
helpful, or to promote themselves, or to reflect discredit somewhere, and they originate or
serve as a transmission belt for information they think the manager should have. Furthermore, it is the nature of the business process that information is generated where it is most
easily reflected and is very scarce in areas or phases where data are not readily available. If
one could project a tape which showed information density through time, he would find areas
of heavy concentration and areas of little or no cloudiness. This means two things: First, people seem to have an inner drive to report available information in many ways, many forms,
and for many users. Note what an accountant or statistician can do with two figures—or a
mathematician without any figures at all! Second, the lack of information in specific areas
means only that it is not available; it does not mean that it is unnecessary. Indeed, the blind
areas may be of the greatest importance for decision-making purposes.*

29. The result of the state of affairs described in the above paragraph would MOST likely be   29.____

    A. inconsequential
    B. an impetus to proper decision-making
    C. high costs and poor decisions
    D. a successful uniform information system

30. The author in this paragraph is PRIMARILY concerned with   30.____

    A. decision-making theory
    B. communications
    C. tape information systems
    D. information gathering by accountants and statisticians

KEY (CORRECT ANSWERS)

1.	B	11.	D	21.	A
2.	A	12.	B	22.	B
3.	A	13.	B	23.	C
4.	A	14.	B	24.	B
5.	A	15.	B	25.	D
6.	C	16.	C	26.	D
7.	A	17.	A	27.	A
8.	A	18.	A	28.	D
9.	B	19.	C	29.	C
10.	C	20.	D	30.	B

TEST 2

DIRECTIONS: Each question or incomplete statement is followed by several suggested answers or completions. Select the one that BEST answers the question or completes the statement. *PRINT THE LETTER OF THE CORRECT ANSWER IN THE SPACE AT THE RIGHT.*

1. It has been decided to make a few important revisions in the methods and procedures of a particular work unit. Of the following, the method of implementing these revisions which would probably be MOST desirable in terms of morale as well as efficiency is to

   1.____

  A. give all the employees in the work unit individual instructions in the revised procedures, making sure that each employee fully understands the changes before instructing the next employee
  B. institute all the revisions at once, followed by on-the-job training for all the employees in the work unit
  C. introduce the revisions one at a time, accompanying each revision with an orientation for the employees
  D. set up a training course for the employees, instructing them in all aspects of the revised procedures prior to their implementation

2. In an administrative survey of a multiple-unit organization, which of the following is it usually MOST important to identify? The

   2.____

  A. data and information used commonly by units, how used and by whom
  B. flow of data and information within a single organization unit
  C. type and volume of data used within individual units and transmitted between units
  D. way data and information are transmitted between units, how used and by whom

3. A noted authority has described a common method of making organizational policy in which the decision-maker tries to find some acceptable level of goal accomplishment short of ultimate fulfillment of all objectives and to frame policies toward such fulfillment. Of the following, this method is BEST termed

   3.____

  A. feedback
  C. satisfying
  B. incrementalism
  D. seriality

4. The managerial grid, as defined by Blake and Mouton, shows two concerns and a range of interaction between them as follows: The horizontal axis indicates a concern for

   4.____

  A. hierarchy, while the vertical axis indicates a concern for people
  B. production, while the vertical axis indicates a concern for people
  C. organization, while the vertical axis indicates a concern for people
  D. people, while the vertical axis indicates a concern for P/L (profit or loss)

5. In the managerial grid, which managerial style is dominant for any given person in any particular situation can be determined by any one or several sets of conditions in combination. The five conditions in CORRECT order are:

   5.____

  A. Organization, management, values, chance, production
  B. Organization, situation, values, personality, chance
  C. Production, situation, personality, chance, individuality
  D. Values, personality, variety, organization, chance

6. The analyst may be faced with a choice of either recommending service contracts or rec-   6.___
ommending on-call service for maintenance of equipment.
In making a decision, the one of the following factors which would mitigate MOST
against the use of on-call service would be that

   A. equipment utilization is not heavy
   B. prompt service when breakdowns occur is seldom essential
   C. regular checkups and servicing are considered desirable based on past equipment
      history
   D. trade-ins are made frequently

7. The type of paper stock MOST commonly used for office forms work is _____ bond.   7.___

   A. cotton content   B. duplicating or mimeo
   C. rag   D. sulphite

8. In laying out an office, according to most authorities, the amount of space which NOR-   8.___
MALLY should be allowed for a clerk would be in the range of _____ square feet.

   A. 10 to 15   B. 25 to 100
   C. 110 to 125   D. 130 to 150

9. A noted behavioral scientist believes that the MOST important element in job satisfac-   9.___
tion, of those listed below, is

   A. job security
   B. responsibility or recognition
   C. salary
   D. type of supervision

10. The point of view that the average human being prefers to be directed, wishes to avoid   10.___
responsibility, has relatively little ambition, and wants security above all has been
described in Douglas MacGregor's classic book on human motivation in business.
He includes this point of view in what he calls

   A. Theory X   B. Theory Y
   C. Theory Z   D. Theory X and Y combined

11. New desk top electronic machines are of two main types-printing or display. Display type   11.___
machines show the results by any of the following methods EXCEPT for

   A. cathode ray tube   B. electro-mechanical
   C. mosaic or liquid crystal   D. nixie

12. The type of chart that is normally MOST useful for studying the work assignments and   12.___
job content of individual positions in a particular organizational unit when making a procedure analysis is the_____ chart.

   A. columnar flow   B. procedure flow
   C. work distribution   D. work process

13. To prepare a work distribution chart, two other types of lists generally must be prepared.   13._____
    In the usual order of preparation, they are FIRST a(n)

    A. flow diagram, then an activity list
    B. skills list, then a task list
    C. task list, then an activity list
    D. activity list, then a task list

14. The critical path is defined as that path (or those paths) through a network   14._____

    A. showing the least number of time units
    B. showing the greatest number of time units
    C. which consists (or consist) entirely of sequential activities
    D. which links (or link) together activities in concurrent relationship to each other

15. A statistical quality control program in the office is valuable in alerting management that   15._____
    the level of quality for particular transactions has deteriorated. It is, however, LEAST
    likely to reveal

    A. when preventive action is necessary
    B. when a variation is due to other than chance
    C. when an assignable cause is present
    D. what the cause of the error is

16. In work measurement, the value of a TMU is _____ min.   16._____

    A. .0001   B. .0006   C. .0036   D. .0100

17. The sheet version of microfilm is NORMALLY referred to as   17._____

    A. microfiche   B. micro-sheet
    C. microdupe   D. microspec

18. While a line and staff organization is generally considered to have the advantages of   18._____
    both a line organization and a functional organization, with the disadvantages of each
    eliminated, disadvantages, nevertheless, do exist.
    Of the following, the one that describes the MOST significant disadvantage of a line
    and staff type of organization is that

    A. fewer opportunities are afforded to match the capacities of personnel with the job,
        since a smaller number of jobs is required
    B. line orders and staff advice, although clearly known to managers, tend to be con-
        fused by non-management members
    C. staff officers may attempt to take over line authority
    D. staff officers may tend to follow the ideas of the line officers and not generate their
        own ideas

19. Which activities take the most time? Are skills being utilized properly? Are employees   19._____
    doing too many unrelated tasks?
    Of the following, the BEST technique to find answers to all of these questions is the

    A. flow diagram   B. skills chart
    C. work count   D. work distribution chart

20. Operator participation in management improvement work is LEAST likely to do which one of the following?

    A. Assure the use of the best available management techniques.
    B. Make installation of new procedures quicker and easier.
    C. Overcome the stigma of the outside expert.
    D. Take advantage of the desire of most operators to seek self-improvement.

20.____

21. Which of the following BEST defines an organization chart? A

    A. chart depicting the informal channels of communications within an organization
    B. chart depicting the major functions of an organization and the normal work flow between subdivisions of the organization
    C. graphic presentation of the arrangement and interrelationships of the subdivisions and functions of an organization as they exist
    D. graphic presentation of the arrangement and relationships of all positions authorized in an organization

21.____

22. Under a PPBS system, fiscal planning is NORMALLY considered to be planning

    A. for anticipated fixed costs only
    B. for present personnel requirements, procurement, and construction
    C. of current income and expenditures
    D. of future budgets

22.____

23. In the selection of space within an office building, LEAST consideration, generally, should be given to which of the following factors?

    A. Future expansion
    B. Proximity to elevators and restrooms
    C. Stability of other tenants on other floors
    D. Ventilation

23.____

24. In office layout, an office unit consisting of a combined desk and file cabinet and small movable partitions may BEST be described as_____ unit.

    A. conference   B. landscaped office
    C. modular office   D. semi-private office

24.____

25. Which of the following is it generally MOST important to consider when allocating office space?

    A. Actual organizational relationships
    B. Lighting requirements
    C. Noise levels
    D. Preferences of employees with over ten years of seniority

25.____

26. In preparing office layouts, the one of the following general factors within the affected unit which should generally receive the LEAST consideration is

    A. lighting levels in the existing area
    B. major work flow–the processing of paper
    C. present and projected growth rate of the unit
    D. traffic patterns of employees and visitors

26.____

27. In reviewing a new office layout, the one of the following questions that should normally receive LEAST consideration is:

    27._____

    A. Have several alternate move day plans been prepared showing possible new locations of each piece of office equipment?
    B. Has expansion been provided for?
    C. Have alternate schemes been adequately explored to try to achieve the best possible layout?
    D. Is there adequate aisle space for ingress and egress?

28. Which of the following is the LEAST important reason for preparing a written study report? The

    28._____

    A. report documents findings and recommendations so that the client can review and comment on them
    B. report is of interest as an historical document
    C. report serves as a document useful in implementing the recommendations
    D. writing process itself helps the analyst structure his thinking and conclusions

29. According to the classic studies by Rensis Likert at the University of Michigan, the GREATEST factor making for good morale and increased productivity was having a

    29._____

    A. good program of employee benefits and wage scales
    B. supervisor who gave his employees free rein, after they were fully trained, and did not interfere with them
    C. supervisor who was interested primarily in production
    D. supervisor who, while also interested in production, was primarily "employee-centered"

30. Organization structure deals with the relationship of functions and the personnel performing these functions. It is usually advisable to think first of functions, then of the individuals performing these functions.
MOST implicit in this approach is the recognition that

    30._____

    A. conditions outside the organization may necessitate changes in the organization structure
    B. functions need not always be coordinated for an organization to effectively carry out its objectives
    C. functions tend to change with time while the interests and abilities of personnel are usually permanent
    D. personnel emphasis often results in unusual combinations of duties that are difficult to manage

———————

KEY (CORRECT ANSWERS)

1.	D	11.	B	21.	C
2.	A	12.	C	22.	D
3.	C	13.	C	23.	C
4.	B	14.	A	24.	C
5.	B	15.	D	25.	A
6.	C	16.	B	26.	A
7.	D	17.	A	27.	A
8.	B	18.	C	28.	B
9.	B	19.	D	29.	D
10.	A	20.	A	30.	D

EXAMINATION SECTION
TEST 1

DIRECTIONS: Each question or incomplete statement is followed by several suggested answers or completions. Select the one that BEST answers the question or completes the statement. *PRINT THE LETTER OF THE CORRECT ANSWER IN THE SPACE AT THE RIGHT.*

1. An executive assigns A, the head of a staff unit, to devise plans for reducing the delay in submittal of reports by a local agency headed by C. The reports are under the supervision of C's subordinate line official B with whom A is to deal directly. In his investigation, A finds: (1) the reasons for the delay; and (2) poor practices which have either been overlooked or condoned by line official B.
   Of the following courses of action A could take, the BEST one would be to

   A. develop recommendations with line official B with regard to reducing the delay and correcting the poor practices and then report fully to his own executive
   B. discuss the findings with C in an attempt to correct the situation before making any formal report on the poor practices
   C. report both findings to his executive, attaching the explanation offered by C
   D. report to his executive on the first finding and discuss the second in a friendly way with line official B
   E. report the first finding to his executive, ignoring the second until his opinion is requested

1._____

2. Drafts of a proposed policy, prepared by a staff committee, are circulated to ten members of the field staff of the organization by route slips with a request for comments within two weeks. Two members of the field staff make extensive comments, four offer editorial suggestions and the remainder make minor favorable comments. Shortly after, it found that the statement needs considerable revision by the field staff.
   Of the following possible reasons for the original failure of the field staff to identify difficulties, the MOST likely is that the

   A. field staff did not take sufficient time to review the material
   B. field staff had not been advised of the type of contribution expected
   C. low morale of the field staff prevented their showing interest
   D. policy statement was too advanced for the staff
   E. staff committee was not sufficiently representative

2._____

3. Operator participation in management improvement work is LEAST likely to

   A. assure the use of best available management technique
   B. overcome the stigma of the outside expert
   C. place responsibility for improvement in the person who knows the job best
   D. simplify installation
   E. take advantage of the desire of most operators to seek self-improvement

3._____

4. In general, the morale of workers in an agency is MOST frequently and MOST significantly affected by the

4._____

A. agency policies of organizational structure and operational procedures
B. distance of the employee's job from his home community
C. fringe benefits
D. number of opportunities for advancement
E. relationship with supervisors

5. Of the following, the PRIMARY function of a work distribution chart is to

5.__

A. analyze the soundness of existing divisions of labor
B. eliminate unnecessary clerical detail
C. establish better supervisory techniques
D. simplify work methods
E. weed out core functions

6. In analyzing a process chart, which one of the following should be asked FIRST?

6.__

A. How   B. When   C. Where   D. Who   E. Why

7. Which one of the following is NOT an advantage of the interview method of collecting data?

7.__

It

A. enables interviewer to judge the person interviewed on such matters as general attitude, knowledge, etc.
B. helps build up personal relations for later installation of changes
C. is a flexible method that can be adjusted to changing circumstances
D. permits the obtaining of *off the record* information
E. produces more accurate information than other methods

8. Which one of the following may be defined as *a regularly recurring appraisal of the manner in which all elements of agency management are being carried out?*

8.__

A. Functional survey   B. Operations audit
C. Organization survey   D. Over-all survey
E. Reconnaissance survey

9. An analysis of the flow of work in a department should begin with the _____ work.

9.__

A. major routine   B. minor routine
C. supervisory   D. technical
E. unusual

10. Which method would MOST likely be used to get first-hand information on complaints from the public?

10.__

A. Study of correspondence
B. Study of work volume
C. Tracing specific transactions through a series of steps
D. Tracing use of forms
E. Worker desk audit

11. People will generally produce the MOST if

11.

A. management exercises close supervision over the work
B. there is strict discipline in the group

C. they are happy in their work
D. they feel involved in their work
E. they follow *the one best way*

12. The normal analysis of which chart listed below is MOST closely related to organizational analysis?
_____ chart.

12.____

A. Layout
B. Operation
C. Process
D. Work count
E. Work distribution

13. The work count would be LEAST helpful in accomplishing which one of the following?

13.____

A. Demonstrating personnel needs
B. Improving the sequence of steps
C. Measuring the value of a step
D. Spotting bottlenecks
E. Stimulating interest in work

14. Which of the following seems LEAST useful as a guide in interviewing an employee in a procedure and methods survey?

14.____

A. Explaining who you are and the purpose of your visit
B. Having a general plan of what you intend to get from the interview
C. Listening carefully and not interrupting
D. Trying out his reactions to your ideas for improvements
E. Trying to analyze his reasons for saying what he says

15. Which one of the following is an advantage of the questionnaire method of gathering facts as compared with the interview method?

15.____

A. Different people may interpret the questions differently.
B. Less *off the record* information is given.
C. More time may be taken in order to give exact answers.
D. Personal relationships with the people involved are not established.
E. There is less need for follow-up.

16. Which one of the following is generally NOT an advantage of the personal observation method of gathering facts?
It

16.____

A. enables staff to use *off the record* information if personally observed
B. helps in developing valid recommendations
C. helps the person making the observation acquire *know how* valuable for later installation and follow-up
D. is economical in time and money
E. may turn up other problems in need of solution

17. Which of the following would MOST often be the best way to minimize resistance to change?

17.____

A. Break the news about the change gently to the people affected.
B. Increase the salary of the people affected by the change.

C. Let the people concerned participate in arriving at the decision to change.
D. Notify all people concerned with the change, both orally and in writing.
E. Stress the advantages of the new system.

18. The functional organization chart   18.___

    A. does not require periodic revision
    B. includes a description of the duties of each organization segment
    C. includes positions and titles for each organization segment
    D. is the simplest type of organization chart
    E. is used primarily by newly established agencies

19. The principle of span of control has frequently been said to be in conflict with the   19.___

    A. principle of unity of command
    B. principle that authority should be commensurate with responsibility
    C. principle that like functions should be grouped into one unit
    D. principle that the number of levels between the top of an organization and the bottom should be small
    E. scalar principle

20. If an executive delegates to his subordinates authority to handle problems of a routine nature for which standard solutions have been established, he may expect that   20.___

    A. fewer complaints will be received
    B. he has made it more difficult for his subordinates to solve these problems
    C. he has opened the way for confusion in his organization
    D. there will be a lack of consistency in the methods applied to the solution of these problems
    E. these routine problems will be handled efficiently and he will have more time for other non-routine work

21. Which of the following would MOST likely be achieved by a change in the basic organization structure from the *process* or *functional* type to the *purpose* or *product* type?   21.___

    A. Easier recruitment of personnel in a tight labor market
    B. Fixing responsibility at a lower level in the organization
    C. Greater centralization
    D. Greater economy
    E. Greater professional development

22. Usually the MOST difficult problem in connection with a major reorganization is   22.___

    A. adopting a pay plan to fit the new structure
    B. bringing the organization manual up-to-date
    C. determining the new organization structure
    D. gaining acceptance of the new plan by the higher level employees
    E. gaining acceptance of the new plan by the lower level employees

23. Which of the following statements MOST accurately describes the work of the chiefs of MOST staff divisions in departments?   23.___
Chiefs

A. focus more on getting the job done than on how it is done
B. are mostly interested in short-range results
C. nearly always advise but rarely if ever command or control
D. usually command or control but rarely advise
E. provide service to the rest of the organization and/or assist the chief executive in planning and controlling operations

24. In determining the type of organization structure of an enterprise, the one factor that might be given relatively greater weight in a small organization than in a larger organization of the same nature is the

24.____

A. geographical location of the enterprise
B. individual capabilities of incumbents
C. method of financing to be employed
D. size of the area served
E. type of activity engaged in

25. Functional foremanship differs MOST markedly from generally accepted principles of administration in that it advocates

25.____

A. an unlimited span of control
B. less delegation of responsibility
C. more than one supervisor for an employee
D. nonfunctional organization
E. substitution of execution for planning

KEY (CORRECT ANSWERS)

1.	A		11.	D
2.	B		12.	E
3.	A		13.	B
4.	E		14.	D
5.	A		15.	C
6.	E		16.	D
7.	E		17.	C
8.	B		18.	B
9.	A		19.	D
10.	A		20.	E

21.	B
22.	D
23.	E
24.	B
25.	C

TEST 2

DIRECTIONS: Each question or incomplete statement is followed by several suggested answers or completions. Select the one that BEST answers the question or completes the statement. *PRINT THE LETTER OF THE CORRECT ANSWER IN THE SPACE AT THE RIGHT*

1. Decentralization of the authority to make decisions is a necessary result of increased complexity in an organization, but for the sake of efficiency and coordination of operations, such decentralization must be planned carefully.
A good general rule is that

   A. any decision should be made at the lowest possible point in the organization where all the information and competence necessary for a sound decision are available
   B. any decision should be made at the highest possible point in the organization, thus guaranteeing the best decision
   C. any decision should be made at the lowest possible point in the organization, but always approved by management
   D. any decision should be made by management and referred to the proper subordinate for comment
   E. no decision should be made by any individual in the organization without approval by a superior

1.___

2. One drawback of converting a conventional consecutive filing system to a terminal digit filing system for a large installation is that

   A. conversion would be expensive in time and manpower
   B. conversion would prevent the proper use of recognized numeric classification systems, such as the Dewey decimal, in classifying files material
   C. responsibility for proper filing cannot be pinpointed in the terminal digit system
   D. the terminal digit system requires considerably more space than a normal filing system
   E. the terminal digit system requires long, specialized training on the part of files personnel

2.__

3. The basic filing system that would ordinarily be employed in a large administrative head-quarters unit is the _____ file system.

   A. alphabetic   B. chronological
   C. mnemonic   D. retention
   E. subject classification

3._

4. A records center is of benefit in a records management program primarily because

   A. all the records of the organization are kept in one place
   B. inactive records can be stored economically in less expensive storage areas
   C. it provides a place where useless records can be housed at little or no cost to the organization
   D. obsolete filing and storage equipment can be utilized out of view of the public
   E. records analysts can examine an organization's files without affecting the unit's operation or upsetting the supervisors

4._

5. In examining a number of different forms to see whether any could be combined or eliminated, which of the following would one be MOST likely to use?

    A. Forms analysis sheet of recurring data
    B. Forms control log
    C. Forms design and approval request
    D. Forms design and guide sheet
    E. Numerical file

5.____

6. The MOST important reason for control of *bootleg* forms is that

    A. they are more expensive than authorized forms
    B. they are usually poorly designed
    C. they can lead to unnecessary procedures
    D. they cannot be reordered as easily as authorized forms
    E. violation of rules and regulations should not be allowed

6.____

7. With a box design of a form, the caption title or question to be answered should be located in the _____ of the box.

    A. center at the bottom   B. center at the top
    C. lower left corner   D. lower right corner
    E. upper left corner

7.____

8. A two-part snapout form would be MOST properly justified if

    A. it is a cleaner operation
    B. it is prepared ten times a week
    C. it saves time in preparation
    D. it is to be filled out by hand rather than by typewriter
    E. proper registration is critical

8.____

9. When deciding whether or not to approve a request for a new form, which reference is normally MOST pertinent?

    A. Alphabetical Forms File
    B. Functional Forms File
    C. Numerical Forms File
    D. Project completion report
    E. Records retention data

9.____

10. Which of the following statements BEST explains the significance of the famed Hawthorne Plant experiments? They showed that

    A. a large span of control leads to more production than a small span of control
    B. morale has no relationship to production
    C. personnel counseling is of relatively little importance in a going organization
    D. the special attention received by a group in an experimental situation has a greater impact on production than changes in working conditions
    E. there is a direct relationship between the amount of illumination and production

10.____

11. Which of the following would most often NOT result from a highly efficient management control system?

11.____

A. Facilitation of delegation
B. Highlighting of problem areas
C. Increase in willingness of people to experiment or to take calculated risks
D. Provision of an objective test of new ideas or new methods and procedures
E. Provision of information useful for revising objectives, programs, and operations

12. The PERT system is a   12.___

    A. method for laying out office space on a modular basis utilizing prefabricated partitions
    B. method of motivating personnel to be continuously alert and to improve their appearance
    C. method of program planning and control using a network or flow plan
    D. plan for expanding reporting techniques
    E. simplified method of cost accounting

13. The term *management control* is MOST frequently used to mean   13.___

    A. an objective and unemotional approach by management
    B. coordinating the efforts of all parts of the organization
    C. evaluation of results in relation to plan
    D. giving clear, precise orders to subordinates
    E. keeping unions from making managerial decisions

14. Which one of the following factors has the MOST bearing on the frequency with which a   14.___
control report should be made?

    A. Degree of specialization of the work
    B. Degree of variability in activities
    C. Expense of the report
    D. Number of levels of supervision
    E. Number of personnel involved

15. The value of statistical records is MAINLY dependent upon the   15.___

    A. method of presenting the material
    B. number of items used
    C. range of cases sampled
    D. reliability of the information used
    E. time devoted to compiling the material

16. When a supervisor delegates an assignment, he should   16.___

    A. delegate his responsibility for the assignment
    B. make certain that the assignment is properly performed
    C. participate in the beginning and final stages of the assignment
    D. retain all authority needed to complete the assignment
    E. oversee all stages of the assignment

17. Assume that the department in which you are employed has never given official sanction   17._____
to a mid-afternoon coffee break. Some bureaus have it and others do not. In the latter
case, some individuals merely absent themselves for about 15 minutes at 3 P.M. while
others remain on the job despite the fatigue which seems to be common among all
employees in this department at that time.
The course of action which you should recommend, if possible, is to

    A.   arrange a schedule of mid-afternoon coffee breaks for all employees
    B.   forbid all employees to take a mid-afternoon coffee break
    C.   permit each bureau to decide for itself whether or not it will have a coffee break
    D.   require all employees who wish a coffee break to take a shorter lunch period
    E.   arrange a poll to discover the consensus of the department

18. The one of the following which is LEAST important in the management of a suggestion   18._____
program is

    A.   giving awards which are of sufficient value to encourage competition
    B.   securing full support from the department's officers and executives
    C.   publicizing the program and the awards given
    D.   holding special conferences to analyze and evaluate some of the suggestions
        needed
    E.   providing suggestion boxes in numerous locations

19. The one of the following which is MOST likely to decrease morale is   19._____

    A.   insistence on strict adherence to safety rules
    B.   making each employee responsible for the tidiness of his work area
    C.   overlooking evidence of hostility between groups of employees
    D.   strong, aggressive leadership
    E.   allocating work on the basis of personal knowledge of the abilities and interests of
        the members of the department

20. Assume that a certain office procedure has been standard practice for many years.   20._____
When a new employee asks why this particular procedure is followed, the supervisor
should FIRST

    A.   explain that everyone does it that way
    B.   explain the reason for the procedure
    C.   inform him that it has always been done that way in that particular office
    D.   tell him to try it for a while before asking questions
    E.   tell him he has never thought about it that way

21. Several employees complain informally to their supervisor regarding some new proce-   21._____
dures which have been instituted. The supervisor should IMMEDIATELY

    A.   explain that management is responsible
    B.   state frankly that he had nothing to do with it
    C.   refer the matter to the methods analyst
    D.   tell the employees to submit their complaint as a formal grievance
    E.   investigate the complaint

22. A new employee asks his supervisor *how he is doing.* Actually, he is not doing well in   22.___
    some phases of the job, but it is felt that he will learn in time.
    The BEST response for the supervisor to make is:

    A. Some things you are doing well, and in others I am sure you will improve
    B. Wait until the end of your probationary period when we will discuss this matter
    C. You are not doing too well
    D. You are doing very well
    E. I'll be able to tell you when I go over your record

23. The PRINCIPAL aim of a supervisor is to   23.___

    A. act as liaison between employee and management
    B. get the work done
    C. keep up morale
    D. train his subordinates
    E. become chief of the department

24. When the work of two bureaus must be coordinated, direct contact between the subordi-   24.___
    nates in each bureau who are working on the problem is

    A. *bad,* because it violates the chain of command
    B. *bad,* because they do not have authority to make decisions
    C. *good,* because it enables quicker results
    D. *good,* because it relieves their superiors of any responsibility
    E. *bad,* because they may work at cross purposes

25. Of the following, the organization defect which can be ascertained MOST readily merely   25.___
    by analyzing an accurate and well-drawn organization chart is

    A. ineffectiveness of an activity
    B. improper span of control
    C. inappropriate assignment of functions
    D. poor supervision
    E. unlawful delegation of authority

KEY (CORRECT ANSWERS)

1.	A		11.	C
2.	A		12.	C
3.	E		13.	C
4.	B		14.	B
5.	A		15.	D
6.	C		16.	B
7.	E		17.	A
8.	E		18.	E
9.	B		19.	C
10.	D		20.	B

21.	E
22.	A
23.	B
24.	C
25.	B

DIRECTIONS: Each question or incomplete statements is followed by several suggested answers or completions. Select the one that BEST answers the question or completes the statement. *PRINT THE LETTER OF THE CORRECT ANSWER IN THE SPACE AT THE RIGHT.*

1. The one of the following which BEST characterizes an agency in which delegation of authority is practiced on an organization-wide level is that the agency is   1.____

  A. autocratic   B. authoritarian
  C. centralized   D. decentralized

2. The concept of the *chain of command* is MOST similar to which one of the following concepts?   2.____

  A. Span of control
  B. Matrix or task-force organization
  C. Scalar principle
  D. Functional departmentation

3. The one of the following techniques which is NOT conducive to the establishment of an effective working relationship between employees and supervisors is   3.____

  A. periodic discussion of job performance with employees
  B. listening to employees when they discuss their job difficulties
  C. observation of employees on the job, in both individual and group situations, in order to help them with job performance
  D. treating all employees the same with respect to job performance and individual behavior

4. Which of the following is a valid, commonly-raised objection to the establishment of work standards for office clerical workers?   4.____

  A. Routine clerical work is not subject to accurate measurement.
  B. Clerical work standards can only lower employee morale by creating undue pressure to produce work rapidly.
  C. Work standards are not effective tools for planning, scheduling, and routing clerical work.
  D. Some phases of many clerical jobs, such as telephone answering or information gathering, cannot be readily or accurately measured.

5. Of the following, the feature which is LEAST characteristic of almost all successful staff relationships with line managers is that the staff employee   5.____

  A. is primarily a representative of his supervisor
  B. receives a salary at least equal to the average salary of his supervisor's direct line subordinates
  C. relies largely on persuasion to get his ideas put into effect
  D. is prepared to submerge his own personality and his own desire for recognition and see others often receive more recognition than he receives

6. The one of the following systems which has, as its principal objective, the storage of items in files so that they may be readily found when needed is called
    A. information retrieval
    B. simulation
    C. critical path
    D. PERT

    6.____

7. A detailed description of the steps to be taken in order to accomplish a job is MOST appropriately called a

    A. policy
    B. rule
    C. procedure
    D. principle

    7.____

8. In choosing the best place in the executive hierarchy to which to assign the task of making a certain type of decision, which one of the following questions should normally be LEAST important?

    A. Who knows the facts on which the decision will be based, or who can obtain them most readily?
    B. Who has the most adequate supply of current forms on which the decision is normally recorded?
    C. Who has the capacity to make sound decisions?
    D. How significant is the decision?

    8.____

9. Of the following, the action which is LEAST likely to be either expressed or implied every time a manager delegates work to a subordinate is that the manager

    A. creates a need for a new class of positions
    B. indicates what work the subordinate is to do
    C. grants the subordinate some authority
    D. creates an obligation for the subordinate who accepts the work to try to complete it

    9.____

10. Of the following, the LEAST appropriate use of organizational charts is to

    A. depict standard operating procedures
    B. indicate lines of responsibility
    C. indicate the relative level of key positions
    D. portray organizations graphically

    10.____

11. The one of the following considerations which is generally LEAST important in deciding whether to automate a management operation by using a computer is whether the computer

    A. possesses a suitable array of programmed actions that might be taken
    B. can draw upon available data for information as to which alternative is best
    C. is already familiar to the staff of the organization
    D. can issue findings in a way that will facilitate the decision-making process

    11.____

12. In evaluating a proposal to establish a library in your agency, it is generally considered LEAST necessary to determine

    A. the average time staff members spend on preparatory research when assigned to projects
    B. how often junior professional and technical staff members are sent out to *look something up* in a local library

    12.____

C. how much time and money agency executives devote to telephoning around the country seeking information before making decisions

D. the quality of the research done by executives and scientists in the agency

13. In determining the number and type of tasks that should be combined into a single job, the one of the following which is normally the LEAST useful factor to consider is the

13.____

A. benefit of functional specialization
B. benefit of tall pyramid organization structures in increasing decentralization
C. need for coordination of tasks with each other
D. effect of the tasks assigned on the morale of the employee

14. Of the following, the one which is LEAST likely to be an objective of systems and procedures analysis is to

14.____

A. eliminate as many unessential forms and records as feasible
B. simplify forms in content and method of preparation
C. mechanize repetitive, routine tasks
D. expand as many of the forms as possible

15. A specific managerial function encompasses all of the following: the establishment of an intentional structure of roles through determination and enumeration of the activities required to achieve the goals of an enterprise and each part of it, the grouping of these activities, the assignment of such groups of activities to a manager, the delegation of authority to carry them out, and provision for coordination of authority and informational relationships horizontally and vertically in the organization structure.
Of the following, the MOST appropriate term for this entire managerial function is

15.____

A. organizing
B. directing
C. controlling
D. staffing

16. The optimum number of subordinates that a supervisor can supervise effectively generally tends to vary INVERSELY with the

16.____

A. percentage of the supervisor's time devoted to supervision rather than operations
B. repetition of activities
C. degree of centralization of decision-making within the supervisor's unit
D. ability of subordinates

17. Under certain circumstances, a top manager may desire to strengthen the position of his staff people by granting them concurring authority, so that no action may be taken in a functional area by subordinate line officials until a designated staff employee agrees to the action. For example, office managers may have to get the approval of the agency personnel officer before hiring a new employee. This approach is likely to be MOST valid under which one of the following conditions?

17.____

A. The top manager refrains from indicating the grounds on which the staff employee may grant or withhold his approval of line proposals.
B. The point of view represented by the staff employee is particularly important, and the possible delay in action will not be serious.
C. It is more important to fix specific accountability for failure to take appropriate action than for wrong actions taken.
D. The top manager gives speed priority over prudence.

18. The inclusion of the *reason why* by a superior in his written orders to his subordinates normally is MOST likely to

18._____

    A. encourage belief by the subordinates in the meaning and intent of the order
    B. be a waste of valuable time for both superior and subordinates
    C. be useful principally where the superior has no power to enforce the order
    D. discourage effective two-way communication between superior and subordinates

19. The one of the following which is generally the BEST justification for an administrator's search for alternative methods of attaining a given objective of the unit he heads is that such-search

19._____

    A. always turns up a better method of attaining objectives than that currently in use
    B. helps to make certain that the best method has a chance to be found and evaluated
    C. helps to insure that his peers realize that the existing method of attaining the objective is not the best
    D. is a good way to train the unit's staff in the organization's operational procedures

20. *Managing-by-Objectives* tends to place PRINCIPAL emphasis upon which of the following?

20._____

    A. Use of primarily qualitative goals at all management levels
    B. Use of trait-appraisal systems based upon personality factors
    C. Use of primarily qualitative goals at lower management levels as contrasted with primarily quantitative goals at higher management levels
    D. Goals which are clear and verifiable

21. Which one of the following BEST identifies the two most important considerations which generally should determine the degree of management decentralization desirable in a given situation?
The

21._____

    A. age of the subordinate executives to whom decisions may be delegated and the number of courses in management that they have completed
    B. number of skills and the competence possessed by subordinate executives and the distribution of the necessary information to the points of decision
    C. ratio of the salary of the superior executives to the salary of the subordinate executives and the number of titles on the executive staff
    D. number of titles in the executive staff and the distribution of information to those various titles

22. Which one of the following is generally LEAST likely to occur at mid-level management as a result of installing an electronic data processing system?

22._____

    A. The time that managers will be required to spend on the controlling function will increase.
    B. The number of contacts that managers will have with subordinates will increase.
    C. Additional time will be needed to train people for managerial positions.
    D. There will be an increase in the volume of information presented to managers for analysis.

23. The concept that the major source of managerial authority is derived from the subordinate's acceptance of the manager's power is MOST closely identified with 23.____

    A. Luther Gulick   B. John D. Mooney
    C. Frederick W. Taylor   D. Chester I. Barnard

24. The one of the following which is generally the principal objection to a pure *functional organization,* as compared with a pure *line organization,* is that 24.____

    A. there is a tendency to overload intermediate and supervisory management at each succeeding level of organization with wide and varied duties
    B. authority flows in an unbroken line from top management to the worker
    C. workers must often report to two or more supervisors
    D. there is a lack of specialization at the supervisory level

25. The appraisal of subordinates and their performance is an integral part of the supervisor's job. There is wide agreement that several basic principles must be taken into account by supervisors involved in the appraisal process in order to perform this function correctly. The one of the statements below which LEAST represents a basic principle of the appraisal process is:
Appraisal(s) 25.____

    A. should be based more on performance of definite tasks than on personality considerations
    B. of long-range potential should rely most heavily on subjective judgment of that potential
    C. involves the use of value judgments by the supervisor and does, therefore, require reference to pre-established standards
    D. should aim at emphasizing subordinates' strengths rather than weaknesses

26. Of the following, the INITIAL step in the decision-making procedure normally is 26.____

    A. evaluation of alternatives
    B. implementing the chosen course of action
    C. listing potential solutions
    D. diagnosis and problem definition

27. Management textbooks are LEAST likely to define coordination as 27.____

    A. a concern for harmonious and unified action directed toward a common objective
    B. the essence of management, since the basic purpose of management is the achievement of harmony of individual effort toward the accomplishment of group goals
    C. the orderly arrangement of group effort to provide unity of action in pursuit of common purpose
    D. the transmittal of messages from senders to receivers, involving acts of persuasion of regulation, or simply the rendering of information

28. A number of important assumptions underlie the modern human relations approach to management and administration. The one of the following which is NOT an assumption integral to the human relations school of thought is that

    A. employee participation is essential to higher productivity
    B. employees are motivated solely by monetary factors
    C. teamwork is indispensable for organization growth and survival
    D. free-flow communications must be established and maintained for organizational effectiveness

28.____

29. Of the following, the MAIN purpose of systematic manpower planning is to

    A. analyze the levels of skill needed by each worker
    B. analyze causes of current vacancies, such as resignations, discharges, retirements, transfers, or promotions
    C. save money by eliminating useless jobs
    D. provide for the continuous and proper staffing of the workforce

29.____

30. A Planning-Programming-Budget System (PPBS) is PRIMARILY intended to do which of the following?

    A. Improve control through a budgeting-by-line-item system
    B. Plan and program budgets by objective rather than by function
    C. Raise money for social welfare programs
    D. Reduce budgets by planning and programming unspent funds

30.____

_____

KEY (CORRECT ANSWERS)

1.	D	11.	C	21.	B
2.	C	12.	D	22.	A
3.	D	13.	B	23.	D
4.	D	14.	D	24.	C
5.	B	15.	A	25.	B
6.	A	16.	C	26.	D
7.	C	17.	B	27.	D
8.	B	18.	A	28.	B
9.	A	19.	B	29.	D
10.	A	20.	D	30.	B

_____

TEST 2

Each question or incomplete statements is followed by several suggested answers or completions. Select the one that BEST answers the question or completes the statement. *PRINT THE LETTER OF THE CORRECT ANSWER IN THE SPACE AT THE RIGHT.*

1. The one of the following which is a basic advantage of microform record system (e.g., microfilm, microfiche) over a conventional filing system is that a microform system

    A. provides a compact method of grouping and systematizing records
    B. provides records which are immediately available without special equipment
    C. eliminates the need for specially trained personnel
    D. eliminates entirely the inadvertent loss of records

1.____

2. In the planning of office space for the various bureaus and divisions of an agency, the one of the following arrangements which is generally considered to be MOST desirable in a conventional layout is to

    A. locate offices where employees do close and tedious work, such as accounting, and also offices of high-level executives away from windows so that distractions will be minimal
    B. locate *housekeeping* offices such as data processing and the mailroom very close to the high executive offices to increase convenience for the executives
    C. locate departments so that the work flow proceeds in an uninterrupted manner
    D. centralize the executive suite for maximum availability and public exposure

2.____

3. Generally, the one of the following that is LEAST likely to be an essential step in a records retention plan is

    A. storing inactive records
    B. checking for accuracy of all records to be retained
    C. classification of all records
    D. making an inventory of all agency records

3.____

4. The PRINCIPAL asset of an office layout diagram, as contrasted with the more abstract organization charts and flowcharts, is that an office layout diagram is

    A. more readily adaptable to strictly conceptual studies
    B. pictorial and therefore easier to understand
    C. suitable for showing both manual and machine processing operations, whereas organization charts and flowcharts may only be used for manual processing operations
    D. better suited for summarizing the number of work units produced at each step

4.____

5. One of the assistants whom you supervise displays apparent familiarity toward a businessman who deals with your agency. This assistant spends more time with this person than the nature of his business would warrant, and you have observed that they are occasionally seen leaving the office together for lunch. In several instances, when this businessman comes into the office and this assistant is not at his desk, the businessman will not deal with any other staff member but will, instead, leave the office and return later when that particular employee is available.
Of the following courses of action, the FIRST one you should take is to

5.____

A. audit the agency's books and records pertaining to this businessman
B. rebuke the assistant for unprofessional conduct at the next staff meeting and warn him of disciplinary action if the practice is not discontinued forthwith
C. advise your agency head of the action by the businessman and the assistant that has been described in the above paragraph
D. reassign the assistant to duties that will not bring him into contact with any businessman

6. The one of the following factors which generally is the BEST justification for keeping higher inventories of supplies and equipment is an expected

    A. decline in demand
    B. price increase
    C. decline in prices
    D. increase in interest charges and storage costs

7. Statistical sampling is often used in administrative operations PRIMARILY because it enables

    A. administrators to determine the characteristics of appointed or elected officials
    B. decisions to be made based on mathematical and scientific fact
    C. courses of action to be determined by scientifically-based computer programs
    D. useful predictions to be made from relatively small samples

8. According to United States Department of Labor figures, the PRINCIPAL source of disabling injuries to office workers is

    A. flying objects and falling objects
    B. striking against equipment
    C. falls and slips
    D. handling materials

9. To expedite the processing of applications issued by your agency, you ask your assistant to design a form that will be used by your typists. After several discussions, he presents you with a draft that requires the typist to use 23 tabular-stop positions.
Such a form would PROBABLY be considered

    A. *undesirable;* typists would now have to soft-roll the platen to make the typing fall on the lines
    B. *desirable;* the fill-in operation by typists would be speeded up
    C. *undesirable;* proper vertical alignment of data would be made difficult by the number of tabular-stop positions required
    D. *desirable;* it would force the typists to utilize the tabular-stop device

Question 10.

DIRECTIONS: Following are five general instructions to file clerks which might appear in the proposed filing manual for an agency:

1. *Follow instructions generally; if you have a suggestion for improvement in the filing methods, install it after notifying the file supervisor who will duly authorize a change in the manual.*

2. *You may discuss the contents of files with fellow employees or outsiders, but do NOT give papers from the file to any person whose duties have no relation to the material requested.*

3. *All special instructions must be given by the file supervisor. Any problems that arise outside the regular routine of filing must be decided by the file supervisor, not by a fellow clerk.*

4. *You will not be held responsible for your own errors; thus, refrain from asking other workers for instructions. No one is more interested in helping you in your training than your file supervisor.*

5. *Speed is the first essential in filing; make it your primary consideration - quick finding of filed material is the real test of your efficiency.*

10. Which of the choices listed below BEST identifies those of the above statements that should or should not be followed by agencies in the functioning of their filing sections? Instruction(s) _____ should be followed; instructions _____ should not be followed.

    A. 1, 2, 3; 4, 5   B. 3; 1, 2, 4, 5
    C. 2, 4; 1, 3, 5   D. 1, 3; 2, 4, 5

10.____

11. Listed below are five steps in the process of staffing:
    I.   Authorization for staffing
    II.   Manpower planning
    III. Development of applicant sources
    IV. Evaluation of applicants
    V.   Employment decisions and offers

The one of the following sequences which is generally the MOST logical arrangement of the above steps is:

    A. I, II, III, IV, V   B. II, I, III, IV, V
    C. III, I, II, IV, V   D. II, III, I, IV, V

11.____

12. Job enrichment is LEAST likely to lead to

    A. fewer employee grievances
    B. increased employee productivity
    C. people acting as adjuncts of increased automation
    D. increased employee morale

12.____

13. Of the following, programmed instruction would usually be MOST effective in teaching

    A. principles of decision-making
    B. technical skills and knowledge
    C. good judgment
    D. executive management ability

13.____

14. Assume that a group has been working effectively with a contributing nonconformist in its midst.

The BEST of the following reasons for the group to retain the nonconformist *generally* is that

    A. nonconformists stimulate groups to think
    B. he may be their boss some day
    C. nonconformists usually are fun to work with
    D. another nonconformist will usurp his role

14.____

15. The *grievance-arbitration* process involves systematic union-management deliberation regarding a complaint that is work-or contract-related. An outcome that does NOT result from this process is

    A. a communications channel from the rank-and-file workers to higher management is developed or improved
    B. the contract is immediately changed to provide justice for both parties
    C. both labor and management identify those parts of the contract that need to be clarified and modified in subsequent negotiations
    D. the language of the agreement is informally translated into understandable terms for the parties bound by it

16. In government, job evaluation is the process of determining the relative worth of the various jobs in an organization so that differential wages can be paid. Job evaluation is based on several basic assumptions.
Of the assumptions listed below, the MOST questionable is that

    A. the cash payments in government should be substantially higher than those in local private industry
    B. it is logical to pay the most for jobs that contribute most to the organization
    C. people feel more fairly treated if wages are based on the relative worth of their jobs
    D. the best way to achieve the goals of the enterprise is to maintain a wage structure based on job worth

17. Of the following, the training method that normally provides the instructor with the LEAST *feedback* from the trainees is

    A. the lecture method
    B. the conference method
    C. simulation or gaming techniques
    D. seminar instruction

18. Insufficient and inappropriate delegation of work assignments is MOST often the fault of

    A. subordinates who are unwilling to accept responsibility for their own mistakes
    B. a paternal attitude on the part of management
    C. the immediate supervisor
    D. subordinates who are too willing to take on extra responsibility

19. As contrasted with expense budgets, capital budgets are MORE likely to

    A. be used for construction of physical facilities
    B. be designed for a shorter time period
    C. include personal service expenditures
    D. include fringe benefits

20. During the first quarter of a year, a division's production rate was 1.26 man-hours per work unit produced. For the second quarter of that year, all other factors (e.g., size of staff, character of work unit, etc.) remained constant, except that the manner of reporting production rate was changed to work units per man-hour instead of man-hours per work unit. During that second quarter, the unit's production rate was .89 work units per man-hour.

On the basis of the above information, it would be MOST NEARLY CORRECT to conclude that the division's production rate during the second quarter was *approximately* _____ than during the first quarter.

A. 30% lower
C. 10% higher

B. 10% lower
D. 30% higher

Questions 21-22.

DIRECTIONS: Answer Questions 21 and 22 on the basis of the following information.

The five bureaus within a department sent the following budget requests to the department head:

> Bureau A - $10 million
> Bureau B - $12 million
> Bureau C - $18 million
> Bureau D - $6 million
> Bureau E - $4 million

After reviewing all of these requests, the department head decided to reduce these requests so that they would total only $40 million. He considered the following two options to accomplish this:

Option I- Reduce the requests of Bureaus A, B, and D by an equal dollar amount. Reduce the dollar amount request of Bureau C by 2 ½ times the dollar amount that he reduces the request of Bureau B. Reduce the dollar amount request of Bureau E by 1/2 of the dollar amount that he reduces the request of Bureau B.

Option II- First, reduce the dollar amount request of all five bureaus by 15%. Then, the remaining reduction required by the entire department would be achieved by further reducing the resulting budget requests of Bureaus B and C by an equal dollar amount each.

21. Under Option I, the dollar amount request for Bureau E, after reduction by the department head, would be MOST NEARLY _____ millions.   21.____

A. $1 2/3   B. $2 1/3   C. $3 1/6   D. $3 1/2

22. Under Option II, the dollar amount of the request of Bureau B, after both reductions were made by the department head, would be MOST NEARLY _____ millions.   22.____

A. $8   B. $9   C. $10   D. $11

23. The Summary of finding of a long management report intended for typical manager Should generally appear   23.____
    A. at the very beginning of the report
    B. at the end of the report
    C. throughout the report
    D. in the middle of the report

24. Of the following, the BIGGEST disadvantage in allowing a free flow of communications in an agency is that such a free flow   24.____

    A. decreases creativity
    B. increases the use of the *grapevine*
    C. lengthens the chain of command
    D. reduces the executive's power to direct the flow of information

25. A downward flow of authority in an organization is one example of _____ communications.   25.___

    A. horizontal   B. informal
    C. circular   D. vertical

26. Workers who belong to a cohesive group are generally thought to   26.___

    A. have more job-related anxieties than those who do not
    B. be less well-adjusted than those who do not
    C. derive little satisfaction from the group
    D. conform to group norms more closely than those in noncohesive groups

27. The one of the following which BEST exemplifies negative motivation is   27.___

    A. a feeling on the part of the worker that the work is significant
    B. monetary rewards offered the worker for high levels of output
    C. reducing or withholding the worker's incentive rewards when performance is mediocre
    D. nonmonetary rewards given the worker, such as publicizing a good suggestion

28. Of the following, the one that would be MOST likely to block effective communication is   28.___

    A. concentration only on the issues at hand
    B. lack of interest or commitment
    C. use of written reports
    D. use of charts and graphs

29. Many functions formerly centralized in a department of personnel have been decentralized, in whole or in part, to operating agencies.   29.___
The one of the following personnel functions which has been LEAST decentralized is

    A. position evaluation
    B. investigation of non-competitive employees
    C. investigation of competitive employees
    D. jurisdictional classification

30. In making a position analysis for a duties classification, the one of the following factors which MUST be considered is the _____the incumbent.   30.___

    A. capabilities of
    B. qualifications of
    C. efficiency attained by
    D. responsibility assigned to

_____

KEY (CORRECT ANSWERS)

1.	A	11.	B	21.	C
2.	C	12.	C	22.	B
3.	B	13.	B	23.	A
4.	B	14.	A	24.	D
5.	C	15.	B	25.	D
6.	B	16.	A	26.	D
7.	D	17.	A	27.	C
8.	C	18.	C	28.	B
9.	C	19.	A	29.	D
10.	B	20.	C	30.	D

EXAMINATION SECTION
TEST 1

DIRECTIONS: Each question or incomplete statement is followed by several suggested answers or completions. Select the one that BEST answers the question or completes the statement. *PRINT THE LETTER OF THE CORRECT ANSWER IN THE SPACE AT THE RIGHT.*

1. The PRIMARY purpose of program analysis as it is used in government is to

    A. replace political judgments with rational programs and policies
    B. help decision-makers to sharpen their judgments about program choices
    C. analyze the impact of past programs on the quality of public services
    D. reduce costs by eliminating waste in public programs and services

1.____

2. While there is no complete method for program analysis that is agreed to by all the experts and is relevant to all types of problems, the MOST important element in program analysis involves the

    A. development of alternatives and the definition of objectives or criteria
    B. collection of information and the construction of a mathematical model
    C. design of experiments and procedures to validate results
    D. collection of expert opinion and the combination of their views

2.____

3. Electronic data processing is a particularly valuable tool of analysis in situations where the analyst has a processing problem involving

    A. *small* input, *few* operations, and *small* output
    B. *large* input, *many* operations, and *small* output
    C. *large* input, *few* operations, and *large* output
    D. *small* input, *many* operations, and *small* output

3.____

4. In order for an analyst to use electronic data processing to solve an analytic problem, the problem must be clearly defined.
The BEST way to prepare material for such definition in electronic data processing is to

    A. discuss the problem with computer programmers in a meeting
    B. prepare a flow diagram outlining the steps in the analysis
    C. write a memorandum with a list of the relevant program issues
    D. write a computer program using FORTRAN, BASIC, or another language

4.____

5. The "growth rate" referred to in current political and economic discussion refers to change from year to year in a country's

    A. investments   B. population
    C. gross national product   D. sale of goods

5.____

6. Interactive or conversational programming is important to the program analyst ESPECIALLY for

    A. preparing analyses leading to management information systems
    B. communicating among analysts in different places

6.____

C. using canned programs in statistical analysis
D. testing trial solutions in rapid sequence

7. Program analysis often calls for recommendation of a choice between competing pro-   7.___
    gram possibilities that differ in the timing of major costs.
    Analysts using the present value technique by setting an interest or discount rate are
    in effect arguing that, other things being equal,

    A. it is inadvisable to defer the start of projects because of rising costs
    B. projects should be completed within a short time period to save money
    C. expenditures should be made out of tax revenues to avoid payment of interest
    D. postponing expenditures is advantageous at some measurable rate

8. Of the following, the formula which is MOST appropriately used to estimate the net need   8.___
    for a given type of service is that net need equals

    A. current clients - anticipated losses + anticipated gains

    B. $\dfrac{\text{current supply}}{\text{Standard}} + \text{current clients}$

    C. (client population x standard) - current supply
    D. current supply - anticipated losses + anticipated gains

9. The purpose of feasibility analysis is to protect the analyst from naive alternatives and,   9.___
    MOST generally, to

    A. identify and quantify technological constraints
    B. carry out a preliminary stage of analysis
    C. anticipate potential blocks to implementation
    D. line up the support of political leadership

Questions 10-11.

DIRECTIONS: Answer Questions 10 and 11 on the basis of the following chart. In a hypothet-
              ical problem involving four criteria and four alternatives, the following data have
              been assembled.

Cost Criterion	Effectiveness Criterion		Timing Criterion		Feasibility Criterion
Alternative					probably
A $500,000	50	units	3	months	feasible
Alternative					probably
B $300,000	100	units	6	months	feasible
Alternative					probably
C $400,000	50	units	12	months	infeasible
Alternative					probably
D $200,000	75	units	3	months	infeasible

10. On the basis of the above data, it appears that the one alternative which is dominated by   10.___
     another alternative is Alternative

     A. A   B. B   C. C   D. D

11. If the feasibility constraint is absolute and fixed, then the critical trade-off is between   11.____

    A. lower cost on the one hand and faster timing and higher effectiveness on the other
    B. lower cost and higher effectiveness on one hand and faster timing on the other
    C. lower cost and faster timing on the one hand and higher effectiveness on the other
    D. lower cost on the one hand and higher effectiveness on the other

12. A classification of an agency's activities in a program structure is MOST useful if it high-   12.____
lights

    A. trade-offs that might not otherwise be considered
    B. ways to improve the efficiency of each activity
    C. the true organizational structure of an agency
    D. bases for insuring that expenditures stay within limits

13. CPM, like PERT, is a useful tool for scheduling large-scale, complex processes.   13.____
In CPM, the critical path is the

    A. path composed of important links
    B. path composed of uncertain links
    C. longest path through the network
    D. shortest path through the network

14. Classical evaluative research calls for the use of control groups. However, there are prac-   14.____
tical difficulties in collecting data on individuals to be used as "controls" in program evalu-
ations.
Researchers may attempt to overcome these difficulties by

    A. using control groups that have no choice such as prison inmates or inmates of
other public institutions or facilities
    B. developing better measures of the inputs, processes, and outputs relevant to public
programs and services
    C. using experimental demonstration projects with participants in the different projects
serving as comparison groups for one another
    D. abandoning attempts at formal evaluation in favor of more qualitative approaches
employing a journalistic style of analysis

15. During the course of an analysis of the remaining "life" of a certain city's landfill for refuse   15.____
disposal, there was a great deal of debate about the impact of changing rates of garbage
generation on the amount of landfill needed and about what rates of garbage generation
to expect over the next decade.
Faced with the need to attempt to resolve this debate, an analyst would construct a
simple model of the refuse disposal system and

    A. project landfill needs without considering refuse generation in the future
    B. conduct a detailed household survey in order to estimate future garbage genera-
tion rates
    C. ask the experts to continue to debate the issue until the argument is won by one
view
    D. do a sensitivity analysis to test the impact of alternative assumptions about refuse
generation

16. The limitations of traditional surveys have fostered the development and use of panels. A panel is a

    A. group of respondents that serves as a continuous source of survey information
    B. group of advisors expert in the design and implementation of surveys
    C. representative sample of respondents at a single point in time
    D. post-survey discussion group composed of former respondents

16.___

17. The difference between sensitivity analysis and risk analysis is that risk analysis

    A. is applicable only to profit and loss situations where the concept of risk is operable
    B. includes an estimate of probabilities of different values of input factors
    C. is applicable to physical problems while sensitivity analysis is applicable to social ones
    D. requires a computer simulation while sensitivity analysis does not

17.___

18. A decision tree, although initially applied to business problems, is a graphic device which is useful to public analysts in

    A. scheduling complex processes
    B. doing long-range forecasting
    C. formulating the structure of alternatives
    D. solving production-inventory problems

18.___

19. The purpose of a management information system in an agency is to

    A. structure data relevant to managerial decision-making
    B. put all of an agency's data in machine-processing form
    C. simplify the record-keeping operations in an agency
    D. keep an ongoing record of management's activities

19.___

20. Assume that an analyst is presented with the following chart for a fire department and supplied also with information indicating a stable size firefighting staff over this time period.

20.___

The analyst could REASONABLY conclude regarding productivity that
    A. productivity over this time period was essentially stable for this firefighting force because the number of responses to real fires during this period was stable, as was the work force
    B. productivity was essentially increasing for this force because the number of total responses was increasing relative to a stable force
    C. productivity was declining because a greater proportion of the total work effort was wasted effort in responding to false alarms
    D. it is impossible to make a judgment about the productivity of the firefighting staff without a judgment about the value of a response to a false alarm

21. In the design of a productivity program for the sanitation department, the BEST measure   21._____
    of productivity would be

    A. tons of refuse collected annually
    B. number of collections made per week
    C. tons of refuse collected per truck shift
    D. number of trucks used per shift

22. The cohort-survival method for estimating future population has been widely employed.   22._____
    In this method,

    A. migration is assumed to be constant over time
    B. net migration within cohorts is assumed to be zero
    C. migration is included as a multiplier factor
    D. net migration within cohorts is assumed to be constant

23. Cost-effectiveness and cost-benefit analysis represent a systematic approach to balanc-   23._____
    ing potential losses against potential gains as a prelude to public action.
    In addition to limitations based on difficulties of measurement and inadequacies in
    data that are typical of systematic program analysis, cost-benefit analysis suffers from
    a serious conceptual flaw in that

    A. the definition of benefit or cost does not typically distinguish to whom benefits or
       costs accrue
    B. a full-scale cost benefit analysis takes too long to do, is too expensive, and needs
       too much data
    C. it has been shown that such analyses are more suitable for defense or water
       resources problems
    D. such analyses are not useful in any problem involving capital and operating costs
       or benefits

24. If you were asked to develop a total cost estimate for one year for a program involving   24._____
    both a capital improvement and operating costs, the BEST way to estimate the capital
    cost component would be to

    A. divide the estimated cost of the capital improvement by the projected operating
       costs over the life of the improvement
    B. multiply the annual operating cost by the projected life of the capital improvement
    C. divide the amortized cost of the capital improvement by the projected life of the
       improvement
    D. multiply the portion of the capital improvement to be completed within the year by
       the cost of the improvement

25. In comparing the costs of two or more alternative programs, it is important to consider all   25._____
    relevant costs.
    The MOST important principle in defining "relevant cost" is that

    A. only marginal or incremental cost should be considered in the estimate
    B. only recurring costs should be considered for each alternative
    C. estimates should include the sunk costs for each alternative
    D. cost estimates need to be as precise as in budget preparation

26. Different techniques for projecting future costs may be suitable in different situations. Assume that it is necessary to estimate the future costs of maintaining garbage collection vehicles.
Under which of the following conditions would it be advisable to develop a cost-estimating equation rather than to use unadjusted current data?

    A. When it is expected that more complex equipment will replace simpler equipment
    B. Whether or not it is expected that the nature of future garbage collection will change
    C. When the current unadjusted data still has to be verified
    D. When the nature of future garbage collection equipment is unknown

26.___

27. The following data has been collected on the costs of two pilot programs, each representing a different approach to the same problem.

	Total cost	Fixed cost	Variable cost	Average unit cost	Number of users
Program A	$45,000	$20,000	$50 per user	$90 per user	500
Program B	$42,000	$ 7,000	$100 per user	$120 per user	350

Assume that the pilot programs are extended city-wide and other factors are constant. Using the above data, what would a cost analyst conclude about the relative costs of the two programs? Program

    A. B would be less costly with fewer than 300 users and Program A would be less costly with more than 300 users
    B. B would be less costly with fewer than 260 users and Program A would be less costly with more than 260 users
    C. A would be less costly without regard to the size of the program
    D. B would be less costly without regard to the size of the program

27.___

Questions 28-30.

DIRECTIONS: Answer Questions 28 through 30 on the basis of the following data assembled for a cost-benefit analysis.

	Cost	Benefit
No program	0	0
Alternative W	$ 3,000	$ 6,000
Alternative X	$10,000	$17,000
Alternative Y	$17,000	$25,000
Alternative Z	$30,000	$32,000

28. From the point of view of pushing public expenditure to the point where marginal benefit equals or exceeds marginal cost, the BEST alternative is Alternative

    A. W   B. X   C. Y   D. Z

28.___

29. From the point of view of selecting the alternative with the best cost-benefit ratio, the BEST alternative is Alternative.

    A. W   B. X   C. Y   D. Z

29.___

30. From the point of view of selecting the alternative with the best measure of net benefit, the BEST alternative is Alternative

    A. W   B. X   C. Y   D. Z

30.___

Questions 31-35.

DIRECTIONS: The set of answers listed below applies to Questions 31 through 35. Each
answer is a type of statistical test.
A. Analysis of variance
B. Pearson Product-Moment Correlation (r)
C. t-test
D. x^2 test (Chi-squared)

Pick the test which is MOST appropriate to the situation described. An answer
may be used more than once.

31.   A comparison between two correlated means obtained from a small sample.   31._____
The CORRECT answer is:

A.   B.   C.   D.

32.   A comparison of three or more means.   32._____
The CORRECT answer is:

A.   B.   C.   D.

33.   A comparison of the divergence of observed frequencies with those expected on the   33._____
hypothesis of equal probability of occurrence.
The CORRECT answer is:

A.   B.   C.   D.

34.   A comparison of the divergence of observed frequencies with those expected on the   34._____
hypothesis of a normal distribution.
The CORRECT answer is:

A.   B.   C.   D.

35.   A comparison between two uncorrelated means obtained from small samples.   35._____
The CORRECT answer is:

A.   B.   C.   D.

36.   There are many different models for evaluative research.   36._____
A time-series design is an example of a _____ experimental design.

A.   field   B.   true   C.   quasi-   D.   pre-

37.   In policy research, as in all kinds of research, it is important to develop research hypoth-   37._____
eses early.
The MAIN purpose of a research hypothesis is to

A.   include the kind of statistical procedures to be used in the research
B.   provide a ready answer in case data is not available for doing research
C.   serve as a guide to the kind of data that must be collected in order to answer the
research question
D.   clarify what is known and what is not known in the research problem

38. While descriptive and causal research are not completely separable, there has been a distinct effort to move in the direction of causal research.
Such an effort is epitomized by the use of

    A. predictive models and measures of deviation from predictions
    B. option and attitudinal surveys in local neighborhoods
    C. community studies and area profiles of localities
    D. individual case histories and group case studies

38.___

39. The one of the following which BEST describes a periodic report is that it

    A. provides a record of accomplishments for a given time span and a comparison with similar time spans in the past
    B. covers the progress made in a project that has been postponed
    C. integrates, summarizes, and perhaps interprets published data on technical or scientific material
    D. describes a decision, advocates a policy or action, and presents facts in support of the writer's position

39.___

40. The PRIMARY purpose of including pictorial illustrations in a formal report is usually to

    A. amplify information which has been adequately treated verbally
    B. present details that are difficult to describe verbally
    C. provide the reader with a pleasant, momentary distraction
    D. present supplementary information incidental to the main ideas developed in the report.

40.___

KEY (CORRECT ANSWERS)

1.	B	11.	B	21.	C	31.	C
2.	A	12.	A	22.	B	32.	A
3.	B	13.	C	23.	A	33.	D
4.	B	14.	C	24.	C	34.	D
5.	C	15.	D	25.	A	35.	C
6.	D	16.	A	26.	A	36.	C
7.	D	17.	B	27.	B	37.	C
8.	C	18.	C	28.	C	38.	A
9.	C	19.	A	29.	A	39.	A
10.	C	20.	D	30.	C	40.	B

TEST 2

1. A measurement procedure is considered to be RELIABLE to the extent that   1.____

   A. independent applications under similar conditions yield consistent results
   B. independent applications under different conditions yield similar results
   C. scores reflect true differences among individuals or situations
   D. scores reflect true differences in the same individual over time

2. Different scales of measurement are distinguished by the feasibility of various empirical   2.____
   operations.
   An ordinal scale of measurement

   A. is not as useful as a ratio or interval scale
   B. is useful in rank-ordering or priority setting
   C. provides the data for addition or subtraction
   D. provides the data for computation of means

3. A widely used approach to sampling is systematic sampling, i.e., selecting every Kth ele-   3.____
   ment in a listing.
   Even with a random start, a DISADVANTAGE in this approach is that

   A. the listing used may contain a cyclical pattern
   B. it is too similar to a simple random sample
   C. the system does not insure a probability sample
   D. it yields an unpredictable sample size

4. A rule of thumb sometimes used in sample size selection is to set sample size equal to   4.____
   five percent of the population size. Other things being equal, this rule

   A. tends to oversample small populations
   B. tends to oversample large populations
   C. provides an accurate rule for sampling
   D. is a relatively inexpensive basis for sampling

5. With regard to a stratified random sample, it may be APPROPRIATE to sample the vari-   5.____
   ous strata in different proportions in order to

   A. approximate the characteristics of a true random sample
   B. establish classes that are internally heterogenous in each case
   C. avoid the necessity of subdividing the cases within each stratum
   D. adequately cover important strata that have small numbers of cases

6. One possible response to the "unknown" or "no answer" category in a tabulation of sur-   6.____
   vey information is to "allocate" the unknown responses, i.e., to estimate the missing data
   on the basis of other known information about the respondents.
   This technique is APPROPRIATE when the unknown category

A.   is very small and is randomly distributed within all subgroups of respondents
B.   is very large and is randomly distributed within all subgroups of respondents
C.   reflects an interviewing failure and a subgroup in the sample tends to produce more unknowns
D.   is a legitimate category and a subgroup in the sample tends to produce more unknowns

7.   In presenting cross-tabulated data showing the relation ship between two variables, it is MOST meaningful to compute percentages   7.____

A.   in both directions in all instances
B.   of each cell in relation to the grand total
C.   in the direction of the smaller number of cells
D.   in the direction of the causal factor

8.   In portraying data based on a sampling operation, it is MOST meaningful and comprehensible to the reader to present   8.____

A.   percentages for the sample and the universe
B.   percentages by themselves
C.   percentages and the base figures
D.   numbers by themselves

9.   A new bridge spanning a river is expected to carry 60,000 cars a day on a rainy day and 80,000 cars a day on other kinds of days.
If there is a $5 toll and one chance in four of a rainy day, the expected value of a day's revenue is   9.____

A. $175,000   B. $375,000   C. $475,000   D. $700,000

10.   The analyst who is asked to estimate the probability of a relatively rare event occurring cannot use the classical frequency measures of probability but rather should   10.____

A.   use a random-numbers table to pick a probability
B.   project historical data into the future
C.   indicate that no probabilistic judgment is possible
D.   make the best possible judgment as to the subjective probability

11.   A useful source of census data for computing annual indicators is the   11.____

A.   Public Use Sample   B.   Continuing Population Survey
C.   Census of Population   D.   Census of Governments

12.   An analyst presented with a set of household records showing age, ethnicity, income, and family status and wishing to study the inter-relationship of all of these variables simultaneously will probably request   12.____

A.   one four-way cross-tabulation
B.   four three-way cross-tabulations
C.   six two-way cross-tabulations
D.   four single tabulations

13. Downward communication, from high management to lower levels in an organization, will often not be fully accepted at the lowest levels of an organization unless high-level management

    13._____

   A. communicates through several levels of mid-level management, where the message can be properly modified and interpreted
   B. communicates directly with the level of the organization it wishes to reach, bypassing any intermediate levels
   C. first establishes an atmosphere in which upward communication is encouraged and listened to
   D. establishes penalties for non-compliance with its communications

14. A top-level manager sometimes has an inaccurate view of the actual lower-level operations of his agency, particularly of those operations which are not running well. Of the following, the MOST frequent cause of this is the

    14._____

   A. general unconcern of top-level management with the way an agency actually operates
   B. tendency of the people at the lowest level in an agency to lie about their actual performance
   C. unwillingness of top-level management to deal with unfavorable information when it is presented
   D. tendency of mid-level management to edit bad news and unpleasant information from reports directed to top management

15. In the conduct of productivity analyses, work measurement is a USEFUL technique for

    15._____

   A. substantiating executive decisions
   B. designing a research study
   C. developing performance yardsticks
   D. preparing a manual of procedure

16. Issue analysis is closely identified with the "fire-fighting" function of management. As such, issue analysis is a(n)

    16._____

   A. systematic assessment over time of an agency's strategic options
   B. annual review of the issues that have come up during the past year
   C. basis for a set of procedures to be followed in an emergency
   D. analysis of a specific policy question often performed in a crisis environment

17. The transportation agency in a large city wishes to study the impact of fare increases on ridership in buses. Rider-ship data for peak hours has been assembled for the same time period for three geographic subareas (A, B and C) with approximately the same socioeconomic characteristics, residential density, and distance from the central business district (CBD). Subarea A had experienced a moderate fare increase on its bus line; Subarea B had had no fare increase; and Subarea C had experienced a major fare increase during the time period.
In the design of this study, the analysis should be framed :

    17._____

   A. Ridership = f (fare level)
   B. Ridership = f (fare level, distance from CBD)
   C. Fare level = f (ridership)
   D. Ridership = f (fare level, socio-economic characteristics, residential density)

18. What organizational concept is illustrated when a group is organized on an *ad hoc* basis to accomplish a specific goal? 18.___

    A. Functional Teamwork   B. Line/staff
    C. Task Force   D. Command

19. The concept of "demand" provides an appropriate theoretical basis for estimating the needs for public services or programs where the service will be on a 19.___

    A. fee basis and involves life-sustaining necessities
    B. free basis and involves life-sustaining necessities
    C. free basis and does not involve life-sustaining necessities
    D. fee basis and does not involve life-sustaining necessities

20. Analysts should be wary of relying exclusively on traditional service standards (e.g., one acre of playground per 1,000 population).
Such standards are often DEFICIENT because they tend to overstate 20.___

    A. the consumer view and understate behavior and values of producers
    B. the producer view and understate behavior and values of users or consumers
    C. local conditions and understate national conditions
    D. behavioral factors and understate practical effects

21. The BEST measure of the performance of a manpower program would be the 21.___

    A. percentage reduction in unemployment by impacted population groups
    B. number of trainees placed in jobs at the beginning of the training program
    C. percentage of students completing a training program
    D. cost per student of the training program and the job placement effort

22. Indices are single figures that measure multi-dimensional concepts.
The critical judgment in the construction of an index involves 22.___

    A. the trade-off between accuracy and simplicity
    B. determination of enough data to do the measurement
    C. avoidance of all possible error
    D. developing a theoretical basis for it

23. Evaluation of public programs is complicated by the reality that programs tend to reflect negotiated compromises among conflicting objectives.
The absence of clear, unitary objectives PARTICULARLY complicates the 23.___

    A. assessment of program input or effort
    B. development of effectiveness criteria
    C. design of new programs to replace the old
    D. diagnosis of a program's processes

24. The basic purpose of the "Super-Agencies" is to 24.___

    A. reduce the number of departments and agencies in the city government
    B. reduce the number of high-level administrators
    C. coordinate agencies reporting to the mayor and supervise agencies in related fields
    D. supervise departments and agencies in unrelated fields

25. In most municipal budgeting systems involving capital and operating budgets, the leasing   25._____
     or renting of facilities is usually shown in

     A. the operating budget   B. the capital budget
     C. a separate schedule   D. either budget

26. New York City's budgeting procedure is unusual in that budget appropriations are consid-   26._____
     ered in two parts, as follows:

     A. Capital budget and income budget
     B. Expense budget and income budget
     C. Revenue budget and expense budget
     D. Expense budget and capital budget

27. The "growth rate" referred to in current political and economic discussion refers to   27._____
     change from year to year in a country's

     A. gross national product   B. population
     C. available labor force   D. capital goods investment

Questions 28-29.

DIRECTIONS: Questions 28 and 29 are based on the following illustration. Assume that the
              figures in the chart are cubes.

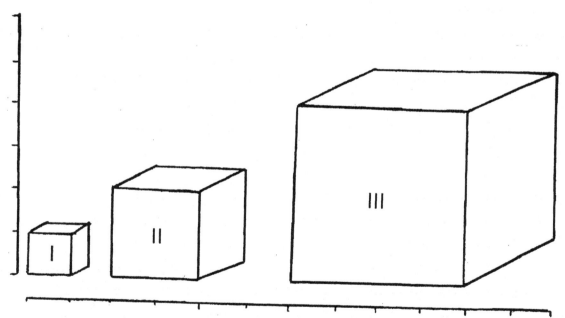

28. In the illustration above, how many times GREATER is the quantity represented by Fig-   28._____
     ure III than the quantity represented by Figure II?

     A. 2   B. 4   C. 8   D. 16

29. The illustration above illustrates a progression in quantity BEST described as   29._____

     A. arithmetic   B. geometric   C. discrete   D. linear

83

Questions 30-35.

DIRECTIONS: Answer Questions 30 through 35 on the basis of the following chart.

In a national study of poverty trends, the following data have been assembled for interpretation.

Persons Below Poverty Level, By Residence

		Number (millions)		Percent	
Item	U.S.	Metropolitan Areas	U.S.	Metropolitan Areas	
2005					
Total	38.8	17.0	22.0	15.3	
Under 25 years	20.0	8.8	25.3	18.1	
65 years & over	5.5	2.5	35.2	26.9	
Black	9.9	5.0	55.1	42.8	
Other	28.3	11.8	18.1	12.0	
2015					
Total	24.3	12.3	12.2	9.5	
Under 25 years	12.2	6.4	13.2	10.4	
65 years & over	4.8	2.3	25.3	20.2	
Black	7.2	3.9	32.3	24.4	
Other	16.7	8.2	9.5	7.3	

30. If no other source of data were available, which of the following groups would you expect to have the HIGHEST rate of poverty?   30.____

    A. Others over 65   B. Others under 65
    C. Blacks over 65   D. Blacks under 65

31. Between 2005 and 2015, the percentage of poor in the United States who were black   31.____

    A. increased from 25.5% to 29.6%
    B. decreased from 55.1% to 32.3%
    C. decreased from 9.9% to 7.2%
    D. stayed the same

32. The data in the second column of the table indicate that, in the metropolitan areas, the number of poor declined by 4.7 million or 36.2% between 2005 and 2015. Yet, the fourth column shows a corresponding decline from 15.3% to 9.5%, or only 5.8%
This apparent discrepancy reflects the fact that the   32.____

    A. metropolitan areas are growing while the number of poor is contracting
    B. two columns in question are based on different sources of information
    C. difference between two percentages is not the same as the percent change in total numbers
    D. tables have inherent errors and must be carefully checked

33. The percentages in each of the last two columns of the table for 1969 and 1979 don't add up to 100%. This is for the reason that   33.____

   A. rounding off each entry to the nearest decimal place caused an error in the total such that the total is not equal to 100%
   B. these columns show the percentage of Blacks, aged, etc. who are poor rather than the percentage of poor who are Black, aged, etc.
   C. there was an error in the construction of the table which was not noticed until the table was already in print
   D. there is double counting in the entries in the table; some people are counted more than once

34. Data such as that presented in the table on persons below poverty level are shown to a single decimal place because   34.____

   A. data in every table should always be shown to a single decimal place
   B. it is the minimal number of decimal places needed to distinguish among table entries
   C. there was no room for more decimal places in the table without crowding
   D. the more accurately a figure is shown the better it is for the user

35. In comparing the poverty of the young (under 25 years) with that of the older population (65 years and over) in 2005 and 2015, one could REASONABLY conclude that   35.____

   A. more young people than old people were poor but older people had a higher rate of poverty
   B. more older people than young people were poor but young people had a higher rate of poverty
   C. there is a greater degree of poverty among the younger population than among the older people
   D. young people and old people have the same rate of poverty

Questions 36-37.

DIRECTIONS: Answer Questions 36 and 37 ONLY on the basis of information given in the passage below.

   Two approaches are available in developing criteria for the evaluation of plans. One approach, designated Approach A, is a review and analysis of characteristics that differentiate successful plans from unsuccessful plans. These criteria are descriptive in nature and serve as a checklist against which the plan under consideration may be judged. These characteristics have been observed by many different students of planning, and there is considerable agreement concerning the characteristics necessary for a plan to be successful.

   A second approach to the development of criteria for judging plans, designated Approach B, is the determination of the degree to which the plan under consideration is economic. The word "economic" is used here in its broadest sense; i.e., effective in its utilization of resources. In order to determine the economic worth of a plan, it is necessary to use a technique that permits the description of any plan in economic terms and to utilize this technique to the extent that it becomes a "way of thinking" about plans.

36. According to _Approach B_, the MOST successful plan is generally one which   36.____

    A. costs least to implement
    B. gives most value for resources expended
    C. uses the least expensive resources
    D. utilizes the greatest number of resources

37. According to _Approach A_, a successful plan is one which is   37.____

    A. descriptive in nature
    B. lowest in cost
    C. similar to other successful plans
    D. agreed upon by many students of planning

Questions 38-40.

DIRECTIONS: Answer Questions 38 through 40 ONLY on the basis of information provided in
              the passage below.

The primary purpose of control reports is to supply information intended to serve as the basis for corrective action if needed. At the same time, the significance of control reports must be kept in proper perspective. Control reports are only a part of the planning-management information system. Control, information includes non-financial as well as financial data that measure performance and isolate variances from standard. Control information also provides feedback so that planning information may be updated and corrected. Whenever possible, control reports should be designed so that they provide feedback for the planning process as well as provide information of immediate value to the control process.

Since the culmination of the control process is the taking of necessary corrective action to bring performance in line with standards, it follows that control information must be directed to the person who is organizationally responsible for taking the required action. Usually the same information, though in a somewhat abbreviated form, is given to the responsible manager's superior. A district sales manager needs a complete daily record of the performance of each of his salesmen; yet, the report forwarded to the regional sales manager summarizes only the performance of each sales district in his region. In preparing reports for higher echelons of management, summary statements and recommendations for action should appear on the first page; substantiating data, usually the information presented to the person directly responsible for the operation, may be included if needed.

38. A control report serves its primary purpose as part of the process which leads   38.____
    DIRECTLY to

    A. better planning for future action
    B. increasing the performance of district salesmen
    C. the establishment of proper performance standards
    D. taking corrective action when performance is poor

39. The one of the following which would be the BEST description of a control report is that a   39.____
    control report is a form of

    A. planning   B. communication
    C. direction   D. organization

40. If control reports are to be effective, the one of the following which is LEAST essential to   40._____
the effectiveness of control reporting is a system of

    A. communication   B. standards
    C. authority   D. work simplification

_____

KEY (CORRECT ANSWERS)

1.	A	11.	B	21.	A	31.	B
2.	B	12.	A	22.	A	32.	C
3.	A	13.	C	23.	B	33.	B
4.	B	14.	D	24.	C	34.	D
5.	D	15.	C	25.	A	35.	A
6.	C	16.	D	26.	D	36.	B
7.	D	17.	A	27.	A	37.	C
8.	C	18.	C	28.	C	38.	D
9.	B	19.	D	29.	B	39.	B
10.	D	20.	B	30.	C	40.	D

_____

EXAMINATION SECTION
TEST 1

DIRECTIONS: Each question or incomplete statement is followed by several suggested answers or completions. Select the one that BEST answers the question or completes the statement. *PRINT THE LETTER OF THE CORRECT ANSWER IN THE SPACE AT THE RIGHT.*

1. Assume that a manager is preparing a list of reasons to justify making a major change in methods and procedures in his agency.
   Which of the following reasons would be LEAST appropriate on such a list?

   A. Improve the means for satisfying needs and wants of agency personnel
   B. Increase efficiency
   C. Intensify competition and stimulate loyalty to separate work groups
   D. Contribute to the individual and group satisfaction of agency personnel

   1.____

2. Many managers recognize the benefits of decentralization but are concerned about the danger of over–relaxation of control as a result of increased delegation.
   Of the following, the MOST appropriate means of establishing proper control under decentralization is for the manager to

   A. establish detailed standards for all phases of operation
   B. shift his attention from operating details to appraisal of results
   C. keep himself informed by decreasing the time span covered by reports
   D. make unilateral decisions on difficult situations that arise in decentralized locations

   2.____

3. In some agencies, the counsel to the agency head is given the right to bypass the chain of command and issue orders directly to the staff concerning matters that involve certain specific processes and practices.
   This situation MOST NEARLY illustrates the principle of

   A. the acceptance theory of authority
   B. multiple–linear authority
   C. splintered authority
   D. functional authority

   3.____

4. Assume that a manager is writing a brief report to his superior outlining the advantages of matrix organization. Of the following, it would be INCORRECT to state that

   A. in matrix organization, a project is emphasized by designating one individual as the focal point for all matters pertaining to it
   B. utilization of manpower can be flexible in matrix organization because a reservoir of specialists is maintained in the line operations
   C. the usual line staff arrangement is generally reversed in matrix organization
   D. in matrix organization, responsiveness to project needs is generally faster due to establishing needed communication lines and decision points

   4.____

5. It is commonly understood that communication is an important part of the administrative process.
   Which of the following is NOT a valid principle of the communication process in administration?

   A. The channels of communication should be spontaneous.
   B. The lines of communication should be as direct and as short as possible.
   C. Communications should be authenticated.
   D. The persons serving in communications centers should be competent.

   5.___

6. The PRIMARY purpose of the quantitative approach in management is to

   A. identify better alternatives for management decision-making
   B. substitute data for judgment
   C. match opinions to data
   D. match data to opinions

   6.___

7. If an executive wants to make a strong case for running his agency as a flat type of structure, he should point out that the PRIMARY advantage of doing so is to

   A. provide less experience in decision-making for agency personnel
   B. facilitate frequent contact between each superior and his immediate subordinates
   C. improve communication and unify attitudes
   D. improve communication and diversify attitudes

   7.___

8. In deciding how detailed his delegation of authority to a subordinate should be, a manager should follow the general principle that

   A. delegation of authority is more detailed at the top of the organizational structure
   B. detailed delegation of authority is associated with detailed work assignments
   C. delegation of authority should be in sufficient detail to prevent overlapping assignments
   D. detailed delegation of authority is associated with broad work assignments

   8.___

9. In recent years, newer and more fluid types of organizational forms have been developed. One of these is a type of free-form organization.
   Another name for this type of organization is the

   A. project organization
   C. naturalistic structure
   B. semimix organization
   D. semipermanent structure

   9.___

10. Which of the following is the MAJOR objective of operational or management systems audits?

    A. Determining the number of personnel needed
    B. Recommending opportunities for improving operating and management practices
    C. Detecting fraud
    D. Determining organization problems

    10.___

11. Assume that a manager observes that conflict exists between his agency and another operating agency of government.
Which of the following statements is the LEAST probable cause of this conflict?

    A. Incompatibility between the agencies' goals but similarity in their resource allocations
    B. Compatibility between agencies' goals and resources
    C. Status differences between agency personnel
    D. Differences in perceptions of each other's policies

11.____

12. Of the following, a MAJOR purpose of brainstorming as a problem-solving technique is to

    A. develop the ability to concentrate
    B. encourage creative thinking
    C. evaluate employees' ideas
    D. develop critical ability

12.____

13. The one of the following requirements which is LEAST likely to accompany regular delegation of work from a manager to a subordinate is a(n)

    A. need to review the organization's workload
    B. indication of what work the subordinate is to do
    C. need to grant authority to the subordinate
    D. obligation for the subordinate who accepts the work to try to complete it

13.____

14. Of the following, the one factor which is generally considered LEAST essential to successful committee operation is

    A. stating a clear definition of the authority and scope of the committee
    B. selecting the committee chairman carefully
    C. limiting the size of the committee to four persons
    D. limiting the subject matter to that which can be handled in group discussion

14.____

15. In using the program evaluation and review technique, the critical path is the path that

    A. requires the shortest time
    B. requires the longest time
    C. focuses most attention on social constraints
    D. focuses most attention on repetitious jobs

15.____

16. Which one of the following is LEAST characteristic of the management-by-objectives approach?

    A. The scope within which the employee may exercise decision-making is broadened
    B. The employee starts with a self-appraisal of his performances, abilities, and potential
    C. Emphasis is placed on activities performed; activities orientation is maximized
    D. Each employee participates in determining his own objectives

16.____

17. The function of management which puts into effect the decisions, plans, and programs   17.___
that have previously been worked out for achieving the goals of the group is MOST
appropriately called

    A. scheduling   B. classifying
    C. budgeting   D. directing

18. In the establishment of a plan to improve office productive efficiency, which of the follow-   18.___
ing guidelines is LEAST helpful in setting sound work standards?

    A. Employees must accept the plan's objectives.
    B. Current production averages must be promulgated as work standards for a group.
    C. The work flow must generally be fairly constant.
    D. The operation of the plan must be expressed in terms understandable to the
         worker.

19. The one of the following activities which, generally speaking, is of *relatively* MAJOR   19.___
importance at the lower-management level and of *somewhat* LESSER importance at
higher-management levels is

    A. actuating   B. forecasting
    C. organizing   D. planning

20. Three styles of leadership exist: democratic, authoritarian, and laissez-faire.   20.___
Of the following work situations, the one in which a democratic approach would normally be the MOST effective is when the work is

    A. routine and moderately complex
    B. repetitious and simple
    C. complex and not routine
    D. simple and not routine

21. Governmental and business organizations *generally* encounter the GREATEST difficul-   21.___
ties in developing tangible measures of which one of the following?

    A. The level of expenditures
    B. Contributions to social welfare
    C. Retention rates
    D. Causes of labor unrest

22. Of the following, a *management-by-objectives* program is BEST described as   22.___

    A. a new comprehensive plan of organization
    B. introduction of budgets and financial controls
    C. introduction of long–range planning
    D. development of future goals with supporting and related progress reviews

23. Research and analysis is probably the most widely used technique for selecting alternatives when major planning decisions are involved.
Of the following, a VALUABLE characteristic of research and analysis is that this technique

    A. places the problem in a meaningful conceptual framework
    B. involves practical application of the various alternatives
    C. accurately analyzes all important tangibles
    D. is much less expensive than other problem-solving methods

23._____

24. If a manager were assigned the task of using a systems approach to designing a new work unit, which of the following should he consider FIRST in carrying out his design?

    A. Networks
    B. Work flows and information processes
    C. Linkages and relationships
    D. Decision points and control loops

24._____

25. The MAIN distinction between Theory X and Theory Y approaches to organization, in accordance with Douglas McGregor's view, is that Theory Y

    A. considers that work is natural to people; Theory X assumes that people are lazy and avoid work
    B. leads to a tall, narrow organization structure, while Theory X leads to one that is flat
    C. organizations motivate people with money; Theory X organizations motivate people with good working conditions
    D. represents authoritarian management, while Theory X management is participative

25._____

KEY (CORRECT ANSWERS)

1.	C		11.	B
2.	B		12.	B
3.	D		13.	A
4.	C		14.	C
5.	A		15.	B
6.	A		16.	C
7.	C		17.	D
8.	B		18.	B
9.	A		19.	A
10.	B		20.	C

21.	B
22.	D
23.	A
24.	B
25.	A

TEST 2

DIRECTIONS: Each question or incomplete statement is followed by several suggested answers or completions. Select the one that BEST answers the question or completes the statement. *PRINT THE LETTER OF THE CORRECT ANSWER IN THE SPACE AT THE RIGHT.*

1. Of the following, the stage in decision-making which is usually MOST difficult is

    A. stating the alternatives
    B. predicting the possible outcome of each alternative
    C. evaluating the relative merits of each alternative
    D. minimizing the undesirable aspects of the alternative selected

    1.____

2. In a department where a clerk is reporting both to a senior clerk in charge of the mail room and also to a supervising clerk in charge of the duplicating section, there may be a breakdown of the management principle called

    A. horizontal specialization   B. job enrichment
    C. unity of command   D. Graicunas' Law

    2.____

3. Of the following, the failure by line managers to accept and appreciate the benefits and limitations of a new program or system VERY frequently can be traced to the

    A. budgetary problems involved
    B. resultant need to reduce staff
    C. lack of controls it engenders
    D. failure of top management to support its implementation

    3.____

4. Although there is general agreement that *management by objectives* has made a major contribution to modern management of large organizations, criticisms of the system during the past few years have resulted in

    A. mounting pressure for relaxation of management goals
    B. renewed concern with human values and the manager's personal needs
    C. over-mechanistic application of the perceptions of the behavioral scientists
    D. disillusionment with *management by objectives* on the part of a majority of managers

    4.____

5. Of the following, which is usually considered to be a MAJOR obstacle to the systematic analysis of potential problems by managers?

    A. Managers have a tendency to think that all the implications of some proposed step cannot be fully understood.
    B. Rewards rarely go to those managers who are most successful at resolving current problems in management.
    C. There is a common conviction of managers that their goals are difficult to achieve.
    D. Managers are far more concerned about correcting today's problems than with preventing tomorrow's.

    5.____

6. Which of the following should generally have the MOST influence on the selection of supervisors?   6.___

    A. Experience within the work unit where the vacancies exist
    B. Amount of money needed to effect the promotion
    C. Personal preferences of the administration
    D. Evaluation of capacity to exercise supervisory responsibilities

7. In questioning a potential administrator for selection purposes, the one of the following practices which is MOST desirable is to   7.___

    A. encourage the job applicant to give primarily *yes* or *no* replies
    B. get the applicant to talk freely and in detail about his background
    C. let the job applicant speak most of the time
    D. probe the applicant's attitudes, motivation, and willingness to accept responsibility

8. In implementing the managerial function of training subordinates, it is USEFUL to know that a widely agreed–upon definition of human learning is that learning   8.___

    A. is a relatively permanent change in behavior that results from reinforced practice or experience
    B. involves an improvement, but not necessarily a change in behavior
    C. involves a change in behavior, but not necessarily an improvement
    D. is a temporary change in behavior which must be subject to practice or experience

9. If a manager were thinking about using a committee of subordinates to solve an operating problem, which of the following would generally NOT be an advantage of such use of the committee approach?   9.___

    A. Improved coordination   B. Low cost
    C. Increased motivation   D. Integrated judgment

10. Which one of the following management approaches MOST often uses model-building techniques to solve management problems?   10.___
    _____ approach

    A. Behavioral   B. Fiscal
    C. Quantitative   D. Process

11. Of the following, the MOST serious risk in using budgets as a tool for management control is the   11.___

    A. probable neglect of other good management practices
    B. likelihood of guesswork because of the need to plan far in advance
    C. possibility of undue emphasis on factors that are easiest to measure
    D. danger of making qualitative rather than quantitative assessments of performance

12. In government budgeting, the problem of relating financial transactions to the fiscal year in which they are budgeted is BEST met by

    A.   determining the cash balance by comparing how much money has been received and how much has been paid out

    B.   applying net revenue to the fiscal year in which they are collected as offset by relevant expenses

    C.   adopting a system whereby appropriations are entered when they are received and expenditures are entered when they are paid out

    D.   entering expenditures on the books when the obligation to make the expenditure is made

12.____

13. If the agency's bookkeeping system records income when it is received and expenditures when the money is paid out, this sytem is USUALLY known as a _____ system.

    A.   cash
    B.   flow–payment
    C.   deferred
    D.   fiscal year income

13.____

14. An audit, as the term applies to budget execution, is MOST NEARLY a

    A.   procedure based on the budget estimates

    B.   control exercised by the executive on the legislature in the establishment of program priorities

    C.   check on the legality of expenditures and is based on the appropriations act

    D.   requirement which must be met before funds can be spent

14.____

15. In government budgeting, there is a procedure known as *allotment*.
Of the following statements which relate to allotment, select the one that is MOST generally considered to be correct.
Allotment

    A.   increases the practice of budget units coming back to the legislative branch for supplemental appropriations

    B.   is simply an example of red tape

    C.   eliminates the requirement of timing of expenditures

    D.   is designed to prevent waste

15.____

16. In government budgeting, the establishment of the schedules of allotments is MOST generally the responsibility of the

    A.   budget unit and the legislature

    B.   budget unit and the executive

    C.   budget unit *only*

    D.   executive and the legislature

16.____

17. Of the following statements relating to preparation of an organization's budget request, which is the MOST generally valid precaution?   17.____

    A. Give specific instructions on the format of budget requests and required supporting data
    B. Because of the complexity of preparing a budget request, avoid argumentation to support the requests
    C. Put requests in whatever format is desirable
    D. Consider that final approval will be given to initial estimates

18. Of the following statements which relate to the budget process in a well–organized government, select the one that is MOST NEARLY correct.   18.____

    A. The budget cycle is the step-by-step process which is repeated each and every fiscal year.
    B. Securing approval of the budget does not take place within the budget cycle.
    C. The development of a new budget and putting it into effect is a two-step process known as the budget cycle.
    D. The fiscal period, usually a fiscal year, has no relation to the budget cycle.

19. If a manager were asked what PPBS stands for, he would be RIGHT if he said   19.____

    A. public planning budgeting system
    B. planning programming budgeting system
    C. planning projections budgeting system
    D. programming procedures budgeting system

Questions 20–21.

DIRECTIONS: Answer Questions 20 and 21 on the basis of the following information.

Sample Budget

Refuse Collection	Amount
Personal Services	$ 30,000
Contractual Services	5,000
Supplies and Materials	5,000
Capital Outlay	10,000
	$ 50,000

Residential Collections	
Dwellings–1 pickup per week	1,000
Tons of refuse collected per year	375
Cost of collections per ton	$ 8
Cost per dwelling pickup per year	$ 3
Total annual cost	$ 3,000

20. The sample budget shown is a simplified example of a _____ budget.

    A. factorial   B. performance
    C. qualitative   D. rational

20._____

21. The budget shown in the sample differs CHIEFLY from line-item and program budgets in that it includes

    A. objects of expenditure but not activities or functions
    B. only activities, functions, and control
    C. activities and functions but not objects of expenditures
    D. levels of service

21._____

Question 22.

DIRECTIONS: Answer Question 22 on the basis of the following information.

Sample Budget

Environmental Safety
    Air Pollution Protection
      Personal Services $20,000,000
      Contractual Services   4,000,000
      Supplies and Materials   4,000,000
      Capital Outlay   2,000,000
        Total Air Pollution Protection $ 30,000,000

    Water Pollution Protection
      Personal Services $23,000,000
      Supplies and Materials   4,500,000
      Capital Outlay   20,500,000
        Total Water Pollution Protection $ 48,000,000

Total Environmental Safety $ 78,000,000

22. Based on the above budget, which is the MOST valid statement?

    A. Environmental Safety, Air Pollution Protection, and Water Pollution Protection could all be considered program elements.
    B. The object listings included water pollution protection and capital outlay.
    C. Examples of the program element listings in the above are personal services and supplies and materials.
    D. Contractual Services and Environmental Safety were the program element listings.

22._____

23. Which of the following is NOT an advantage of a program budget over a line-item budget?
A program budget

    A. allows us to set up priority lists in deciding what activities we will spend our money on
    B. gives us more control over expenditures than a line-item budget
    C. is more informative in that we know the broad purposes of spending money
    D. enables us to see if one program is getting much less money than the others

23._____

24. If a manager were trying to explain the fundamental difference between traditional   24.___
accounting theory and practice and the newer practice of managerial accounting, he
would be MOST accurate if he said that

   A. traditional accounting practice focused on providing information for persons outside organizations, while managerial accounting focuses on providing information
   for people inside organizations
   B. traditional accounting practice focused on providing information for persons inside
   organizations while managerial accounting focuses on providing information for
   persons outside organizations
   C. managerial accounting is exclusively concerned with historical facts while traditional accounting stresses future projections exclusively
   D. traditional accounting practice is more budget-focused than managerial accounting

25. Which of the following formulas is used to determine the number of days required to pro-   25.___
cess work?

   A. $\dfrac{\text{Employees x Daily Output}}{\text{Volume}}$ = Days to Process Work

   B. $\dfrac{\text{Volume x Daily Output}}{\text{Employees}}$ = Days to Process Work

   C. $\dfrac{\text{Volume}}{\text{Employees x Daily Output}}$ = Days to Process Work

   D. $\dfrac{\text{Employees x Volume}}{\text{Daily Output}}$ = Days to Process Work

KEY (CORRECT ANSWERS)

1.	C	11.	C
2.	C	12.	D
3.	D	13.	A
4.	B	14.	C
5.	D	15.	D
6.	D	16.	C
7.	D	17.	A
8.	A	18.	A
9.	B	19.	B
10.	C	20.	B

21. D
22. A
23. B
24. A
25. C

TEST 3

DIRECTIONS: Each question or incomplete statement is followed by several suggested answers or completions. Select the one that BEST answers the question or completes the statement. *PRINT THE LETTER OF THE CORRECT ANSWER IN THE SPACE AT THE RIGHT.*

1. Electronic data processing equipment can produce more information faster than can be generated by any other means.
   In view of this, the MOST important problem faced by management at present is to   1.___

   A. keep computers fully occupied
   B. find enough computer personnel
   C. assimilate and properly evaluate the information
   D. obtain funds to establish appropriate information systems

2. A well-designed management information system ESSENTIALLY provides each executive and manager the information he needs for   2.___

   A. determining computer time requirements
   B. planning and measuring results
   C. drawing a new organization chart
   D. developing a new office layout

3. It is generally agreed that management policies should be periodically reappraised and restated in accordance with current conditions.
   Of the following, the approach which would be MOST effective in determining whether a policy should be revised is to   3.___

   A. conduct interviews with staff members at all levels in order to ascertain the relationship between the policy and actual practice
   B. make proposed revisions in the policy and apply it to current problems
   C. make up hypothetical situations using both the old policy and a revised version in order to make comparisons
   D. call a meeting of top level staff in order to discuss ways of revising the policy

4. Every manager has many occasions to lead a conference or participate in a conference of some sort.
   Of the following statements that pertain to conferences and conference leadership, which is generally considered to be MOST valid?   4.___

   A. Since World War II, the trend has been toward fewer shared decisions and more conferences.
   B. The most important part of a conference leader's job is to direct discussion.
   C. In providing opportunities for group interaction, management should avoid consideration of its past management philosophy.
   D. A good administrator cannot lead a good conference if he is a poor public speaker.

5. Of the following, it is usually LEAST desirable for a conference leader to   5.___

   A. turn the question to the person who asked it
   B. summarize proceedings periodically
   C. make a practice of not repeating questions
   D. ask a question without indicating who is to reply

6. The behavioral school of management thought bases its beliefs on certain assumptions. 6.____
Which of the following is NOT a belief of this school of thought?

    A. People tend to seek and accept responsibility.
    B. Most people can be creative in solving problems.
    C. People prefer security above all else.
    D. Commitment is the most important factor in motivating people.

7. The one of the following objectives which would be LEAST appropriate as a major goal of 7.____
research in the field of human resources management is to

    A. predict future conditions, events, and manpower needs
    B. evaluate established policies, programs, and practices
    C. evaluate proposed policies, programs, and practices
    D. identify deficient organizational units and apply suitable penalties

8. Of the following general interviewing methods or techniques, the one that is USUALLY 8.____
considered to be effective in counseling, grievances, and appraisal interviews is the
_____ interview.

    A. directed   B. non-directed
    C. panel   D. patterned

9. The ESSENTIAL first phase of decision-making is 9.____

    A. finding alternative solutions
    B. making a diagnosis of the problem
    C. selecting the plan to follow
    D. analyzing and comparing alternative solutions

10. Assume that, in a certain organization, a situation has developed in which there is little 10.____
difference in status or authority between individuals.
Which of the following would be the MOST likely result with regard to communication in
this organization?

    A. Both the accuracy and flow of communication will be improved.
    B. Both the accuracy and flow of communication will substantially decrease.
    C. Employees will seek more formal lines of communication.
    D. Neither the flow nor the accuracy of communication will be improved over the
       former hierarchical structure.

11. The main function of many agency administrative offices is *information management.* 11.____
Information that is received by an administrative officer may be classified as active or
passive, depending upon whether or not it requires the recipient to take some action.
Of the following, the item received which is clearly the MOST active information is

    A. an appointment of a new staff member
    B. a payment voucher for a new desk
    C. a press release concerning a past city event
    D. the minutes of a staff meeting

103

12. Which one of the following sets BEST describes the general order in which to teach an   12.___
operation to a new employee?

    A. Prepare, present, tryout, follow-up
    B. Prepare, test, tryout, re-test
    C. Present, test, tryout, follow-up
    D. Test, present, follow-up, re-test

13. Of the following, public employees may be separated from public service   13.___

    A. for the same reasons which are generally acceptable for discharging employees in private industry
    B. only under the most trying circumstances
    C. under procedures that are neither formalized nor subject to review
    D. solely in extreme cases involving offenses of gravest character

14. Of the following, the one LEAST considered to be a communication barrier is   14.___

    A. group feedback   B. charged words
    C. selective perception   D. symbolic meanings

15. Of the following ways for a manager to handle his appointments, the BEST way, accord-   15.___
ing to experts in administration, generally is to

    A. schedule his own appointments and inform his secretary not to reserve his time without his approval
    B. encourage everyone to make appointments through his secretary and tell her when he makes his own appointments
    C. see no one who has not made a previous appointment
    D. permit anyone to see him without an appointment

16. Assume that a manager decides to examine closely one of five units under his supervi-   16.___
sion to uncover problems common to all five.
His research technique is MOST closely related to the method called

    A. experimentation   B. simulation
    C. linear analysis   D. sampling

17. If one views the process of management as a dynamic process, which one of the follow-   17.___
ing functions is NOT a legitimate part of that process?

    A. Communication   B. Decision-making
    C. Organizational slack   D. Motivation

18. Which of the following would be the BEST statement of a budget-oriented purpose for a   18.___
government administrator? To

    A. provide 200 hours of instruction in basic reading for 3500 adult illiterates at a cost of $1 million in the next fiscal year
    B. inform the public of adult educational programs
    C. facilitate the transfer to a city agency of certain functions of a federally-funded program which is being phased out
    D. improve the reading skills of the adult citizens in the city

19. Modern management philosophy and practices are changing to accommodate the expectations and motivations of organization personnel.
Which of the following terms INCORRECTLY describes these newer managerial approaches?

    A. Rational management
    C. Decentralization
    B. Participative management
    D. Democratic supervision

19._____

20. Management studies support the hypothesis that, in spite of the tendency of employees to censor the information communicated to their supervisor, subordinates are MORE likely to communicate problem-oriented information upward when they have

    A. a long period of service in the organization
    B. a high degree of trust in the supervisor
    C. a high educational level
    D. low status on the organizational ladder

20._____

KEY (CORRECT ANSWERS)

1.	C	11.	A
2.	B	12.	A
3.	A	13.	A
4.	B	14.	A
5.	A	15.	B
6.	C	16.	D
7.	D	17.	C
8.	B	18.	A
9.	B	19.	A
10.	D	20.	B

EXAMINATION SECTION
TEST 1

DIRECTIONS: Each question or incomplete statement is followed by several suggested answers or completions. Select the one that BEST answers the question or completes the statement. *PRINT THE LETTER OF THE CORRECT ANSWER IN THE SPACE AT THE RIGHT.*

1. Several employees complain informally to their supervisor regarding some new procedures which have been instituted. The supervisor should immediately

    A. explain that management is responsible
    B. investigate the complaint
    C. refer the matter to the methods analyst
    D. tell the employees to submit their complaint as a formal grievance

1.____

2. The PRINCIPAL aim of an administrator is to

    A. act as liaison between employee and management
    B. get the work done
    C. keep up morale
    D. train his subordinates

2.____

3. Work measurement can be applied to operations where workload can be related to

    A. available personnel for the implementation of assigned tasks
    B. follow-up programs for continued progress
    C. cost abatement and optimum efficiency
    D. man hour utilization on assigned tasks

3.____

4. The one of the following which is NOT a primary advantage of a work measurement program is

    A. the selection of informed personnel
    B. knowledge of personnel needs
    C. support of personnel requests
    D. setting of approximate unit costs

4.____

5. A program of work measurement would be LEAST likely to

    A. point up the need for management research
    B. keep workload and personnel on an even keel
    C. measure the performance in exceptional operations
    D. evaluate the status of operations

5.____

6. *Generally speaking, there are two kinds of work measurement:*
(1) the traditional industrial engineering kind where performance standards are determined by time study or other engineering techniques, and (2) the statistical kind where yardsticks (so-called to distinguish them from engineered standards) are developed from a statistical analysis of past performance data. These data consist essentially of periodic reports in which work performed, expressed in identifiable work units, is related to the time required to perform it, usually expressed in man-hours.
The ESSENTIAL difference between the two kinds of work measurement is that

6.____

A. the statistical type is based on past, current, and future determinants of a diversent nature, while engineered standards are restrictive
B. yardsticks are less restrictive than engineered standards
C. time study standards employ a higher ratio of manhour data than do statistical standards
D. engineered standards are more costly as well as more accurate than routine time study methods

7. Government has favored the use of the statistical type of work measurement over the industrial type MAINLY because 7.___

A. government is an institution rarely hampered by money seeking techniques
B. as the statistical type of work measurement is broadly based, it is more capable of filling the wide expanse of government's needs
C. employees might object vehemently against speed-ups, thereby sapping work measurement's force
D. the former appears to be just as effective and less expensive than the latter

8. A work measurement program is a system by which a 8.___

A. periodic account is kept of individual and group performance
B. recurring account is kept of group performance
C. periodic account is kept of performance by an individual
D. periodic account is kept of performance by a group

9. Statistical standards developed during the early stages of a work measurement program are 9.___

A. changed too rapidly and thus are of little value in the final program
B. subject to change as the program moves forward
C. incorporated into the final program, ultimately for research studies
D. abandoned before the effective date of the final program

10. It is NOT an objective of a work measurement program to 10.___

A. furnish a basis for procedural control
B. provide a true basis for management control
C. furnish a genuine basis for budget control
D. provide a basis for management planning

11. The MOST valid of the following concepts of management control is that it examines 11.___

A. the method with which work assignments have been accomplished in accordance with preconceived plans and policies
B. preconceived plans and policies to determine their ultimate value
C. results to determine how well work assignments have been accomplished in accordance with preconceived plans and policies
D. the work of individual employees to get an acceptable standard, so as not to endanger the entire control program

12. Of the following, the LEAST likely area in which a deficiency in operations would be revealed by a work measurement program is

    A. improper personnel utilization
    B. inadequate equipment
    C. distribution of work
    D. personnel rating

12._____

13. The MOST accurate of the following statements regarding the standard as used in a work measurement program is:

    A. standard rates of performance should not be established until the effectiveness of an operation has been determined
    B. the measure of effectiveness should be kept separate and distinct from the application of standards to actual performance
    C. standards should not be used as guides in planning
    D. standard rates of performance must be established before effectiveness of an operation can be determined

13._____

14. The first and most important basic consideration in instituting a program of work measurement is the

    A. indoctrination of personnel
    B. establishment of a uniform technology
    C. selection of the time unit
    D. selection of a standard

14._____

15. A _____ is an item or a group of items, generally physical, which, when taken in the aggregate, serve to measure amounts of work.

    A. Therblig   B. function
    C. operation   D. work unit

15._____

16. Which of the following epitomizes the *raison d'etre* of work simplification?

    A. Waste elimination   B. Empirical costs
    C. Time study speed-ups   D. Charting techniques

16._____

17. A process charting analysis is likely to be of little value in the event of

    A. a major change in the department's activity
    B. a new supervisor from the outside coming in to head the unit
    C. increase in volume of work
    D. sizable personnel turnover

17._____

18. Staff or functional supervision in an organization

    A. is least justified at the operational level
    B. is contrary to the principle of Unity of Command
    C. is more effective than authoritative supervision
    D. normally does not give the right to take direct disciplinary action

18._____

19. The correlation between a flow process chart and a flow diagram is BEST described by   19.____
    which of the following statements?

    A. A flow process chart is supportive machinery to the flow diagram.
    B. In essence, the flow process chart exhibits time, distance, and location using stan-
       dard symbols, whereas the flow diagram exhibits flow lines and uses classifica-
       tional symbols.
    C. Much of the information on the flow process chart is reproduced from the flow dia-
       gram.
    D. The flow diagram is complementary to the flow process chart.

20. Indicate which statement is LEAST apt to clarify the underlying distinction between work   20.____
    simplification and other methods of betterment procedures.
    Work simplification

    A. is dependent on supervisory participation
    B. is designed for employee participation
    C. emphasizes group participation
    D. emphasizes the ideas of experts

21. In describing the process of administrative management, the LEAST valid description is   21.____
    that it

    A. is composed of interdependent functions
    B. is comprised of related parts
    C. is cyclical
    D. consists of independent parts

22. Work activity, as to type, individual performance, and time expenditure, is BEST illus-   22.____
    trated by a _____ chart.

    A. flow process   B. work flow
    C. work distribution   D. operations

23. Neither the work distribution nor the flow process chart furnishes adequate intelligence   23.____
    as to

    A. methods   B. activities
    C. nature of work activity   D. unit prices

24. A graphic presentation of the steps and distribution through which each copy of a multi-   24.____
    ple copy office form travels is a(n)

    A. work distribution chart   B. flow process chart
    C. flow diagram   D. operations chart

25. A CHIEF target of work simplification is   25.____

    A. the achievement of greater productivity with the same work effort
    B. obtaining the same work accomplishment with less effort
    C. employee participation and little resistance to change
    D. all of the above

KEY (CORRECT ANSWERS)

1.	B		11.	C
2.	B		12.	D
3.	D		13.	D
4.	A		14.	B
5.	C		15.	D
6.	B		16.	A
7.	D		17.	B
8.	B		18.	D
9.	B		19.	D
10.	A		20.	D

21.	D
22.	C
23.	D
24.	C
25.	C

———

TEST 2

Each question or incomplete statement is followed by several suggested answers or completions. Select the one that BEST answers the question or completes the statement. *PRINT THE LETTER OF THE CORRECT ANSWER IN THE SPACE AT THE RIGHT.*

1. In conducting a work simplification program, which of the following office problems is the MOST likely to be solved by the use of the flow process chart?
   1._____

   A. Are the employees deluged with unrelated tasks?
   B. What activities are the most costly, in terms of time consumed?
   C. Is the proper sequence of work activity employed?
   D. Is there an even distribution of work among the employees?

2. In the matter of procedural analysis, which question should be asked FIRST?
   2._____

   A. When should the step be performed?
   B. Who should perform the step?
   C. What is the significance of the step?
   D. Where can this be improved upon?

3. Storage on a movement diagram is represented by
   3._____

   A. ◇   B. ▽
   C. □   D. none of the above

4. The use of a flow process chart is LEAST desirable in indicating
   4._____

   A. the time rate for each step
   B. distance travelled
   C. equipment-facilities layout
   D. sequence of activities

5. Division of work is BEST delineated by means of a _____ chart.
   5._____

   A. work methods   B. flow process
   C. work distribution   D. flow authority

6. In seeking to conduct a work simplification analysis, the MOST appropriate first step would be to
   6._____

   A. chart the procedures
   B. survey the facilities as to spatial access
   C. make problem area determination
   D. set up composition of forms analysis

7. The conception of a standard is BEST denoted as a
   7._____

   A. hypothetical level
   B. circumscribed level of work activity
   C. level of comparing
   D. quintessential ideal

8. With reference to office work simplification, it could be considered expedient to

    A. first simplify the procedure and then the individual methods
    B. simplify the individual methods first, then the procedure
    C. concurrently, simplify the methods and the procedure
    D. none of the above

8.____

9. The MOST valid precept relative to work analysis is

    A. the volume of work is inversely proportional to the distribution or sequence of work
    B. in meeting production standards, the sequence of work transcends its distribution
    C. work sequence and work distribution should be analyzed in relation to work volume
    D. work sequence and work distribution should be examined for work validation concepts

9.____

10. The flow process chart is PRINCIPALLY used

    A. as a useful tool to train new employees
    B. to ascertain the effectiveness of the organization's employees
    C. to pinpoint *bottlenecks* affecting an operation
    D. to determine the visibility of organizational relationships

10.____

11. The work distribution chart would generally be of little value in answering which of the following questions?

    A. In what order are the activities being carried out?
    B. Which activities consume the most time?
    C. Is a work balance maintained among the employees?
    D. Are the employees laboring under a plethora of unrelated tasks?

11.____

12. A worthwhile analytical tool in work simplification is the flow process chart. The MOST valid description is that

    A. a flow process chart is generally reliable without review for a period of a year
    B. the flow process chart should be reviewed and possibly revised at six-month intervals
    C. the flow process chart is an ad hoc instrument
    D. the value of a flow process chart is not determined by time

12.____

13. In the analysis of a method of procedure in a work simplification program, a competent analyst should FIRST focalize on the clearance or diminution of

    A. verifications
    C. inspections
    B. transportations
    D. storages

13.____

14. Which one of the following statements BEST distinguishes a method from a procedure?

    A. A method is a consistent sequence of procedures.
    B. A procedure comprises a sequence of related methods, performed in most instances by a single person.
    C. A series of related methods comprise a procedure.
    D. In breadth, a method takes precedence over a procedure.

14.____

15. The data provided by the flow process chart in a work simplification program is INADE-   15.___
QUATE to answer which one of the following questions?

    A. What is being performed?
    B. In what manner should the work be performed?
    C. What is the quantity of work performed?
    D. Who should perform the work?

Questions 16-17.

DIRECTIONS: Questions 16 and 17 are to be answered on the basis of the following pas-
                sage.

    Ideally, then, the process of budget formulation would consist of a flow of directives down
the organization, and a reverse flow of recommendations in terms of alternatives among
which selection would be made at every level. Ideally, also, a change in the recommendations
at any level would require reconsideration and revision at all lower levels. By a process of
successive approximation, everything would be taken into account and all points of view har-
monized. Such a process, however, would be ideal only if the future could be foreseen clearly
and time did not matter. As it is, in a complicated organization like the Federal government,
the initial policy objectives established for the budget become out-of-date, before such a procedure could be carried through. While this difficulty does not in any way impugn the principle
that the budget should be considered in terms of alternatives, it may call for short-cut methods of estimation rather than long drawn-out ones.

16. According to the above passage,   16.___

    A. the ideal method for estimating purposes is a short one
    B. the ideal method is not ideal for use in the Federal government
    C. directives should flow up and down via short methods
    D. the Federal government needs to speed up its reverse flow of recommendations for
       greater budgetary estimates

17. A suitable title for the above passage would be   17.___

    A. FORMULATING THE FEDERAL GOVERNMENT'S BUDGETARY PRINCIPLES
    B. DIRECTIVES AND RECOMMENDATIONS: BUDGETARY FLOW
    C. THE PROCESS OF BUDGET FORMULATION
    D. THE APPLICATION OF THE IDEAL ESTIMATE TO THE FEDERAL GOVERN-
       MENT

Questions 18-19.

DIRECTIONS: Questions 18 and 19 are to be answered in accordance with the following pas-
                sage.

    For purposes of budget formulation, the association of budgeting with accounting is less
fortunate. Preparing for the future and recording the past do not necessarily require the same
aptitudes or attitudes. The task of the accountant is to record past transactions in meticulous
detail. Budgeting involves estimates of an uncertain future. But, because of the influence of
accounts, government's budgets are prepared in a degree of detail that is quite unwarranted
by the uncertain assumptions on which the estimates are based. A major source of government waste could be eliminated if estimates were prepared in no greater detail than was justified by their accuracy.

18. The author of the above paragraph

    A. is undermining the accounting profession
    B. believes accountants dwell solely in the past and cannot deal with the future efficiently
    C. wants the accountants out of government unless they become more accurate in their findings
    D. wishes to redirect the accountants' handling of budget procedures

18.____

19. The author's attitude appears to be

    A. tongue-in-cheek
    C. strident
    B. morose
    D. constructive

19.____

20. The idea that classic organizational structure tends to create work situations having requirements counter to those for psychological success and self-esteem, sometimes called the *organizational dilemma,* is MOST closely associated with

    A. Argyris   B. Taylor   C. Gulick   D. Maslow

20.____

Questions 21-25.

DIRECTIONS: Questions 21 through 25 contain incorrectly used words which change the meaning of the statement. Identify the word in the statement that is incorrect and select the choice that would make the sentence correct.

21. Standards of production performance are necessary to reveal the quantities of material, the number of hours of labor, the machine hours, and quantities of service (as, for example, power, steam, etc.) necessary to perform the various production operations. The establishment of such standards is an engineering rather than an accounting task, but it should be emphasized that such standards are needless to the development of the budgetary procedure—at least insofar as the budget is to serve as a tool of control. Such standards serve not only in the development of the budget and in measuring efficiency of production performance, but also in developing purchase requirements and in estimating costs.

    A. Manifest
    C. Essential.
    B. Evaluation
    D. Function

21.____

22. Where standard costs are not available or their use is impracticable due to uncertainty of prices, estimates of the costs must be made on the basis of past experience and expected conditions. Ability to use standards largely eliminates the use of the budget for purposes of control of costs but its value remains for purposes of coordination of the program with purchases and finance.

    A. Failure
    C. Culmination
    B. Current
    D. Apparent

22.____

23. While one of the first objectives of the labor budget is to provide the highest practicable degree of regularity of employment, consideration must also be given to the estimating and perdurability of labor cost. Regularity of employment in itself effects some reduction in labor cost, but when carried beyond the point of practicability, it may increase other costs. For example, additional sales effort may be required to expand sales volume or to develop new products for slack periods; the cost of carrying inventories and the dangers of obsolescence and price declines must also be considered. A proper balance must be secured.

   23.____

  A. Material   B. Control   C. Futures   D. To

24. The essentials of budgeting perhaps can be summarized in this manner:

   24.____

    1. Develop a sound business program.
    2. Report on the progress in achieving that program.
    3. Take necessary action as to all variances which are inevitable.
    4. Revise the program to meet the changing conditions as required.

  A. Perfect   B. Plans
  C. Controllable   D. Secure

25. If a planning and control procedure is considered worthwhile, then it is a syllogism that preparation for the installation should be adequate. Time devoted to this educational aspect ordinarily will prove quite rewarding. The management to be involved with the budget, and particularly the middle management, must have a clear understanding of the budgetary procedure.

   25.____

  A. Acquired   B. Remedial
  C. Monetary   D. Truism

KEY (CORRECT ANSWERS)

1.	D		11.	A
2.	C		12.	D
3.	D		13.	D
4.	C		14.	C
5.	C		15.	C
6.	C		16.	B
7.	C		17.	C
8.	A		18.	D
9.	C		19.	D
10.	C		20.	A

21.	C
22.	B
23.	B
24.	C
25.	D

TEST 3

DIRECTIONS: Each question or incomplete statement is followed by several suggested answers or completions. Select the one that BEST answers the question or completes the statement. *PRINT THE LETTER OF THE CORRECT ANSWER IN THE SPACE AT THE RIGHT.*

1. The MOST important element in job satisfaction is

    A. job security
    B. responsibility or recognition
    C. salary
    D. type of supervision

1.____

2. The point of view that the average person wishes to avoid responsibility, wishes to be directed, has little ambition, and wants security above all, is described by Douglas MacGregor as Theory

    A. X
    C. Z
    B. Y
    D. X and Y combined

2.____

3. To prepare a work distribution chart, two other types of lists must generally be prepared. In usual order of preparation, they are a(n) _____ and a(n) _____ list.

    A. flow chart; activity
    C. task list; activity
    B. skills list; task
    D. activity list; task

3.____

4. A statistical control program in an office is valuable to detect deterioration in operations. It is, however, LEAST likely to reveal

    A. when preventative action is needed
    B. when a variation is due to chance
    C. when an assignable cause is present
    D. what the cause of error or deterioration is

4.____

5. Which of the following BEST defines an organization chart?
An organizational chart

    A. depicts informal channels of communication within an organization
    B. depicts the major functions of an organization and the normal work flow between subdivisions of the organization
    C. presents graphically the arrangement and interrelationships of the subdivisions and the functions of the organization as they exist
    D. presents graphically the arrangement and relationships of all the positions authorized in an organization

5.____

6. In considering an office layout for a unit, which of the following factors should generally receive the LEAST consideration?

    A. Lighting levels in the existing area
    B. Major work flow—the processing of paper
    C. Present and projected growth rate of the unit
    D. Traffic patterns of employees and visitors

6.____

7. The BEST way to secure effective management is usually to   7.___

    A. allow staff to help solve administrative problems of line management
    B. provide a good organization structure
    C. select capable managers
    D. set up conservative spans of control

8. Which of the following is NOT an advantage of oral instructions as compared with written   8.___
instructions?
Oral

    A. instructions can be easily changed
    B. instructions are superior in transmitting complex directives
    C. instructions facilitate exchange of information between a superior and his subordinate(s)
    D. discussions are possible with oral instructions, making it easier to ascertain understanding

9. Which organization principle is MOST closely related to procedural analysis and   9.___
improvement?

    A. Duplication, overlapping, and conflict should be eliminated.
    B. The objectives of the organization should be clearly defined.
    C. Managerial authority should be clearly defined.
    D. Top management should be freed of burdensome details.

10. Of the following control techniques, a _____ is MOST useful on large, complex projects.   10.___

    A. general work plan   B. Gantt chart
    C. monthly progress report   D. PERT chart

11. Work is organized so that the work is broken down into a series of jobs. Each unit of work   11.___
moves progressively from position to position until completion.
This paragraph BEST describes a

    A. parallel plan of work subdivision
    B. serial plan
    C. unit assembly plan
    D. unit process plan

12. According to the classic studies of Rensis Likert, the GREATEST factor making for good   12.___
morale and increased productivity was having a

    A. good program of employee benefits and wage scales
    B. supervisor who gave his employees free rein after they were fully trained and did
not interfere with them
    C. supervisor who was primarily interested in production
    D. supervisor who, while interested in production, was primarily *employee-centered*

13. The managerial grid shows two concerns and a range of interaction between them.   13.___
In this grid, the horizontal axis indicates a concern for _____ and the vertical axis
indicates a concern for_____.

    A. production; people   B. hierarchy; people
    C. organization; people   D. people; costs

14. It has been decided to make a few important revisions in the methods and procedures of a particular work unit. Of the following, which method of implementing these revisions would probably be the MOST desirable in terms of morale and of efficiency?

    A. Give all employees in unit individual instructions in the revised procedures and make sure each employee knows them before instructing the next.
    B. Institute all revisions at once, followed by on-the-job training for all members of the work unit.
    C. Introduce the revisions one at a time and accompany each revision with an orientation for employees.
    D. Set up a training course for the employees which instructs them in all aspects of the revised procedures prior to their implementation.

14.____

15. An operations research technique which would be employed to determine the optimum number of window clerks or interviewers to have in an agency serving the public would MOST likely be the use of

    A. line of balance
    C. simulation
    B. queueing theory
    D. work sampling

15.____

16. Douglas MacGregor's theory of human motivation classifies worker behavior into two distinct categories: Theory X and Theory Y. Theory X, the traditional view, states that the average man dislikes working and will avoid work if he can, unless coerced. Theory Y holds essentially the opposite view.
The manager can apply both of these theories to worker behavior BEST if he

    A. follows an *open-door* policy only with respect to his immediate subordinates
    B. recognizes his subordinates' mental and social needs as well as agency needs
    C. recognizes that executive responsibility is primarily limited to fulfillment of agency productivity goals
    D. directs his subordinate managers to follow a policy of close supervision

16.____

17. In interpersonal communications, it is important to ascertain whether oral directions and instruction are understood.
One of the MOST important sources of such information is known as

    A. the *halo* effect
    C. feedback
    B. evaluation
    D. quantitative analysis

17.____

18. The *grapevine* MOST often provides a useful service by

    A. correcting some of the deficiencies of the formal communication system
    B. rapidly conveying a true picture of events
    C. involving staff in current organizational changes
    D. interfering with the operation of the formal communication system

18.____

19. People who are in favor of a leadership style in which the subordinates help make decisions contend that it produces favorable effects in a work unit.
According to these people, which of the following is NOT likely to be an effect of such *participative management*?

19.____

A. Reduced turnover
B. Accelerated learning of duties
C. Greater acceptance of change
D. Reduced acceptance of the work unit's goals

20. Employees of a public service agency will be MOST likely to develop meaningful goals for both the agency and the employee and become committed to attaining them if supervisors   20.___

A. allow them unilaterally to set their own goals
B. provide them with a clear understanding of the premises underlying the agency's goals
C. encourage them to concentrate on setting only short-range goals for themselves
D. periodically review the agency's goals in order to suggest changes in accordance with current conditions

———

KEY (CORRECT ANSWERS)

1.	B		11.	B
2.	A		12.	D
3.	C		13.	A
4.	D		14.	D
5.	C		15.	B
6.	A		16.	B
7.	B		17.	C
8.	B		18.	A
9.	A		19.	D
10.	D		20.	B

———

EXAMINATION SECTION
TEST 1

DIRECTIONS: Each question or incomplete statement is followed by several suggested answers or completions. Select the one that BEST answers the question or completes the statement. *PRINT THE LETTER OF THE CORRECT ANSWER IN THE SPACE AT THE RIGHT.*

1. Assume that a civil service list has been established for a position in an agency which had provisional appointees serving in three permanent vacancies. One of these provisionals is on the eligible list, but was discharged because permanent appointments were accepted by three eligibles who were higher on the list. The former provisional has complained to the agency head, alleging that special efforts were made to appoint these eligibles. The personnel officer of the agency should advise the agency head that

    A. the court could compel him to appoint the former provisional appointee
    B. he is required by civil service law to appoint the higher ranking eligibles from the list
    C. the human rights commission could compel him to appoint the former provisional appointee
    D. he should attempt conciliation

1.____

2. Assume that two accountants working in a section under your supervision were appointed from the same eligible list. Accountant Jones received a higher score on the competitive examination than Accountant Doe; Jones was third on the eligible list and Doe was fifth. Jones was told to report to work on March 15 but Doe, who was working under a provisional appointment, was given permanent status as of March 1. For economy reasons, your agency head is considering abolishing one position of accountant and requests guidance from you before making any decision.
    It would be BEST to tell him that

    A. if he decides to abolish one position of accountant, he should lay off Jones because Doe was given permanent status before Jones
    B. under the rule of *one in three* Doe could not have been reached for appointment before Jones, so that Doe would have to be laid off first
    C. if he decides to abolish one position of accountant, he should lay off Doe because Doe's provisional appointment was in violation of the Civil Service Law
    D. he should evaluate the performance of Jones and Doe before making any determination as to which accountant to lay off

2.____

3. An employee who has been on the job for a number of years became a problem drinker during the past year. The supervisor and this employee are good friends.
    Because this problem has been affecting the work of the unit adversely, it would be BEST for the supervisor to

    A. attempt to cover up the problem by moving the subordinate's desk to a corner of the office where he would not be noticed so readily
    B. refer the employee for counseling to the employee counseling service
    C. reassign some of the problem drinker's responsibilities to other employees
    D. send the employee home in a tactful manner whenever he reports for duty in an unfit condition

3.____

4. In a strike situation, a member of the striking union reports for work but abstains from the full performance of his duties in his normal manner.
According to the state civil service law, it is *accurate* to say that the

    A. employee should be presumed to have engaged in a strike
    B. employee should not be presumed to have engaged in a strike
    C. city must bear the burden of proving that the employee engaged in a strike
    D. city may deny the employee the opportunity to rebut any charge that he engaged in a strike

4.____

5. Assume that, as a manager in a health agency which is establishing a *management-by-objectives* program, you are asked to review and make recommendations on the following goals set by the agency head for the coming year.
Which one of these objectives should you recommend dropping because of difficulty in verifying the degree to which the goal has been attained?

    A. Establishing night clinics in two preventive health care centers
    B. Informing more people of available health services
    C. Preparing a training manual for data-processing personnel
    D. Producing a 4-page health news bulletin to be distributed monthly to employees

5.____

6. The MAIN purpose of the *management-by-objectives* system is to

    A. develop a method of appraising the performance of managerial employees against verifiable objectives rather than against subjective appraisals and personal supervision
    B. decentralize managerial decision-making more effectively by setting goals for personnel all the way down to each first-line supervisor as well as to staff people
    C. increase managerial accountability and improve managerial effectiveness
    D. enable top level managerial employees to impose quantitative goals which will focus attention on the relevant trends that may affect the future

6.____

7. Certain city and state employees are on one year's probation for violating the strike provisions of the state civil service law.
According to a ruling by the state attorney general, in the event of layoffs during their year of probation, the status of these employees should be considered

    A. *permanent,* with retention rights based on original date of appointment
    B. *probationary,* subject to layoff before permanent employees
    C. *permanent,* to be credited with one year less service than indicated by the original date of appointment
    D. *probationary,* subject to layoff before other employees in the layoff unit except for those with one year's seniority

7.____

8. Assume that, as a senior supervisor conducting a training course for a group of newly-assigned first-line supervisors, you emphasize that an effective supervisor should encourage employee suggestions. One member of the group dissents, asserting that many employees come up with worthless, time-wasting ideas.
The one of the following which would be the MOST appropriate response for you to make is that

8.____

122

A. the supervisor's attitude is wrong, because no suggestion is entirely without merit
B. the supervisor must remember that encouragement of employee suggestions is the major part of any employee development program
C. even if a suggestion seems worthless, the participation of the employee helps to increase his identification with the agency
D. even if a suggestion seems worthless, the supervisor may be able to save it for future use

9. The *grapevine* is an informal channel of communication which exists among employees in an organization as a natural result of their social interaction, and their desire to be kept posted on the latest information. Some information transmitted through the grapevine is truth, some half-truth, and some just rumor.
Which one of the following would be the MOST appropriate attitude for a member of a management team to have about the grapevine?

    9.____

A. The grapevine often carries false, malicious, and uncontrollable rumors and management should try to stamp it out by improving official channels of communication.
B. There are more important problems; normally only a small percentage of employees are interested in information transmitted through the grapevine.
C. The grapevine can give management insight into what employees think and feel and can help to supplement the formal communication systems.
D. The grapevine gives employees a harmless outlet for their imagination and an opportunity to relieve their fears and tensions in the form of rumors.

10. Although there are no formal performance appraisal mechanisms for non-managerial employees, managers nevertheless make informal appraisals because some method is needed to measure progress and to let employees know how they are doing.
The MOST important recent trend in making performance appraisals is toward judging the employee *primarily* on the extent to which he has

    10.____

A. tried to perform his assigned tasks
B. demonstrated personal traits which are accepted as necessary to do the job satisfactorily
C. accomplished the objectives set for his job
D. followed the procedures established for the job

11. The proof of a successful human relations program in an organization is the morale crises that never happen.
Of the following, the implication for managers that follows MOST directly from this statement is that they should

    11.____

A. review and initiate revisions in all organization policies which may have an adverse effect on employee morale
B. place more emphasis on ability to anticipate and prevent morale problems than on ability to resolve an actual crisis
C. see that first-line supervisors work fairly and understandingly with employees
D. avoid morale crises at all costs, since even the best resolution leaves scars, suspicions, and animosities

12. Suppose that you are conducting a conference on a specific problem. One employee   12._____
makes a suggestion which you think is highly impractical.
Of the following, the way for you to respond to this suggestion is FIRST to

    A. be frank and tell the employee that his solution is wrong
    B. ask the employee in what way his suggestion will solve the problem under discussion
    C. refrain from any comment on it, and ask the group whether they have any other solutions to offer
    D. ask another participant to point out what is wrong with the suggestion

13. Suppose that a manager notices continuing deterioration in the work, conduct, and inter-   13._____
personal relationships of one of his immediate subordinates, indicating that this
employee has more than a minor emotional problem. Although the manager has made
an attempt to help this employee by talking over his problems with him on several occasions, the employee has shown little improvement.
Of the following, generally the MOST constructive action for the manager to take at
this point would be to

    A. continue to be supportive by sympathetic listening and counseling
    B. show tolerance toward the performance of the disturbed employee
    C. discuss the employee's deteriorating condition with him and suggest that he seek professional help
    D. consider whether the needs of this employee and the agency would be best served by his transfer to another division

14. A manager has a problem involving conflict between two employees concerning a   14._____
method of performing a work assignment. He does not know the reasons for this conflict.
The MOST valuable communications method he can use to aid him in resolving the
problem is

    A. a formal hearing for each employee
    B. a staff meeting
    C. disciplinary memoranda
    D. an informal interview with each employee

15. As a training technique, role-playing is generally considered to be MOST successful   15._____
when it results in

    A. uncovering the underlying causes of conflict so that any recurrences are prevented
    B. recreating an actual work situation which involves conflict among people and in which members of the group simulate specific personalities
    C. freeing people from patterns of rigid thinking and enabling them to look at themselves and others in a new way
    D. increasing the participants' powers of logic and reasoning

16. In conducting a disciplinary interview, a supervisor finds that he must ask some highly   16._____
personal questions which are relevant to the problem at hand.
The interviewer is MOST likely to get *truthful* answers to these questions if he asks
them

A. early in the interview, before the interviewee has had a chance to become emotional
B. in a manner so that the interviewee can answer them with a simple *yes* or *no*
C. well into the interview, after rapport and trust have been established
D. just after the close of the interview, so that the questions appear to be off the record

17. Suppose that, as a newly assigned manager, you observe that a supervisor in your division uses autocratic methods which are causing resentment among his subordinates. Of the following, the MOST likely reason for this supervisor's using such methods is that he   17.____

A. was probably exposed to this type of supervision himself
B. does not have an intuitive sense of tact, diplomacy, and consideration and no amount of training can change this
C. received approval for use of such methods from his former subordinates
D. does not understand the basic concept of rewards and punishments in the practice of supervision

18. A newly appointed employee, Mr. Jones, was added to the staff of a supervisor who, because of the pressure of other work, turned him over to an experienced subordinate by saying, *Show Mr. Jones around and give him something to do.*
On the basis of this experience, Mr. Jones' FIRST impression of his new position was most likely to have been   18.____

A. *negative,* mainly because it appeared that his job was not worth his supervisor's attention
B. *negative,* mainly because the more experienced subordinate would tend to emphasize the unpleasant aspects of the work
C. *positive,* mainly because his supervisor wasted no time in assigning him to a subordinate
D. *positive,* mainly because he saw himself working for a dynamic supervisor who expected immediate results

19. An employee who stays in one assignment for a number of years often develops a feeling of possessiveness concerning his knowledge of the job which may develop into a problem.
Of the following, the BEST way for a supervisor to remedy this difficulty is to   19.____

A. give the employee less important work to do
B. point out minor errors as often as possible
C. raise performance standards for all employees
D. rotate the employee to a different assignment

20. A supervisor who tends to be supportive of his subordinates, in contrast to a supervisor who relies upon an authoritarian style of leadership, is more likely, in dealing with his staff, to have to listen to complaints, to have to tolerate emotionally upset employees, and even have to hear unreasonable and insulting remarks.
Compared to the authoritarian supervisor, he is MORE likely to   20.____

A. be unconsciously fearful of failure
B. have an overriding interest in production
C. have subordinates who are better educated
D. receive accurate feedback information

KEY (CORRECT ANSWERS)

1.	B		11.	B
2.	B		12.	B
3.	B		13.	C
4.	A		14.	D
5.	B		15.	C
6.	C		16.	C
7.	B		17.	A
8.	C		18.	A
9.	C		19.	D
10.	C		20.	D

———

TEST 2

DIRECTIONS: Each question or incomplete statement is followed by several suggested answers or completions. Select the one that BEST answers the question or completes the statement. *PRINT THE LETTER OF THE CORRECT ANSWER IN THE SPACE AT THE RIGHT.*

1. Assume that one of your subordinates, a supervisor in charge of a small unit in your bureau, asks your advice in handling a situation which has just occurred in his unit. On returning from a meeting the supervisor notices that Jane Jones, the unit secretary, is not at her regular work location. Another employee had become faint, and the secretary accompanied this employee outdoors for some fresh air. It is a long-standing rule that no employee is permitted to leave the building during office hours except on official business or with the unit head's approval. Quite recently another employee was reprimanded by the supervisor for going out at 10 A.M. for a cup of coffee.
Of the following, it would be BEST for you to advise the supervisor to

    A. circulate a memo within the unit, restating the department's regulation concerning leaving the building during office hours
    B. overlook this rule violation in view of the extenuating circumstances
    C. personally reprimand the unit secretary since all employees must be treated in the same way when official rules are broken
    D. tell the unit secretary that you should reprimand her, but that you've decided to overlook the rule infraction this time

1.____

2. Of the following, the MOST valid reason why the application of behavioral modification techniques to management of large organizations is not yet widely accepted by managers is that these techniques are

    A. based mainly on research conducted under highly controlled conditions
    B. more readily adaptable to training unskilled employees
    C. incompatible with the validated *management-by-objectives* approach
    D. manipulative and incompatible with the democratic approach

2.____

3. Because of intensive pressures which have developed since the onset of the city's financial problems, the members of a certain bureau have begun to file grievances about their working conditions. These protests are accumulating at a much greater rate than normal and faster than they can be disposed of under the current state of affairs. Concerned about the possible effect of these unresolved matters on the productivity of the bureau at such a critical time, the administrator in charge decides to take immediate action to improve staff relationships. With this intention in mind, he should

    A. explain to the staff why their grievances cannot be handled at the present time; then inform them that there will be a moratorium on the filing of additional grievances until the current backlog has been eliminated
    B. assemble all grievants at a special meeting and assure them that their problems will be handled in due course, but the current pressures preclude the prompt settling of their grievances

3.____

    C. assign the assistant directors of the bureau to immediately schedule and conduct hearings on the accumulated grievances until the backlog is eliminated

    D. suggest that the grievants again confer with their supervisors about their problems, orally rather than in writing, with direct appeal to him for such cases as are not resolved in this manner

4. A supervisor is attending a staff meeting with other accounting supervisors during which the participants are to propose various possible methods of dealing with a complex operational problem.
The one of the following procedures which will MOST likely produce an acceptable proposal for solving this problem at this meeting is for the

    A. group to agree at the beginning of the meeting on the kinds of approaches to the problem that are most likely to succeed

    B. conference leader to set a firm time limit on the period during which the participants are to present whatever ideas come to mind

    C. group to discuss each proposal fully before the next proposal is made

    D. conference leader to urge every participant in the meeting to present at least one proposal

5. Which one of the following types of communication systems would foster an authoritarian atmosphere in a large agency?
A communication system which

    A. is restricted to organizational procedures and specific job instructions

    B. provides information to employees about the rationale for their jobs

    C. informs employees about their job performance

    D. provides information about the relationship of employees' work to the agency's goals

6. According to most management experts, the one of the following which would generally have SERIOUS shortcomings as a component of a performance evaluation program is

    A. rating the performance of each subordinate against the performance of other subordinates

    B. limiting the appraisal to an evaluation of current performance

    C. rating each subordinate in terms of clearly stated, measurable job goals

    D. interviewing the subordinate to discuss present job performance and ways of improvement

7. Which of the following is consistent with the management-by-objectives approach as used in a fiscal affairs division of a large city agency?

    A. Performance goals for the division are established by the administrator, who requires daily progress reports for each accounting unit.

    B. Each subordinate accountant participates in setting his own short term performance goals.

    C. A detailed set of short-term performance goals for each accountant is prepared by his supervisor.

    D. Objectives are established and progress evaluated by a committee of administrative accountants.

Questions 8-11.

DIRECTIONS: Questions 8 through 11 are to be answered on the basis of the information
given below.

Assume that you are the director of a small bureau, organized into three divisions. The
bureau has a total of twenty employees: fourteen in professional titles and six in clerical titles.
Each division has a chief who reports directly to you and who supervises five employees.

For Questions 8 through 11, you are to select the MOST appropriate training method,
from the four choices given, based on the situation in the question:
   A.   Lecture, with a small blackboard available
   B.   Lecture, with audio-visual aids
   C.   Conference
   D.   Buddy system (experienced worker is accompanied by worker to be trained)

8.   A major reorganization of your department was completed. You have decided to conduct   8._____
a training session of about one hour's duration for all your subordinates in order to
acquaint them with the new departmental structure as well as the new responsibilities
which have been assigned to the divisions of your bureau.

9.   Three assistant supervisors, each with one year of service in your department, are trans-   9._____
ferred to your bureau as part of the process of strengthening the major activity of your
bureau. In connection with their duties, they are required to do field visits to business
firms located in the various industrial areas of the city.

10.   The work of your bureau requires that various forms be processed sequentially through   10._____
each of three divisions. In recent weeks, you have received complaints from the division
chiefs that their production is being impeded by a lack of cooperation from the chiefs and
workers in the other divisions.

11.   In order to improve the efficiency of the department, your department head has directed   11._____
that all bureaus hold weekly, thirty-minute-long training sessions for all employees, to
review relevant work procedures.

12.   Which one of the following actions is usually MOST appropriate for a manager to take in   12._____
order to encourage and develop coordination of effort among different units or individuals
within an organization?

   A.   Providing rewards to the most productive employees
   B.   Giving employees greater responsibility and the authority to exercise it
   C.   Emphasizing to the employees that it is important to coordinate their efforts
   D.   Explaining the goals of the organization to the employees and how their jobs relate
to those goals

13.   The management of time is one of the critical aspects of any supervisor's performance.   13._____
Therefore, in evaluating a subordinate from the viewpoint of how he manages time, a
supervisor should rate HIGHEST the subordinate who

A. concentrates on each task as he undertakes it
B. performs at a standard and predictable pace under all circumstances
C. takes shortened lunch periods when he is busy
D. tries to do two things simultaneously

14. A MAJOR research finding regarding employee absenteeism is that   14.____

A. absenteeism is likely to be higher on hot days
B. male employees tend to be absent more than female employees
C. the way an employee is treated has a definite bearing on absenteeism
D. the distance employees have to travel is one of the most important factors in absenteeism

15. Of the following, the supervisory behavior that is of GREATEST benefit to the organiza-   15.____
tion is exhibited by supervisors who

A. are strict with subordinates about following rules and regulations
B. encourage subordinates to be interested in the work
C. are willing to assist with subordinates' work on most occasions
D. get the most done with available staff and resources

16. In order to maintain a proper relationship with a worker who is assigned to staff rather   16.____
than line functions, a line supervisor should

A. accept all recommendations of the staff worker
B. include the staff worker in the conferences called by the supervisor for his subordi-
nates
C. keep the staff worker informed of developments in the area of his staff assignment
D. require that the staff worker's recommendations be communicated to the supervi-
sor through the supervisor's own superior

17. Of the following, the GREATEST disadvantage of placing a worker in a staff position   17.____
under the direct supervision of the supervisor whom he advises is the possibility that the

A. staff worker will tend to be insubordinate because of a feeling of superiority over
the supervisor
B. staff worker will tend to give advice of the type which the supervisor wants to hear
or finds acceptable
C. supervisor will tend to be mistrustful of the advice of a worker of subordinate rank
D. supervisor will tend to derive little benefit from the advice because to supervise
properly he should know at least as much as his subordinate

18. One factor which might be given consideration in deciding upon the optimum span of   18.____
control of a supervisor over his immediate subordinates is the position of the supervisor
in the hierarchy of the organization. It is generally considered proper that the number of
subordinates immediately supervised by a higher, upper echelon, supervisor

A. is unrelated to and tends to form no pattern with the number supervised by lower
level supervisors
B. should be about the same as the number supervised by a lower level supervisor
C. should be larger than the number supervised by a lower level supervisor
D. should be smaller than the number supervised by a lower level supervisor

19. Assume that you are a supervisor and have been assigned to assist the head of a large agency unit. He asks you to prepare a simple, functional organization chart of the unit. Such a chart would be USEFUL for

    A. favorably impressing members of the public with the important nature of the agency's work
    B. graphically presenting staff relationships which may indicate previously unknown duplications, overlaps, and gaps in job duties
    C. motivating all employees toward better performance because they will have a better understanding of job procedures
    D. subtly and inoffensively making known to the staff in the unit that you are now in a position of responsibility

19.____

20. In some large organizations, management's traditional means of learning about employee dissatisfaction has been the *open door policy.*
This policy *usually* means that

    A. management lets it be known that a management representative is generally available to discuss employees' questions, suggestions, and complaints
    B. management sets up an informal employee organization to establish a democratic procedure for orderly representation of employees
    C. employees are encouraged to attempt to resolve dissatisfactions at the lowest possible level of authority
    D. employees are provided with an address or box so that they may safely and anonymously register complaints

20.____

KEY (CORRECT ANSWERS)

1.	B		11.	A
2.	A		12.	D
3.	D		13.	A
4.	B		14.	C
5.	A		15.	D
6.	A		16.	C
7.	B		17.	B
8.	B		18.	D
9.	D		19.	B
10.	C		20.	A

READING COMPREHENSION
UNDERSTANDING AND INTERPRETING WRITTEN MATERIAL
EXAMINATION SECTION
TEST 1

DIRECTIONS: Each question or incomplete statement is followed by several suggested answers or completions. Select the one that BEST answers the question or completes the statement. *PRINT THE LETTER OF THE CORRECT ANSWER IN THE SPACE AT THE RIGHT.*

Questions 1-5.

DIRECTIONS: Questions 1 through 5 are to be answered SOLELY on the basis of the following passage.

The most effective control mechanism to prevent gross incompetence on the part of public employees is a good personnel program. The personnel officer in the line departments and the central personnel agency should exert positive leadership to raise levels of performance. Although the key factor is the quality of the personnel recruited, staff members other than personnel officers can make important contributions to efficiency. Administrative analysts, now employed in many agencies, make detailed studies of organization and procedures, with the purpose of eliminating delays, waste, and other inefficiencies. Efficiency is, however, more than a question of good organization and procedures; it is also the product of the attitudes and values of the public employees. Personal motivation can provide the will to be efficient. The best management studies will not result in substantial improvement of the performance of those employees who feel no great urge to work up to their abilities.

1. The above passage indicates that the KEY factor in preventing gross incompetence of public employees is the

    A. hiring of administrative analysts to assist personnel people
    B. utilization of effective management studies
    C. overlapping of responsibility
    D. quality of the employees hired

1.____

2. According to the above passage, the central personnel agency staff SHOULD

    A. work more closely with administrative analysts in the line departments than with personnel officers
    B. make a serious effort to avoid jurisdictional conflicts with personnel officers in line departments
    C. contribute to improving the quality of work of public employees
    D. engage in a comprehensive program to change the public's negative image of public employees

2.____

3. The above passage indicates that efficiency in an organization can BEST be brought about by

    A. eliminating ineffective control mechanisms
    B. instituting sound organizational procedures

3.____

C. promoting competent personnel
D. recruiting people with desire to do good work

4. According to the above passage, the purpose of administrative analysis in a public agency is to

4.___

A. prevent injustice to the public employee
B. promote the efficiency of the agency
C. protect the interests of the public
D. ensure the observance of procedural due process

5. The above passage implies that a considerable rise in the quality of work of public employees can be brought about by

5.___

A. encouraging positive employee attitudes toward work
B. controlling personnel officers who exceed their powers
C. creating warm personal associations among public employees in an agency
D. closing loopholes in personnel organization and procedures

Questions 6-8.

DIRECTIONS: Questions 6 through 8 are to be answered SOLELY on the basis of the following passage on Employee Needs.

EMPLOYEE NEEDS

The greatest waste in industry and in government may be that of human resources. This waste usually derives not from employees' unwillingness or inability, but from management's ineptness to meet the maintenance and motivational needs of employees. Maintenance needs refer to such needs as providing employees with safe places to work, written work rules, job security, adequate salary, employer-sponsored social activities, and with knowledge of their role in the overall framework of the organization. However, of greatest significance to employees are the motivational needs of job growth, achievement, responsibility, and recognition.

Although employee dissatisfaction may stem from either poor maintenance or poor motivation factors, the outward manifestation of the dissatisfaction may be very much alike, i.e., negativism, complaints, deterioration of performance, and so forth. The improvement in the lighting of an employee's work area or raising his level of pay won't do much good if the source of the dissatisfaction is the absence of a meaningful assignment. By the same token, if an employee is dissatisfied with what he considers inequitable pay, the introduction of additional challenge in his work may simply make matters worse.

It is relatively easy for an employee to express frustration by complaining about pay, washroom conditions, fringe benefits, and so forth; but most people cannot easily express resentment in terms of the more abstract concepts concerning job growth, responsibility, and achievement.

It would be wrong to assume that there is no interaction between maintenance and motivational needs of employees. For example, conditions of high motivation often overshadow poor maintenance conditions. If an organization is in a period of strong growth and expansion, opportunities for job growth, responsibility, recognition, and achievement are usually abundant, but the rapid growth may have outrun the upkeep of maintenance factors. In this situation, motivation may be high, but only if employees recognize the poor maintenance conditions as unavoidable and temporary. The subordination of maintenance factors cannot go on indefinitely, even with the highest motivation.

Both maintenance and motivation factors influence the behavior of all employees, but employees are not identical and, furthermore, the needs of any individual do not remain constant. However, a broad distinction can be made between employees who have a basic orientation toward maintenance factors and those with greater sensitivity toward motivation factors.

A highly maintenance-oriented individual, preoccupied with the factors peripheral to his job rather than the job itself, is more concerned with comfort than challenge. He does not get deeply involved with his work but does with the condition of his work area, toilet facilities, and his time for going to lunch. By contrast, a strongly motivation-oriented employee is usually relatively indifferent to his surroundings and is caught up in the pursuit of work goals.

Fortunately, there are few people who are either exclusively maintenance-oriented or purely motivation-oriented. The former would be deadwood in an organization, while the latter might trample on those around him in his pursuit to achieve his goals.

6. With respect to employee motivational and maintenance needs, the management policies of an organization which is growing rapidly will probably result   6.____

    A. more in meeting motivational needs rather than maintenance needs
    B. more in meeting maintenance needs rather than motivational needs
    C. in meeting both of these needs equally
    D. in increased effort to define the motivational and maintenance needs of its employees

7. In accordance with the above passage, which of the following CANNOT be considered as an example of an employee maintenance need for railroad clerks?   7.____

    A. Providing more relief periods
    B. Providing fair salary increases at periodic intervals
    C. Increasing job responsibilities
    D. Increasing health insurance benefits

8. Most employees in an organization may be categorized as being interested in   8.____

    A. maintenance needs *only*
    B. motivational needs *only*
    C. both motivational and maintenance needs
    D. money only, to the exclusion of all other needs

Questions 9-11.

DIRECTIONS: Questions 9 through 11 are to be answered SOLELY on the basis of the following passage on Good Employee Practices.

GOOD EMPLOYEE PRACTICES

As a city employee, you will be expected to take an interest in your work and perform the duties of your job to the best of your ability and in a spirit of cooperation. Nothing shows an interest in your work more than coming to work on time, not only at the start of the day but also when returning from lunch. If it is necessary for you to keep a personal appointment at lunch hour which might cause a delay in getting back to work on time, you should explain the situation to your supervisor and get his approval to come back a little late before you leave for lunch.

You should do everything that is asked of you willingly and consider important even the small jobs that your supervisor gives you. Although these jobs may seem unimportant, if you forget to do them or if you don't do them right, trouble may develop later.

Getting along well with your fellow workers will add much to the enjoyment of your work. You should respect your fellow workers and try to see their side when a disagreement arises. The better you get along with your fellow workers and your supervisor, the better you will like your job and the better you will be able to do it.

9. According to the above passage, in your job as a city employee, you are expected to   9.___

    A. show a willingness to cooperate on the job
    B. get your supervisor's approval before keeping any personal appointments at lunch hour
    C. avoid doing small jobs that seem unimportant
    D. do the easier jobs at the start of the day and the more difficult ones later on

10. According to the above passage, getting to work on time shows that you   10.___

    A. need the job
    B. have an interest in your work
    C. get along well with your fellow workers
    D. like your supervisor

11. According to the above passage, the one of the following statements that is NOT true is   11.___

    A. if you do a small job wrong, trouble may develop
    B. you should respect your fellow workers
    C. if you disagree with a fellow worker, you should try to see his side of the story
    D. the less you get along with your supervisor, the better you will be able to do your job

Questions 12-15.

DIRECTIONS: Questions 12 through 15 are to be answered SOLELY on the basis of the following passage on Employee Suggestions.

EMPLOYEE SUGGESTIONS

To increase the effectiveness of the city government, the city asks its employees to offer suggestions when they feel an improvement could be made in some government operation. The Employees' Suggestions Program was started to encourage city employees to do this.

Through this Program, which is only for city employees, cash awards may be given to those whose suggestions are submitted and approved. Suggestions are looked for not only from supervisors but from all city employees as any city employee may get an idea which might be approved and contribute greatly to the solution of some problem of city government

Therefore, all suggestions for improvement are welcome, whether they be suggestions on how to improve working conditions, or on how to increase the speed with which work is done, or on how to reduce or eliminate such things as waste, time losses, accidents or fire hazards. There are, however, a few types of suggestions for which cash awards cannot be given. An example of this type would be a suggestion to increase salaries or a suggestion to change the regulations about annual leave or about sick leave. The number of suggestions sent in has increased sharply during the past few years. It is hoped that it will keep increasing in the future in order to meet the city's needs for more ideas for improved ways of doing things.

12. According to the above passage, the MAIN reason why the city asks its employees for suggestions about government operations is to   12._____

    A. increase the effectiveness of the city government
    B. show that the Employees' Suggestion Program is working well
    C. show that everybody helps run the city government
    D. have the employee win a prize

13. According to the above passage, the Employees' Suggestion Program can approve awards ONLY for those suggestions that come from   13._____

    A. city employees
    B. city employees who are supervisors
    C. city employees who are not supervisors
    D. experienced employees of the city

14. According to the above passage, a cash award cannot be given through the Employees' Suggestion Program for a suggestion about   14._____

    A. getting work done faster
    B. helping prevent accidents on the job
    C. increasing the amount of annual leave for city employees
    D. reducing the chance of fire where city employees work

15. According to the above passage, the suggestions sent in during the past few years have   15._____

    A. all been approved
    B. generally been well written
    C. been mostly about reducing or eliminating waste
    D. been greater in number than before

Questions 16-18.

DIRECTIONS: Questions 16 through 18 are to be answered SOLELY on the basis of the following passage.

The supervisor will gain the respect of the members of his staff and increase his influence over them by controlling his temper and avoiding criticizing anyone publicly. When a mistake is made, the good supervisor will talk it over with the employee quietly and privately. The supervisor will listen to the employee's story, suggest the better way of doing the job, and offer help so the mistake won't happen again. Before closing the discussion, the supervisor should try to find something good to say about other parts of the employee's work. Some praise and appreciation, along with instruction, is more likely to encourage an employee to improve in those areas where he is weakest.

16. A good title that would show the meaning of the above passage would be   16.__

    A. HOW TO CORRECT EMPLOYEE ERRORS
    B. HOW TO PRAISE EMPLOYEES
    C. MISTAKES ARE PREVENTABLE
    D. THE WEAK EMPLOYEE

17. According to the above passage, the work of an employee who has made a mistake is   17.__
more likely to improve if the supervisor

    A. avoids criticizing him
    B. gives him a chance to suggest a better way of doing the work
    C. listens to the employee's excuses to see if he is right
    D. praises good work at the same time he corrects the mistake

18. According to the above passage, when a supervisor needs to correct an employee's mis-   18.__
take, it is important that he

    A. allow some time to go by after the mistake is made
    B. do so when other employees are not present
    C. show his influence with his tone of voice
    D. tell other employees to avoid the same mistake

Questions 19-23.

DIRECTIONS: Questions 19 through 23 are to be answered SOLELY on the basis of the fol-
                lowing passage.

In studying the relationships of people to the organizational structure, it is absolutely nec-essary to identify and recognize the informal organizational structure. These relationships are necessary when coordination of a plan is attempted. They may be with *the boss,* line supervi-sors, staff personnel, or other representatives of the formal organization's hierarchy, and they may include the *liaison men* who serve as the leaders of the informal organization. An acquaintanceship with the people serving in these roles in the organization, and its formal counterpart, permits a supervisor to recognize sensitive areas in which it is simple to get a conflict reaction. Avoidance of such areas, plus conscious efforts to inform other people of his own objectives for various plans, will usually enlist their aid and support. Planning *without people* can lead to disaster because the individuals who must act together to make any plan a success are more important than the plans themselves.

19. Of the following titles, the one that MOST clearly describes the above passage is   19

    A. COORDINATION OF A FUNCTION
    B. AVOIDANCE OF CONFLICT
    C. PLANNING WITH PEOPLE
    D. PLANNING OBJECTIVES

20. According to the above passage, attempts at coordinating plans may fail unless   20._____

    A. the plan's objectives are clearly set forth
    B. conflict between groups is resolved
    C. the plans themselves are worthwhile
    D. informal relationships are recognized

21. According to the above passage, conflict   21._____

    A. may, in some cases, be desirable to secure results
    B. produces more heat than light
    C. should be avoided at all costs
    D. possibilities can be predicted by a sensitive supervisor

22. The above passage implies that   22._____

    A. informal relationships are more important than formal structure
    B. the weakness of a formal structure depends upon informal relationships
    C. liaison men are the key people to consult when taking formal and informal structures into account
    D. individuals in a group are at least as important as the plans for the group

23. The above passage suggests that   23._____

    A. some planning can be disastrous
    B. certain people in sensitive areas should be avoided
    C. the supervisor should discourage acquaintanceships in the organization
    D. organizational relationships should be consciously limited

Questions 24-25.

DIRECTIONS: Questions 24 and 25 are to be answered SOLELY on the basis of the following passage.

Good personnel relations of an organization depend upon mutual confidence, trust, and good will. The basis of confidence is understanding. Most troubles start with people who do not understand each other. When the organization's intentions or motives are misunderstood, or when reasons for actions, practices, or policies are misconstrued, complete cooperation from individuals is not forthcoming. If management expects full cooperation from employees, it has a responsibility of sharing with them the information which is the foundation of proper understanding, confidence, and trust. Personnel management has long since outgrown the days when it was the vogue to *treat them rough and tell them nothing.* Up-to-date personnel management provides all possible information about the activities, aims, and purposes of the organization. It seems altogether creditable that a desire should exist among employees for such information which the best-intentioned executive might think would not interest them and which the worst-intentioned would think was none of their business.

24. The above passage implies that one of the causes of the difficulty which an organization   24._____
might have with its personnel relations is that its employees

    A. have not expressed interest in the activities, aims, and purposes of the organization
    B. do not believe in the good faith of the organization

C. have not been able to give full cooperation to the organization
D. do not recommend improvements in the practices and policies of the organization

25. According to the above passage, in order for an organization to have good personnel relations, it is NOT essential that

    25.____

A. employees have confidence in the organization
B. the purposes of the organization be understood by the employees
C. employees have a desire for information about the organization
D. information about the organization be communicated to employees

---

KEY (CORRECT ANSWERS)

1.	D		11.	D
2.	C		12.	A
3.	D		13.	A
4.	B		14.	C
5.	A		15.	D
6.	A		16.	A
7.	C		17.	D
8.	C		18.	B
9.	A		19.	C
10.	B		20.	D

21.	D
22.	D
23.	A
24.	B
25.	C

TEST 2

DIRECTIONS: Questions 1 through 8 are to be answered SOLELY on the basis of the following passage.

Important figures in education and in public affairs have recommended development of a private organization sponsored in part by various private foundations which would offer installment payment plans to full-time matriculated students in accredited colleges and universities in the United States and Canada. Contracts would be drawn to cover either tuition and fees, or tuition, fees, room and board in college facilities, from one year up to and including six years. A special charge, which would vary with the length of the contract, would be added to the gross repayable amount. This would be in addition to interest at a rate which would vary with the income of the parents. There would be a 3% annual interest charge for families with total income, before income taxes, of $50,000 or less. The rate would increase by 1/10 of 1% for every $1,000 of additional net income in excess of $50,000 up to a maximum of 10% interest. Contracts would carry an insurance provision on the life of the parent or guardian who signs the contract; all contracts must have the signature of a parent or guardian. Payment would be scheduled in equal monthly installments.

1. Which of the following students would be eligible for the payment plan described in the above passage? A

    A. matriculated student taking six semester hours toward a graduate degree
    B. matriculated student taking seventeen semester hours toward an undergraduate degree
    C. graduate matriculated at the University of Mexico taking eighteen semester hours toward a graduate degree
    D. student taking eighteen semester hours in a special pre-matriculation program

1.____

2. According to the above passage, the organization described would be sponsored in part by

    A. private foundations
    B. colleges and universities
    C. persons in the field of education
    D. persons in public life

2.____

3. Which of the following expenses could NOT be covered by a contract with the organization described in the above passage?

    A. Tuition amounting to $20,000 per year
    B. Registration and laboratory fees
    C. Meals at restaurants near the college
    D. Rent for an apartment in a college dormitory

3.____

4. The total amount to be paid would include ONLY the

    A. principal
    B. principal and interest
    C. principal, interest, and special charge
    D. principal, interest, special charge, and fee

4.____

5. The contract would carry insurance on the   5.__

    A. life of the student
    B. life of the student's parents
    C. income of the parents of the student
    D. life of the parent who signed the contract

6. The interest rate for an annual loan of $25,000 from the organization described in the   6.__
above passage for a student whose family's net income was $55,000 should be

    A. 3%   B. 3.5%   C. 4%   D. 4.5%

7. The interest rate for an annual loan of $35,000 from the organization described in the   7.__
above passage for a student whose family's net income was $100,000 should be

    A. 5%   B. 8%   C. 9%   D. 10%

8. John Lee has submitted an application for the installment payment plan described in the   8.__
above passage. John's mother and father have a store which grossed $500,000 last
year, but the income which the family received from the store was $90,000 before taxes.
They also had $5,000 income from stock dividends. They paid $10,000 in income taxes.
The amount of income upon which the interest should be based is

    A. $85,000   B. $90,000   C. $95,000   D. $105,000

Questions 9-13.

DIRECTIONS: Questions 9 through 13 are to be answered SOLELY on the basis of the following passage.

    Since an organization chart is pictorial in nature, there is a tendency for it to be drawn in
an artistically balanced and appealing fashion, regardless of the realities of actual organizational structure. In addition to being subject to this distortion, there is the difficulty of commu-
nicating in any organization chart the relative importance or the relative size of various
component parts of an organizational structure. Furthermore, because of the need for sim-
plicity of design, an organization chart can never indicate the full extent of the interrelation-
ships among the component parts of an organization.

    These interrelationships are often just as vital as the specifications which an organization
chart endeavors to indicate. Yet, if an organization chart were to be drawn with all the wide
variety of criss-crossing communication and cooperation networks existent within a typical
organization, the chart would probably be much more confusing than informative. It is also
obvious that no organization chart as such can prove or disprove that the organizational
structure it represents is effective in realizing the objectives of the organization. At best, an
organization chart can only illustrate some of the various factors to be taken into consideration in understanding, devising, or altering organizational arrangements.

9. According to the above passage, an organization chart can be expected to portray the   9.

    A. structure of the organization along somewhat ideal lines
    B. relative size of the organizational units quite accurately
    C. channels of information distribution within the organization graphically
    D. extent of the obligation of each unit to meet the organizational objectives

10. According to the above passage, those aspects of internal functioning which are NOT shown on an organization chart

    A. can be considered to have little practical application in the operations of the organization

    B. might well be considered to be as important as the structural relationships which a chart does present

    C. could be the cause of considerable confusion in the operations of an organization which is quite large

    D. would be most likely to provide the information needed to determine the overall effectiveness of an organization

10.___

11. In the above passage, the one of the following conditions which is NOT implied as being a defect of an organization chart is that an organization chart may

    A. present a picture of the organizational structure which is different from the structure that actually exists

    B. fail to indicate the comparative size of various organizational units

    C. be limited in its ability to convey some of the meaningful aspects of organizational relationships

    D. become less useful over a period of time during which the organizational facts which it illustrated have changed

11.___

12. The one of the following which is the MOST suitable title for the above passage is

    A. THE DESIGN AND CONSTRUCTION OF AN ORGANIZATION CHART

    B. THE INFORMAL ASPECTS OF AN ORGANIZATION CHART

    C. THE INHERENT DEFICIENCIES OF AN ORGANIZATION CHART

    D. THE UTILIZATION OF A TYPICAL ORGANIZATION CHART

12.___

13. It can be INFERRED from the above passage that the function of an organization chart is to

    A. contribute to the comprehension of the organization form and arrangements

    B. establish the capabilities of the organization to operate effectively

    C. provide a balanced picture of the operations of the organization

    D. eliminate the need for complexity in the organization's structure

13.___

Questions 14-16.

DIRECTIONS: Questions 14 through 16 are to be answered SOLELY on the basis of the following passage.

In dealing with visitors to the school office, the school secretary must use initiative, tact, and good judgment. All visitors should be greeted promptly and courteously. The nature of their business should be determined quickly and handled expeditiously. Frequently, the secretary should be able to handle requests, receipts, deliveries, or passes herself. Her judgment should determine when a visitor should see members of the staff or the principal. Serious problems or doubtful cases should be referred to a supervisor.

14. In general, visitors should be handled by the   14.___

    A. school secretary   B. principal
    C. appropriate supervisor   D. person who is free

15. It is wise to obtain the following information from visitors: 15.___

    A. Name   B. Nature of business
    C. Address   D. Problems they have

16. All visitors who wish to see members of the staff should   16.___

    A. be permitted to do so
    B. produce identification
    C. do so for valid reasons only
    D. be processed by a supervisor

Questions 17-19.

DIRECTIONS: Questions 17 through 19 are to be answered SOLELY on the basis of the following passage.

Information regarding payroll status, salary differentials, promotional salary increments, deductions, and pension payments should be given to all members of the staff who have questions regarding these items. On occasion, if the secretary is uncertain regarding the information, the staff member should be referred to the principal or the appropriate agency. No question by a staff member regarding payroll status should be brushed aside as immaterial or irrelevant. The school secretary must always try to handle the question or pass it on to the person who can handle it.

17. If a teacher is dissatisfied with information regarding her salary status, as given by the   17._
school secretary, the matter should be

    A. dropped
    B. passed on to the principal
    C. passed on by the secretary to proper agency or the principal
    D. made a basis for grievance procedures

18. The following is an adequate summary of the above passage: 18._

    A. The secretary must handle all payroll matters
    B. The secretary must handle all payroll matters or know who can handle them
    C. The secretary or the principal must handle all payroll matters
    D. Payroll matters too difficult to handle must be followed up until they are solved

19. The above passage implies that   19._

    A. many teachers ask immaterial questions regarding payroll status
    B. few teachers ask irrelevant pension questions
    C. no teachers ask immaterial salary questions
    D. no question regarding salary should be considered irrelevant

Questions 20-22.

DIRECTIONS: Questions 20 through 22 are to be answered SOLELY on the basis of the following passage.

The necessity for good speech on the part of the school secretary cannot be overstated. The school secretary must deal with the general public, the pupils, the members of the staff, and the school supervisors. In every situation which involves the general public, the secretary serves as a representative of the school. In dealing with pupils, the secretary's speech must serve as a model from which students may guide themselves. Slang, colloquialisms, malapropisms, and local dialects must be avoided.

20. The above passage implies that the speech pattern of the secretary must be

    A. perfect
    B. very good
    C. average
    D. on a level with that of the pupils

20.____

21. The last sentence indicates that slang

    A. is acceptable
    B. occurs in all speech
    C. might be used occasionally
    D. should be shunned

21.____

22. The above passage implies that the speech of pupils

    A. may be influenced
    C. is generally good
    B. does not change readily
    D. is generally poor

22.____

Questions 23-25.

DIRECTIONS: Questions 23 through 25 are to be answered SOLELY on the basis of the following passage.

The school secretary who is engaged in the task of filing records and correspondence should follow a general set of rules. Items which are filed should be available to other secretaries or to supervisors quickly and easily by means of the application of a modicum of common sense and good judgment. Items which, by their nature, may be difficult to find should be cross-indexed. Folders and drawers should be neatly and accurately labeled. There should never be a large accumulation of papers which have not been filed.

23. A good general rule to follow in filing is that materials should be

    A. placed in folders quickly
    B. neatly stored
    C. readily available
    D. cross-indexed

23.____

24. Items that are filed should be available to

    A. the secretary charged with the task of filing
    B. secretaries and supervisors
    C. school personnel
    D. the principal

24.____

25. A modicum of common sense means _____ common sense.

    A.   an average amount of   B.   a great deal of
    C.   a little   D.   no

25.____

KEY (CORRECT ANSWERS)

1.	B		11.	D
2.	A		12.	C
3.	C		13.	A
4.	C		14.	A
5.	D		15.	B
6.	B		16.	C
7.	B		17.	C
8.	C		18.	B
9.	A		19.	D
10.	B		20.	B

21.	D
22.	A
23.	C
24.	B
25.	C

TEST 3

Questions 1-4.

DIRECTIONS: Questions 1 through 4 are to be answered SOLELY on the basis of the following passage.

The proposition that administrative activity is essentially the same in all organizations appears to underlie some of the practices in the administration of private higher education. Although the practice is unusual in public education, there are numerous instances of industrial, governmental, or military administrators being assigned to private institutions of higher education and, to a lesser extent, of college and university presidents assuming administrative positions in other types of organizations. To test this theory that administrators are interchangeable, there is a need for systematic observation and classification. The myth that an educational administrator must first have experience in the teaching profession is firmly rooted in a long tradition that has historical prestige. The myth is bound up in the expectations of the public and personnel surrounding the administrator. Since administrative success depends significantly on how well an administrator meets the expectations others have of him, the myth may be more powerful than the special experience in helping the administrator attain organizational and educational objectives. Educational administrators who have risen through the teaching profession have often expressed nostalgia for the life of a teacher or scholar, but there is no evidence that this nostalgia contributes to administrative success

1. Which of the following statements as completed is MOST consistent with the above passage? The greatest number of administrators has moved from

    A. industry and the military to government and universities
    B. government and universities to industry and the military
    C. government, the armed forces, and industry to colleges and universities
    D. colleges and universities to government, the armed forces, and industry

1.____

2. Of the following, the MOST reasonable inference from the above passage is that a specific area requiring further research is the

    A. place of myth in the tradition and history of the educational profession
    B. relative effectiveness of educational administrators from inside and outside the teaching profession
    C. performance of administrators in the administration of public colleges
    D. degree of reality behind the nostalgia for scholarly pursuits often expressed by educational administrators

2.____

3. According to the above passage, the value to an educational administrator of experience in the teaching profession

    A. lies in the firsthand knowledge he has acquired of immediate educational problems
    B. may lie in the belief of his colleagues, subordinates, and the public that such experience is necessary
    C. has been supported by evidence that the experience contributes to administrative success in educational fields
    D. would be greater if the administrator were able to free himself from nostalgia for his former duties

3.____

4. Of the following, the MOST suitable title for the above passage is   4.___

    A. EDUCATIONAL ADMINISTRATION, ITS PROBLEMS
    B. THE EXPERIENCE NEEDED FOR EDUCATIONAL ADMINISTRATION
    C. ADMINISTRATION IN HIGHER EDUCATION
    D. EVALUATING ADMINISTRATIVE EXPERIENCE

Questions 5-6.

DIRECTIONS: Questions 5 and 6 are to be answered SOLELY on the basis of the following
                passage.

Management by objectives (MBO) may be defined as the process by which the superior
and the subordinate managers of an organization jointly define its common goals, define
each individual's major areas of responsibility in terms of the results expected of him and use
these measures as guides for operating the unit and assessing the contribution of each of its
members.

The MBO approach requires that after organizational goals are established and communicated, targets must be set for each individual position which are congruent with organizational goals. Periodic performance reviews and a final review using the objectives set as
criteria are also basic to this approach.

Recent studies have shown that MBO programs are influenced by attitudes and percep-
tions of the boss, the company, the reward-punishment system, and the program itself. In
addition, the manner in which the MBO program is carried out can influence the success of
the program. A study done in the late sixties indicates that the best results are obtained when
the manager sets goals which deal with significant problem areas in the organizational unit,
or with the subordinate's personal deficiencies. These goals must be clear with regard to
what is expected of the subordinate. The frequency of feedback is also important in the success of a management-by-objectives program. Generally, the greater the amount of feedback, the more successful the MBO program.

5. According to the above passage, the expected output for individual employees should be   5.___
    determined

    A. after a number of reviews of work performance
    B. after common organizational goals are defined
    C. before common organizational goals are defined
    D. on the basis of an employee's personal qualities

6. According to the above passage, the management-by-objectives approach requires   6.___

    A. less feedback than other types of management programs
    B. little review of on-the-job performance after the initial setting of goals
    C. general conformance between individual goals and organizational goals
    D. the setting of goals which deal with minor problem areas in the organization

Questions 7-10.

DIRECTIONS: Questions 7 through 10 are to be answered SOLELY on the basis of the follow-
                ing passage.

Management, which is the function of executive leadership, has as its principal phases the planning, organizing, and controlling of the activities of subordinate groups in the accomplishment of organizational objectives. Planning specifies the kind and extent of the factors, forces, and effects, and the relationships among them, that will be required for satisfactory accomplishment. The nature of the objectives and their requirements must be known before determinations can be made as to what must be done, how it must be done and why, where actions should take place, who should be responsible, and similar problems pertaining to the formulation of a plan. Organizing, which creates the conditions that must be present before the execution of the plan can be undertaken successfully, cannot be done intelligently without knowledge of the organizational objectives. Control, which has to do with the constraint and regulation of activities entering into the execution of the plan, must be exercised in accordance with the characteristics and requirements of the activities demanded by the plan.

7. The one of the following which is the MOST suitable title for the above passage is   7._____

   A. THE NATURE OF SUCCESSFUL ORGANIZATION
   B. THE PLANNING OF MANAGEMENT FUNCTIONS
   C. THE IMPORTANCE OF ORGANIZATIONAL FUNCTIONS
   D. THE PRINCIPLE ASPECTS OF MANAGEMENT

8. It can be inferred from the above passage that the one of the following functions whose   8._____
   existence is essential to the existence of the other three is the

   A. regulation of the work needed to carry out a plan
   B. understanding of what the organization intends to accomplish
   C. securing of information of the factors necessary for accomplishment of objectives
   D. establishment of the conditions required for successful action

9. The one of the following which would NOT be included within any of the principal phases   9._____
   of the function of executive leadership as defined in the above passage is

   A. determination of manpower requirements
   B. procurement of required material
   C. establishment of organizational objectives
   D. scheduling of production

10. The conclusion which can MOST reasonably be drawn from the above passage is that   10._____
    the control phase of managing is most directly concerned with the

   A. influencing of policy determinations
   B. administering of suggestion systems
   C. acquisition of staff for the organization
   D. implementation of performance standards

Questions 11-12.

DIRECTIONS: Questions 11 and 12 are to be answered SOLELY on the basis of the following
               passage.

Under an open-and-above-board policy, it is to be expected that some supervisors will gloss over known shortcomings of subordinates rather than face the task of discussing them face-to-face. It is also to be expected that at least some employees whose job performance is below par will reject the supervisor's appraisal as biased and unfair. Be that as it may, these are inescapable aspects of any performance appraisal system in which human beings are involved. The supervisor who shies away from calling a spade a spade, as well as the employee with a chip on his shoulder, will each in his own way eventually be revealed in his true light--to the benefit of the organization as a whole.

11. The BEST of the following interpretations of the above passage is that ___11.___

    A. the method of rating employee performance requires immediate revision to improve employee acceptance
    B. substandard performance ratings should be discussed with employees even if satisfactory ratings are not
    C. supervisors run the risk of being called unfair by their subordinates even though their appraisals are accurate
    D. any system of employee performance rating is satisfactory if used properly

12. The BEST of the following interpretations of the above passage is that ___12.___

    A. supervisors generally are not open-and-above-board with their subordinates
    B. it is necessary for supervisors to tell employees objectively how they are performing
    C. employees complain when their supervisor does not keep them informed
    D. supervisors are afraid to tell subordinates their weaknesses

Questions 13-15.

DIRECTIONS: Questions 13 through 15 are to be answered SOLELY on the basis of the following passage.

During the last decade, a great deal of interest has been generated around the phenomenon of *organizational development,* or the process of developing human resources through conscious organization effort. Organizational development (OD) stresses improving interpersonal relationships and organizational skills, such as communication, to a much greater degree than individual training ever did. The kind of training that an organization should emphasize depends upon the present and future structure of the organization. If future organizations are to be unstable, shifting coalitions, then individual skills and abilities, particularly those emphasizing innovativeness, creativity, flexibility, and the latest technological knowledge, are crucial and individual training is most appropriate.

But if there is to be little change in organizational structure, then the main thrust of training should be group-oriented or organizational development. This approach seems better designed for overcoming hierarchical barriers, for developing a degree of interpersonal relationships which make communication along the chain of command possible, and for retaining a modicum of innovation and/or flexibility.

13. According to the above passage, group-oriented training is MOST useful in ___13.___

    A. developing a communications system that will facilitate understanding through the chain of command
    B. highly flexible and mobile organizations
    C. preventing the crossing of hierarchical barriers within an organization
    D. saving energy otherwise wasted on developing methods of dealing with rigid hierarchies

14. The one of the following conclusions which can be drawn MOST appropriately from the   14.____
above passage is that

    A. behavioral research supports the use of organizational development training methods rather than individualized training
    B. it is easier to provide individualized training in specific skills than to set up sensitivity training programs
    C. organizational development eliminates innovative or flexible activity
    D. the nature of an organization greatly influences which training methods will be most effective

15. According to the above passage, the one of the following which is LEAST important for   15.____
large-scale organizations geared to rapid and abrupt change is

    A. current technological information
    B. development of a high degree of interpersonal relationships
    C. development of individual skills and abilities
    D. emphasis on creativity

Questions 16-18.

DIRECTIONS: Questions 16 through 18 are to be answered SOLELY on the basis of the following passage.

The increase in the extent to which each individual is personally responsible to others is most noticeable in a large bureaucracy. No one person *decides* anything; each decision of any importance, is the product of an intricate process of brokerage involving individuals inside and outside the organization who feel some reason to be affected by the decision, or who have special knowledge to contribute to it. The more varied the organization's constituency, the more outside *veto-groups* will need to be taken into account. But even if no outside consultations were involved, sheer size would produce a complex process of decision. For a large organization is a deliberately created system of tensions into which each individual is expected to bring work-ways, viewpoints, and outside relationships markedly different from those of his colleagues. It is the administrator's task to draw from these disparate forces the elements of wise action from day to day, consistent with the purposes of the organization as a whole.

16. The above passage is essentially a description of decision making as   16.____

    A. an organization process
    B. the key responsibility of the administrator
    C. the one best position among many
    D. a complex of individual decisions

17. Which one of the following statements BEST describes the responsibilities of an adminis-   17.____
trator?

    A. He modifies decisions and goals in accordance with pressures from within and outside the organization.
    B. He creates problem-solving mechanisms that rely on the varied interests of his staff and *veto-groups.*
    C. He makes determinations that will lead to attainment of his agency's objectives.
    D. He obtains agreement among varying viewpoints and interests.

18. In the context of the operations of a central public personnel agency, a *veto group* would LEAST likely consist of 18.____

    A. employee organizations
    B. professional personnel societies
    C. using agencies
    D. civil service newspapers

Questions 19-25.

DIRECTIONS: Questions 19 through 25 are to be answered SOLELY on the basis of the following passage, which is an extract from a report prepared for Department X, which outlines the procedure to be followed in the case of transfers of employees.

Every transfer, regardless of the reason therefore, requires completion of the record of transfer, Form DT 411. To denote consent to the transfer, DT 411 should contain the signatures of the transferee and the personnel officer(s) concerned, except that, in the case of an involuntary transfer, the signatures of the transferee's present and prospective supervisors shall be entered in Boxes 8A and 8B, respectively, since the transferee does not consent. Only a permanent employee may request a transfer; in such cases, the employee's attendance record shall be duly considered with regard to absences, latenesses, and accrued overtime balances. In the case of an inter-district transfer, the employee's attendance record must be included in Section 8A of the transfer request, Form DT 410, by the personnel officer of the district from which the transfer is requested. The personnel officer of the district to which the employee requested transfer may refuse to accept accrued overtime balances in excess of ten days.

An employee on probation shall be eligible for transfer. If such employee is involuntarily transferred, he shall be credited for the period of time already served on probation. However, if such transfer is voluntary, the employee shall be required to serve the entire period of his probation in the new position. An employee who has occurred a disability which prevents him from performing his normal duties may be transferred during the period of such disability to other appropriate duties. A disability transfer requires the completion of either Form DT 414 if the disability is job-connected, or Form DT 415 if it is not a job-connected disability. In either case, the personnel officer of the district from which the transfer is made signs in Box 6A of the first two copies and the personnel officer of the district to which the transfer is made signs in Box 6B of the last two copies, or, in the case of an intra-district disability transfer, the personnel officer must sign in Box 6A of the first two copies and Box 6B of the last two copies.

19. When a personnel officer consents to an employee's request for transfer from his district, this procedure requires that the personnel officer sign Form(s) 19.__

    A. DT 411
    B. DT 410 and DT 411
    C. DT 411 and either Form DT 414 or DT 415
    D. DT 410 and DT 411, and either Form DT 414 or DT 415

20. With respect to the time record of an employee transferred against his wishes during his probationary period, this procedure requires that 20.__

    A. he serve the entire period of his probation in his present office
    B. he lose his accrued overtime balance

C. his attendance record be considered with regard to absences and latenesses
D. he be given credit for the period of time he has already served on probation

21. Assume you are a supervisor and an employee must be transferred into your office against his wishes. According to the this procedure, the box you must sign on the record of transfer is

21.____

A. 6A   B. 8A   C. 6B   D. 8B

22. Under this procedure, in the case of a disability transfer, when must Box 6A on Forms DT 414 and DT 415 be signed by the personnel officer of the district to which the transfer is being made?

22.____

A. In all cases when either Form DT 414 or Form DT 415 is used
B. In all cases when Form DT 414 is used and only under certain circumstances when Form DT 415 is used
C. In all cases when Form DT 415 is used and only under certain circumstances when Form DT 414 is used
D. Only under certain circumstances when either Form DT 414 or Form DT 415 is used

23. From the above passage, it may be inferred MOST correctly that the number of copies of Form DT 414 is

23.____

A. no more than 2
B. at least 3
C. at least 5
D. more than the number of copies of Form DT 415

24. A change in punctuation and capitalization only which would change one sentence into two and possibly contribute to somewhat greater ease of reading this report extract would be MOST appropriate in the

24.____

A. 2nd sentence, 1st paragraph
B. 3rd sentence, 1st paragraph
C. next to he last sentence, 2nd paragraph
D. 2nd sentence, 2nd paragraph

25. In the second paragraph, a word that is INCORRECTLY used is

25.____

A. *shall* in the 1st sentence
B. *voluntary* in the 3rd sentence
C. *occurred* in the 4th sentence
D. *intra-district* in the last sentence

KEY (CORRECT ANSWERS)

1.	C	11.	C
2.	B	12.	B
3.	B	13.	A
4.	B	14.	D
5.	B	15.	B
6.	C	16.	A
7.	D	17.	C
8.	B	18.	B
9.	C	19.	A
10.	D	20.	D

21.	D
22.	D
23.	B
24.	B
25.	C

INTERPRETING STATISTICAL DATA
GRAPHS, CHARTS AND TABLES
TEST 1

DIRECTIONS: Each question or incomplete statement is followed by several suggested answers or completions. Select the one that BEST answers the question or completes the statement. *PRINT THE LETTER OF THE CORRECT ANSWER IN THE SPACE AT THE RIGHT.*

Questions 1-5.

DIRECTIONS: Questions 1 through 5 are to be answered SOLELY on the basis of the following chart.

DUPLICATION JOBS

JOB. NO.	DATES Submitted	DATES Required	DATES Completed	PROCESS	NO. OF ORIGINALS	NO. OF COPIES OF EACH ORIGINAL	REQUEST-ING UNIT
324	6/22	6/25	6/25	Xerox	14	25	Research
325	6/25	6/27	6/28	Kodak	10	125	Training
326	6/25	6/25	6/25	Xerox	12	11	Budget
327	6/25	6/27	6/26	Press	17	775	Admin. Div. H
328	6/28	ASAP*	6/25	Press	5	535	Personnel
329	6/26	6/26	6/27	Xerox	15	8	Admin. Div. G

*ASAP - As soon as possible

1. The unit whose job was to be xeroxed but was NOT completed by the date required is

   A. Administrative Division H
   B. Administrative Division G
   C. Research
   D. Training

1.____

2. The job with the LARGEST number of original pages to be xeroxed is job number

   A. 324   B. 326   C. 327   D. 329

2.____

3. Jobs were completed AFTER June 26, for

    A.   Training and Administrative Division G
    B.   Training and Administrative Division H
    C.   Research and Budget
    D.   Administrative Division G *only*

4. Which one of the following units submitted a job which was completed SOONER than required?

    A.   Training
    B.   Administrative Division H
    C.   Personnel
    D.   Administrative Division G

5. The jobs which were submitted on different days but were completed on the SAME day and used the SAME process had job numbers

    A.   324 and 326
    B.   327 and 328
    C.   324, 326, and 328
    D.   324, 326, and 329

KEY (CORRECT ANSWERS)

1. B
2. D
3. A
4. B
5. A

TEST 2

DIRECTIONS: Questions 1 through 10 are to be answered SOLELY on the basis of the Production Record table shown below for the Information Unit in Agency X for the work week ended Friday, December 6. The table shows, for each employee, the quantity of each type of work performed and the percentage of the work week spent in performing each type of work.

NOTE: Assume that each employee works 7 hours a day and 5 days a week, making a total of 35 hours for the work week.

PRODUCTION RECORD - INFORMATION UNIT IN AGENCY X
(For the work week ended Friday, December 6)

NUMBER OF

	Papers Filed	Sheets Proofread	Visitors Received	Envelopes Addressed
Miss Agar	3120	33	178	752
Mr. Brun	1565	59	252	724
Miss Case	2142	62	214	426
Mr. Dale	4259	29	144	1132
Miss Earl	2054	58	212	878
Mr. Farr	1610	69	245	621
Miss Glen	2390	57	230	790
Mr. Hope	3425	32	176	805
Miss Iver	3726	56	148	650
Mr. Joad	3212	55	181	495

PERCENTAGE OF WORK WEEK SPENT ON

	Filing Papers	Proof-reading	Receiving Visitors	Addressing Envelopes	Performing Miscellaneous Work
Miss Agar	30%	9%	34%	11%	16%
Mr. Brun	13%	15%	52%	10%	10%
Miss Case	23%	18%	38%	6%	15%
Mr. Dale	50%	7%	17%	16%	10%
Miss Earl	24%	14%	37%	14%	11%
Mr. Farr	16%	19%	48%	8%	9%
Miss Glenn	27%	12%	42%	12%	7%
Mr. Hope	38%	8%	32%	13%	9%
Miss Iver	43%	13%	24%	9%	11%
Mr. Joad	33%	11%	36%	7%	13%

1. For the week, the average amount of time which the employees spent in proofreading was MOST NEARLY _____ hours.   1.____

    A. 3.1   B. 3.6   C. 4.4   D. 5.1

2. The average number of visitors received daily by an employee was MOST NEARLY   2.____

    A. 40   B. 57   C. 198   D. 395

3. Of the following employees, the one who addressed envelopes at the FASTEST rate was   3.____

    A. Miss Agar   B. Mr. Brun   C. Miss Case   D. Mr. Dale

4. Mr. Farr's rate of filing papers was MOST NEARLY _____ pages per minute.   4.____

    A. 2   B. 1.7   C. 5   D. 12

5. The average number of hours that Mr. Brun spent daily on receiving visitors exceeded the average number of hours that Miss Iver spent daily on the same type of work by MOST NEARLY _____ hours.   5.____

    A. 2   B. 3   C. 4   D. 5

6. Miss Earl worked at a FASTER rate than Miss Glen in   6.____

    A. filing papers   B. proofreading sheets
    C. receiving visitors   D. addressing envelopes

7. Mr. Joad's rate of filing papers _____ Miss Iver's rate of filing papers by APPROXI-MATELY _____ .   7.____

    A. was less than; 10%   B. exceeded; 33%
    C. was less than; 16%   D. exceeded; 12%

8. Assume that in the following week Miss Case is instructed to increase the percentage of her time spent on filing papers to 35%.   8.____
    If she continued to file papers at the same rate as she did for the week ended December 6, the number of additional papers that she filed the following week was MOST NEARLY

    A. 3260   B. 5400   C. 250   D. 1120

9. Assume that in the following week Mr. Hope increased his weekly total of envelopes addressed to 1092.   9.____
    If he continued to spend the same amount of time on this assignment as he did for the week ended December 6, the increase in his rate of addressing envelopes the following week was MOST NEARLY _____ envelopes per hour.

    A. 15   B. 65   C. 155   D. 240

10. Assume that in the following week Miss Agar and Mr. Dale spent 3 and 9 hours less, respectively, on filing papers than they had spent for the week ended December 6, without changing their rates of work.
The total number of papers filed during the following week by both Miss Agar and Mr. Dale was MOST NEARLY

    A. 4235   B. 4295   C. 4315   D. 4370

10.____

KEY (CORRECT ANSWERS)

1. C
2. A
3. B
4. C
5. A
6. C
7. D
8. D
9. B
10. B

TEST 3

Questions 1-6.

DIRECTIONS: Questions 1 through 6 are to be answered SOLELY on the basis of the chart below.

EMPLOYMENT ERRORS

	Allan	Barry	Cary	David
July	5	4	1	7
Aug.	8	3	9	8
Sept.	7	8	7	5
Oct.	3	6	5	3
Nov.	2	4	4	6
Dec.	5	2	8	4

1. The clerk with the HIGHEST number of errors for the 6-month period was   1.___

   A. Allan   B. Barry   C. Cary   D. David

2. If the number of errors made by Allan in the six months shown represented one-eighth of   2.___
   the total errors made by the unit during the entire year, what was the TOTAL number of
   errors made by the unit for the year?

   A. 124   B. 180   C. 240   D. 360

3. The number of errors made by David in November was what fraction of the total errors   3.___
   made in November?

   A. 1/3   B. 1/6   C. 378   D. 3/16

4. The average number of errors made per month per clerk was MOST NEARLY   4.___

   A. 4   B. 5   C. 6   D. 7

5. Of the total number of errors made during the six-month period, the percentage made in   5.___
   August was MOST NEARLY

   A. 2%   B. 4%   C. 23%   D. 44%

6. If the number of errors in the unit were to decrease in the next six months by 30%, what   6.___
   would be MOST NEARLY the total number of errors for the unit for the next six months?

   A. 87   B. 94   C. 120   D. 137

KEY (CORRECT ANSWERS)

1. C
2. C
3. C
4. B
5. C
6. A

TEST 4

Questions 1-5.

DIRECTIONS: Questions 1 through 5 are to be answered SOLELY on the basis of the data given below. These data show the performance rates of the employees in a particular division for a period of six months.

Employee	Jan.	Feb.	Mar.	April	May	June
A	96	53	64	48	76	72
B	84	58	69	56	67	79
C	73	68	71	54	59	62
D	98	74	79	66	86	74
E	89	78	67	74	75	77

1. According to the above data, the average monthly performance for a worker is MOST NEARLY

   A. 66   B. 69   C. 72   D. 75

1.____

2. According to the above data, the mean monthly performance for the division is MOST NEARLY

   A. 350   B. 358   C. 387   D. 429

2.____

3. According to the above data, the employee who shows the LEAST month-to-month variation in performance is

   A. A   B. B   C. C   D. D

3.____

4. According to the above data, the employee who shows the GREATEST range in performance is

   A. A   B. B   C. C   D. D

4.____

5. According to the above data, the median employee with respect to performance for the six-month period is

   A. A   B. B   C. C   D. D

5.____

KEY (CORRECT ANSWERS)

1. C
2. B
3. C
4. A
5. B

TEST 5

Questions 1-5.

DIRECTIONS: Questions 1 through 5 are to be answered SOLELY on the basis of the chart below, which shows the absences in Unit A for the period November 1 through November 15.

ABSENCE RECORD - UNIT A
November 1-15

Date:	1	2	3	4	5	6	7	8	9	10	11	12	13	14	15
Employee:															
Ames	X	s	H					X			H			X	X
Bloom	X		H			X	X	S	s		H	S	S		X
Deegan	X	J	H	J	J	J	X	X			H				X
Howard	X		H					X			H			X	X
Jergens	X	M	H	M	M	M		X			H			X	X
Lange	X		H			S	X	X							X
Morton	X						X	X	V	V	H				X
O'Shea	X		H			0		X			H	X		X	X

CODE FOR TYPES OF ABSENCE
X - Saturday or Sunday
H - Legal Holiday
P - Leave without pay
M - Military Leave
J - Jury duty
V - Vacation
S - Sick Leave
O - Other leave of absence

NOTE: If there is no entry against an employee's name under a date, the employee worked on that date.

1. According to the above chart, NO employee in Unit A was absent on   1.____

   A. leave without pay   B. military leave
   C. other leave of absence   D. vacation

2. According to the above chart, all but one of the employees in Unit A were present on the   2.____

   A. 3rd   B. 5th   C. 9th   D. 13th

3. According to the above chart, the ONLY employee who worked on a legal holiday when   3.____
   the other employees were absent are

   A. Deegan and Morton   B. Howard and O'Shea
   C. Lange and Morton   D. Morton and O'Shea

162

4. According to the above chart, the employee who was absent ONLY on a day that was a
Saturday, Sunday, or legal holiday was

    A. Bloom   B. Howard   C. G. Morton   D. O'Shea

4.____

5. The employees who had more absences than anyone else are

    A. Bloom and Deegan
    B. Bloom, Deegan, and Jergens
    C. Deegan and Jergens
    D. Deegan, Jergens, and O'Shea

5.____

KEY (CORRECT ANSWERS)

    1. A
    2. D
    3. C
    4. B
    5. B

TEST 6

Questions 1-7.

DIRECTIONS: Questions 1 through 7 are to be answered SOLELY on the basis of the time sheet and instructions given below.

	MON.		TUBS.		WED.		THURS .		FRI.	
	IN	OUT	IN	OUT	IN	OUT	IN	OUT	IN	OUT
Walker	8:45	5:02	9:20	5:00	9:00	5:02	Annual Lv.		9:04	5:05
Jones	9:01	5:00	9:03	5:02	9:08	5:01	8:55	5:04	9:00	5:00
Rubins	8:49	5:04	Sick Lv.		9:05	5:04	9:03	5:03	9:04	3:30(PB)
Brown	9:00	5:01	8:55	5:03	9:00	5:05	9:04	5:07	9:05	5:03
Roberts	9:30 (PA)	5:08	8:43	5:07	9:05	5:05	9:09	12:30 (PB)	8:58	5:04

The above time sheet indicates the arrival and leaving times of five telephone operators who punched a time clock in a city agency for the week of April 14. The times they arrived at work in the mornings are indicated in the columns labeled *IN* and the times they left work are indicated in the columns labeled *OUT*. The letters (PA) mean prearranged lateness, and the letters (PB) mean personal business. Time lost for these purposes is charged to annual leave.

The operators are scheduled to arrive at 9:00. However, they are not considered late unless they arrive after 9:05. If they prearrange a lateness, they are not considered late. Time lost through lateness is charged to annual leave. A full day's work is eight hours, from 9:00 to 5:00.

1. Which operator worked the entire week WITHOUT using any annual leave or sick leave time?

    A. Jones   B. Brown
    C. Roberts   D. None of the above

1.___

2. On which days was NONE of the operators considered late?

    A. Monday and Wednesday   B. Monday and Friday
    C. Wednesday and Thursday   D. Wednesday and Friday

2.___

3. Which operator clocked out at a different time each day of the week?

    A. Roberts   B. Jones   C. Rubins   D. Brown

3.___

4. How many of the operators were considered late on Wednesday?

    A. 0   B. 1   C. 2   D. 3

4.___

5. What was the TOTAL number of charged latenesses for the week of April 14?

    A. 1   B. 3   C. 5   D. 7

5.___

6. Which day shows the MOST time charged to all types of leave by all the operators?

    A. Monday   B. Tuesday   C. Wednesday   D. Thursday

6.___

7. What operators were considered ON TIME all week?　　　　　　　　7.____

    A. Jones and Rubins   B. Rubins and Brown
    C. Brown and Roberts   D. Walker and Brown

_____

KEY (CORRECT ANSWERS)

    1. B
    2. B
    3. A
    4. B
    5. B
    6. D
    7. B

_____

TEST 7

Questions 1-10.

DIRECTIONS: Questions 1 through 10 are to be answered SOLELY on the basis of the information and code tables given below.

In accordance with these code tables, each employee in the department is assigned a code number consisting of ten digits arranged from left to right in the following order:

    I. Division in Which Employed
    II. Title of Position
    III. Annual Salary
    IV. Age
    V. Number of Years Employed in Department

EXAMPLE: A clerk is 21 years old, has been employed in the department for three years, and is working in the Supply Division at a yearly salary of $25,000. His code number is 90-115-13-02-2.

DEPARTMENTAL CODE

TABLE I		TABLE II		TABLE III		TABLE IV		TABLE V	
Code	Division No. in Which Employed	Code	Title No. of Position	Code	Annual No. Salary	Code	No. Age	Code	No. of No. Years Employee in Dept.
10	Accounting	115	Clerk	11	$18,000 or less	01	Under 20 yrs.	1	Less than 1 yr.
20	Construction	155	Typist	12	$18,001 to $24,000	02	20 to 29 yrs.	2	1 to 5 yrs.
30	Engineering	175	Stenographer	13	$24,001 to $30,000	03	30 to 39 yrs.	3	6 to 10 yrs.
40	Information	237	Bookkeeper	14	$30,001 to $36,000	04	40 to 49 yrs.	4	11 to 15 yrs.
50	Maintenance	345	Statistician	15	$36,001 to $45,000	05	50 to 59 yrs.	5	16 to 25 yrs.
60	Personnel	545	Storekeeper	16	$45,001 to $60,000	06	60 to 69 yrs.	6	26 to 35 yrs.
70	Record	633	Draftsman	17	$60,001 to $70,000	07	70 yrs. or over	7	36 yrs. or over
80	Research	665	Civil Engineer	18	$70,001 or over				
90	Supply	865	Machinist						
		915	Porter						

1. A draftsman employed in the Engineering Division at a yearly salary of $34,800 is 36 years old and has been employed in the department for 9 years.
   He should be coded

   A. 20-633-13-04-3
   C. 20-665-14-04-4
   B. 30-865-13-03-4
   D. 30-633-14-03-3

   1.____

2. A porter employed in the Maintenance Division at a yearly salary of $28,800 is 52 years old and has been employed in the department for 6 years.
   He should be coded

   A. 50-915-12-03-3
   C. 50-915-13-05-3
   B. 90-545-12-05-3
   D. 90-545-13-03-3

   2.____

3. Richard White, who has been employed in the department for 12 years, receives $50,000 a year as a civil engineer in the Construction Division. He is 38 years old.
   He should be coded

   A. 20-665-16-03-4
   C. 20-633-14-04-2
   B. 20-665-15-02-1
   D. 20-865-15-02-5

   3.____

4. An 18-year-old clerk appointed to the department six months ago is assigned to the Record Division. His annual salary is $21,600.
   He should be coded

   A. 70-115-11-01-1
   C. 70-115-12-02-1
   B. 70-115-12-01-1
   D. 70-155-12-01-1

   4.____

5. An employee has been coded 40-155-12-03-3.
   Of the following statements regarding this employee, the MOST accurate one is that he is

   A. a clerk who has been employed in the department for at least 6 years
   B. a typist who receives an annual salary which does not exceed $24,000
   C. under 30 years of age and has been employed in the department for at least 11 years
   D. employed in the Supply Division at a salary which exceeds $18,000 per annum

   5.____

6. Of the following statements regarding an employee who is coded 60-175-13-01-2, the LEAST accurate statement is that this employee

   A. is a stenographer in the Personnel Division
   B. has been employed in the department for at least one year
   C. receives an annual salary which exceeds $24,000
   D. is more than 20 years of age

   6.____

7. The following are the names of four employees of the department with their code numbers:

   James Black, 80-345-15-03-4
   William White, 30-633-14-03-4
   Sam Green, 80-115-12-02-3
   John Jones, 10-237-13-04-5

   If a salary increase is to be given to the employees who have been employed in the department for 11 years or more and who earn less than $36,001 a year, the two of the above employees who will receive a salary increase are

   7.____

167

A. John Jones and William White
B. James Black and Sam Green
C. James Black and William White
D. John Jones and Sam Green

8. Code number 50-865-14-02-6, which has been assigned to a machinist, contains an obvious inconsistency.
This inconsistency involves the figures

   A. 50-865   B. 865-14   C. 14-02   D. 02-6

8.___

9. Ten employees were awarded merit prizes for outstanding service during the year. Their code numbers were:

80-345-14-04-4	40-155-12-02-2
40-155-12-04-4	10-115-12-02-2
10-115-13-03-2	80-115-13-02-2
80-175-13-05-5	10-115-13-02-3
10-115-12-04-3	30-633-14-04-4

Of these outstanding employees, the number who were clerks employed in the Accounting Division at a salary ranging from $24,001 to $30,000 per annum is

   A. 1   B. 2   C. 3   D. 4

9.___

10. The MOST accurate of the following statements regarding the ten outstanding employees listed in the previous question is that

A. fewer than half of the employees were under 40 years of age
B. there were fewer typists than stenographers
C. four of the employees were employed in the department 11 years or more
D. two of the employees in the Research Division receive annual salaries ranging from $30,001 to $36,000

10.___

KEY (CORRECT ANSWERS)

1. D
2. C
3. A
4. B
5. B
6. D
7. A
8. D
9. B
10. C

INTERPRETING STATISTICAL DATA
GRAPHS, CHARTS AND TABLES

TEST 1

DIRECTIONS: Each question or incomplete statement is followed by several suggested answers or completions. Select the one that BEST answers the question or completes the statement. *PRINT THE LETTER OF THE CORRECT ANSWER IN THE SPACE AT THE RIGHT.*

Questions 1-5.

DIRECTIONS: Questions 1 through 5 are to be answered SOLELY on the basis of the following table.

ANNUAL SALARIES PAID TO SELECTED CLERICAL TITLES IN FIVE MAJOR CITIES IN 2012 AND 2014

2014

	Clerk	Typist	Steno	Legal Steno	Computer Operator
Newton	$33,900	$34,800	$36,300	$43,800	$35,400
Barton	$32,400	$34,200	$35,400	$43,500	$34,200
Phelton	$32,400	$32,400	$34,200	$42,000	$33,000
Washburn	$33,600	$34,800	$35,400	$43,800	$34,800
Biltmore	$33,000	$34,200	$35,100	$43,500	$34,500

2012

	Clerk	Typist	Steno	Legal Steno	Computer Operator
Newtown	$31,800	$33,600	$35,400	$41,400	$34,500
Barton	$30,000	$31,500	$33,000	$39,600	$31,500
Phelton	$29,400	$30,600	$31,800	$37,800	$31,200
Washburn	$30,600	$32,400	$31,800	$37,800	$31,200
Biltmore	$30,000	$31,800	$33,000	$39,600	$32,100

1. Assume that the value of the fringe benefits offered to clerical employees in 2014 amounted to 14% of their annual salaries in Newton, 17% in Barton, 18% in Phelton, 15% in Washburn, and 16% in Biltmore.
The total cost of employing a computer operator for 2014 was GREATEST in

   A. Newtown   B. Barton   C. Phelton   D. Washburn

1.____

2. During negotiations for their 2015 contract, the stenographers of Biltmore are demanding that their rate of pay be fixed at 85% of the legal stenographer salary.
If this demand is granted and if the legal stenographer salary increases by 7% in 2015, the 2015 stenographer salary will be MOST NEARLY

   A. $36,972   B. $37,560   C. $39,564   D. $40,020

2.____

3. Of the following, the GREATEST percentage increase in salary from 2012 to 2014 was gained by   3._____

    A. clerks in Newtown
    B. stenographers in Barton
    C. legal stenographers in Washburn
    D. computer operators in Biltmore

4. The title which achieved the SMALLEST average percentage increase in salary from 2012 to 2014 was   4._____

    A. clerk   B. typist
    C. stenographer   D. legal stenographer

5. Assume that, in 2014, clerks accounted for 60% of the clerical work force in Barton. The   5._____
clerical work force consists of 140 employees. In 2012, the clerks accounted for 65% of the clerical work force in Barton. The clerical work force then consisted of 120 employees.
The difference between the 2012 and 2014 payroll for clerks in Barton is MOST NEARLY

    A. $120,000   B. $240,000   C. $360,000   D. $480,000

―――――――

KEY (CORRECT ANSWERS)

    1. A
    2. C
    3. C
    4. C
    5. C

―――――――

TEST 2

Questions 1-9.

DIRECTIONS: Questions 1 through 9 are to be answered SOLELY on the basis of the facts given in the table below, which contains certain information about employees in a city bureau.

			RECORD OF EMPLOYEES IN A CITY BUREAU		
NAME	TITLE	AGE	ANNUAL SALARY	YEARS OF SERVICE	EXAMINATION RATING
Jones	Clerk	34	$20,400	10	82
Smith	Stenographer	25	19,200	2	72
Black	Typist	19	14,400	1	71
Brown	Stenographer	36	25,200	12	88
Thomas	Accountant	49	41,200	21	91
Gordon	Clerk	31	30,000	8	81
Johnson	Stenographer	26	26,400	5	75
White	Accountant	53	36,000	30	90
Spencer	Clerk	42	27,600	19	85
Taylor	Typist	24	21,600	5	74
Simpson	Accountant	37	50,000	11	87
Reid	Typist	20	12,000	2	72
Fulton	Accountant	55	55,000	31	100
Chambers	Clerk	22	15,600	4	75
Calhoun	Stenographer	48	28,800	16	80

1. The name of the employee whose salary would be the middle one if all the salaries were ranked in order of magnitude is   1.____

   A. White   B. Johnson   C. Brown   D. Spencer

2. The combined monthly salary of all the stenographers EXCEEDS the combined monthly salary of all the clerks by   2.____

   A. $6,000   B. $500   C. $22,800   D. $600

3. The age of the employee who received the HIGHEST rating in the examination among those who have less than 10 years of service is _____ years.   3.____

   A. 22   B. 31   C. 55   D. 34

4. The average examination rating of those employees who had 15 years of service or more as compared with the average examination rating of those employees who had 5 years of service or less is MOST NEARLY _____ points _____.   4.____

   A. 16; greater   B. 7; greater
   C. 10; less   D. 25; greater

5. The name of the youngest employee whose monthly salary is more than $1,000 per month and who has more than one year of service is   5.____

   A. Reid   B. Black   C. Chambers   D. Taylor

6. The name of the employee who received an examination rating of over 85%, who has more than 15 years of service, and who earns a yearly salary of more than $25,000 but less than $40,000 is   6.____

   A. Thomas   B. Spencer   C. Calhoun   D. White

7. The annual salary of the HIGHEST paid stenographer is 7.____

    A. more than twice as great as the salary of the youngest employee
    B. greater than the salary of the oldest typist but not as great as the salary of the oldest clerk
    C. greater than the salary of the highest paid typist but not as great as the salary of the lowest paid accountant
    D. less than the combined salaries of the two youngest typists

8. The number of employees whose annual salary is more than $15,600 but less than $28,800 and who have at least 5 years of service is 8.____

    A. 11   B. 8   C. 6   D. 5

9. Of the following, it would be MOST accurate to state that the 9.____

    A. youngest employee is lowest with respect to number of years of service, examination rating, and salary
    B. oldest employee is highest with respect to number of years of service, examination rating, but not with respect to salary
    C. annual salary of the youngest clerk is $1,200 more than the annual salary of the youngest typist and $2,400 less than the annual salary of the youngest stenographer
    D. difference in age between the youngest and oldest typist is less than one-fourth the difference in age between the youngest and oldest stenographer

_____

KEY (CORRECT ANSWERS)

1. B
2. B
3. B
4. A
5. C
6. D
7. C
8. D
9. D

_____

TEST 3

DIRECTIONS: Questions 1 through 10 are to be answered SOLELY on the basis of the Personnel Record of Division X shown below.

Employee	Bureau In Which Employed	Title	Annual Salary	No. of Days Absent On Vacation	No. of Days Absent On Sick Leave	No. of Times Late
Abbott	Mail	Clerk	$31,200	18	0	1
Barnes	Mail	Clerk	25,200	25	3	7
Davis	Mail	Typist	24,000	21	9	2
Adams	Payroll	Accountant	42,500	10	0	2
Bell	Payroll	Bookkeeper	31,200	23	2	5
Duke	Payroll	Clerk	27,600	24	4	3
Gross	Payroll	Clerk	21,600	12	5	7
Lane	Payroll	Stenographer	26,400	19	16	20
Reed	Payroll	Typist	22,800	15	11	11
Arnold	Record	Clerk	32,400	6	15	9
Cane	Record	Clerk	24,500	14	3	4
Fay	Record	Clerk	21,100	20	0	4
Hale	Record	Typist	25,200	18	2	7
Baker	Supply	Clerk	30,000	20	3	2
Clark	Supply	Clerk	27,600	25	6	5
Ford	Supply	Typist	22,800	25	4	22

Table title: DIVISION X — PERSONNEL RECORD - CURRENT YEAR

1. The percentage of the total number of employees who are clerks is MOST NEARLY   1._____

   A.   25%   B.   33%   C.   38%   D.   56%

2. Of the following employees, the one who receives a monthly salary of $2,100 is   2._____

   A.   Barnes   B.   Gross   C.   Reed   D.   Clark

3. The difference between the annual salary of the highest paid clerk and that of the lowest paid clerk is   3._____

   A. $6,000   B. $8,400   C. $11,300   D. $20,900

4. The number of employees receiving more than $25,000 a year but less than $40,000 a year is   4._____

   A.   6   B.   9   C.   12   D.   15

5. The TOTAL annual salary of the employees of the Mail Bureau is _____ the total annual salary of the employees of the _____.   5._____

   A.   one-half of; Payroll Bureau
   B.   less than; Record Bureau by $21,600
   C.   equal to; Supply Bureau
   D.   less than; Payroll Bureau by $71,600

6. The average annual salary of the employees who are not clerks is MOST NEARLY   6._____

    A. $23,700   B. $25,450   C. $26,800   D. $27,850

7. If all the employees were given a 10% increase in pay, the annual salary of Lane would   7._____
then be

    A. *greater* than that of Barnes by $1,320
    B. *less* than that of Bell by $4,280
    C. *equal* to that of Clark
    D. *greater* than that of Ford by $3,600

8. Of the clerks who earned less than $30,000 a year, the one who was late the FEWEST   8._____
number of times was late _____ time(s).

    A. 1   B. 2   C. 3   D. 4

9. The bureau in which the employees were late the FEWEST number of times on an aver-   9._____
age is the _____ Bureau.

    A. Mail   B. Payroll   C. Record   D. Supply

10. The MOST accurate of the following statements is that   10._____

    A. Reed was late more often than any other typist
    B. Bell took more time off for vacation than any other employee earning $30,000 or
more annually
    C. of the typists, Ford was the one who was absent the fewest number of times
because of sickness
    D. three clerks took no time off because of sickness

KEY (CORRECT ANSWERS)

1. D
2. A
3. C
4. B
5. C
6. D
7. A
8. C
9. A
10. B

TEST 4

DIRECTIONS: Questions 1 through 10 are to be answered SOLELY on the basis of the Weekly Payroll Record shown below of Bureau X in a public agency. In answering these questions, note that gross weekly salary is the salary before deductions have been made; take-home pay is the amount remaining after all indicated weekly deductions have been made from the gross weekly salary. In answering questions involving annual amounts, compute on the basis of 52 weeks per year.

BUREAU X
WEEKLY PAYROLL PERIOD

Unit In Which Employed	Employee	Title	Gross Weekly Salary (Before Deductions)	Weekly Deductions From Gross Salary		
				Medical Insurance	Income Tax	Pension System
Accounting	Allen	Accountant	$950	$14.50	$125.00	$53.20
Accounting	Barth	Bookkeeper	720	19.00	62.00	40.70
Accounting	Keller	Clerk	580	6.50	82.00	33.10
Accounting	Peters	Typist	560	6.50	79.00	35.30
Accounting	Simons	Stenographer	610	14.50	64.00	37.80
Information	Brown	Clerk	560	13.00	56.00	42.20
Information	Smith	Clerk	590	14.50	61.00	58.40
Information	Turner	Typist	580	13.00	59.00	62.60
Information	Williams	Stenographer	620	19.00	44.00	69.40
Mail	Conner	Clerk	660	13.00	74.00	55.40
Mail	Farrell	Typist	540	6.50	75.00	34.00
Mail	Johnson	Stenographer	580	19.00	36.00	37.10
Records	Dillon	Clerk	640	6.50	94.00	58.20
Records	Martin	Clerk	540	19.00	29.00	50.20
Records	Standish	Typist	620	14.50	67.00	60.10
Records	Wilson	Stenographer	690	6.50	101.00	75.60

1. Dillon's annual take-home pay is MOST NEARLY

   A. $25,000   B. $27,000   C. $31,000   D. $33,000

2. The difference between Turner's gross annual salary and his annual take-home pay is MOST NEARLY

   A. $3,000   B. $5,000   C. $7,000   D. $9,000

3. Of the following, the employee whose weekly take-home pay is CLOSEST to that of Keller's is

   A. Peters   B. Brown   C. Smith   D. Turner

4. The average gross annual salary of the typists is

   A. less than $27,500
   B. more than $27,500 but less than $30,000
   C. more than $30,000 but less than $32,500
   D. more than $32,500

1.____

2.____

3.____

4.____

5. The average gross weekly salary of the stenographers EXCEEDS the gross weekly sal-   5.____
ary of the clerks by

    A. $20   B. $30   C. $40   D. $50

6. Of the following employees in the Accounting Unit, the one who pays the HIGHEST per-   6.____
centage of his gross weekly salary for the Pension System is

    A. Barth   B. Keller   C. Peters   D. Simons

7. For all of the Accounting Unit employees, the total annual deductions for Medical Insur-   7.____
ance are less than the total annual deductions for the Pension System by MOST
NEARLY

    A. $6,000   B. $7,000   C. $8,000   D. $9,000

8. Of the following, the employee whose total weekly deductions are MOST NEARLY 27%   8.____
of his gross weekly salary is

    A. Barth   B. Brown   C. Martin   D. Wilson

9. The total amount of the gross weekly salaries of all the employees in the Records Unit is   9.____
MOST NEARLY

    A. 95% of the total amount of the gross weekly salaries of all the employees in the
         Information Unit
    B. 10% greater than the total amount of the gross weekly salaries of all the employ-
         ees in the Mail Unit
    C. 75% of the total amount of the gross weekly salaries of all the employees in the
         Accounting Unit
    D. four times as great as the total amount deducted weekly for tax for all the employ-
         ees in the Records Unit

10. For the employees in the Information Unit, the AVERAGE weekly deductions for Income   10.____
Tax _____ the average weekly deduction for _____.

    A. exceeds; Income Tax for the employees in the Records Unit
    B. is less than; the Pension System for the employees in the Mail Unit
    C. exceeds; Income Tax for the employees in the Accounting Unit
    D. is less than; the Pension System for the employees in the Records Unit

KEY (CORRECT ANSWERS)

1. A
2. C
3. C
4. B
5. B
6. C
7. B
8. D
9. C
10. D

_____

TEST 5

Questions 1-9.

DIRECTIONS: Questions 1 through 9 are to be answered SOLELY on the basis of the following information.

Assume that the following rules for computing service ratings are to be used experimen-
tally in determining the service ratings of seven permanent city employees. (Note that these
rules are hypothetical and are NOT to be confused with the existing method of computing service ratings for city employees.) The personnel record of each of these seven employees is
given in Table II. You are to determine the answer to each of the questions on the basis of the
rules given below for computing service ratings and the data contained in the personnel
records of these seven employees.

All computations should be made as of the close of the rating period ending March 31,
2017.

Service Rating
The service rating of each permanent competitive class employee shall be computed by
adding the following three scores: (1) a basic score, (2) the employee's seniority score, and
(3) the employee's efficiency score.

Seniority Score
An employee's seniority score shall be computed by crediting him with 1/2% per year for
each year of service starting with the date of the employee's entrance as a permanent
employee into the competitive class, up to a maximum of 15 years (7 1/2%).

A residual fractional period of eight months or more shall be considered as a full year
and credited with 1/2%. A residual fraction of from four to, but not including, eight months
shall be considered as a half-year and credited with 1/4%. A residual fraction of less than four
months shall receive no credit in the seniority score.

For example, a person who entered the competitive class as a permanent employee on
August 1, 2014 would, as of March 31, 2017, be credited with a seniority score of 1 1/2% for
his 2 years and 8 months of service.

Efficiency Score
An employee's efficiency score shall be computed by adding the annual efficiency ratings
received by him during his service in his present position. (Where there are negative efficiency ratings, such ratings shall be subtracted from the sum of the positive efficiency ratings.) An employee's annual efficiency rating shall be based on the grade he receives from
his supervisor for his work performance during the annual efficiency rating period.

Basic Score
A basic score of 70% shall be given to each employee upon permanent appointment to a
competitive class position.

An employee shall receive a grade of A for performing work of the highest quality and
shall be credited with an efficiency rating of plus (+) 3%. An employee shall receive a grade of
F for performing work of the lowest quality and shall receive an efficiency rating of minus (-)
2%. Table I, entitled BASIS FOR DETERMINING ANNUAL EFFICIENCY RATINGS, lists the
six grades of work performance with their equivalent annual efficiency ratings. Table I also

lists the efficiency ratings to be assigned for service in a position for less than a year during the annual efficiency rating period.

The annual efficiency rating period shall run from April 1 to March 31, inclusive.

TABLE I – BASIS FOR DETERMINING ANNUAL EFFICIENCY RATINGS				
			Annual Efficiency Rating for Service in a Position For:	
Quality of Work Performed	Grade Assigned	8 months to a full year	At least 4 months but less than 8 months	Less than 4 months
Highest	A	+3%	+1 1/2%	0%
Good	B	+2%	+1%	0%
Standard	C	+1%	+1/2%	0%
Substandard	D	0%	0%	0%
Poor	E	-1%	-4%	0%
Lowest	F	-2%	-1%	0%

Appointment or Promotion During an Efficiency Rating Period

An employee who has been appointed or promoted during an efficiency rating period shall receive for that period an efficiency rating only for work performed by him during the portion of the period that he served in the position to which he was appointed or promoted. His efficiency rating for the period shall be determined in accordance with Table I.

Sample Computation of Service Rating

John Smith entered the competitive class as a permanent employee on December 1, 2012 and was promoted to his present position as a Clerk, Grade 3, on November 1, 2015. As a Clerk, Grade 3, he received a grade of B for work performed during the five-month period extending from November 1, 2015 to March 31, 2016 and a grade of C for work performed during the full annual period extending from April 1, 2016 to March 31, 2017.

On the basis of the RULES FOR COMPUTING SERVICE RATINGS, John Smith should be credited with:

70%   Basic Score
2 1/4%.   Seniority Score - for 4 years and 4 months of service (from 12/1/12 to 3/31/17)
2%   Efficiency Score - for 5 months of B service and a full _____ year of C service
74 1/4%

TABLE II
PERSONNEL RECORD OF SEVEN PERMANENT
COMPETITIVE CLASS EMPLOYEES

Employee	Present Position	Date of Appointment or Promotion To Present Position	Date of Entry as Permanent Employee in Competitive Class
Allen	Clerk, Gr. 5	6-1-13	7-1-00
Brown	Clerk, Gr. 4	1-1-15	7-1-17
Cole	Clerk, Gr. 3	9-1-13	11-1-10
Fox	Clerk, Gr. 3	10-1-13	9-1-08
Green	Clerk, Gr. 2	12-1-11	12-1-11
Hunt	Clerk, Gr. 2	7-1-12	7-1-12
Kane	Steno, Gr. 3	11-16-14	3-1-11

GRADES RECEIVED ANNUALLY FOR WORK
PERFORMED IN PRESENT POSITION

Employee	4-1-11 to 3-31-12	4-1-12 to 3-31-13	4-1-13 to 3-31-14	4-1-14 to 3-31-15	4-1-15 to 3-31-16	4-1-16 to 3-31-17
Allen			C*	C	B	C
Brown				C*	C	B
Cole			A*	B	C	C
Fox			C*	C	D	C
Green	C*	D	C	D	C	C
Hunt		C*	C	E	C	C
Kane				B*	B	C

EXPLANATORY NOTES:
*   Served in present position for less than a full year during this rating period. (Note date of appointment, or promotion, to present position.)
    All seven employees have served continuously as permanent employees since their entry into the competitive class.

Questions 1 through 9 refer to the employees listed in Table II. You are to answer these questions SOLELY on the basis of the preceding RULES FOR COMPUTING SERVICE RATINGS and on the information concerning these seven employees given in Table II. You are reminded that all computations are to be made as of the close of the rating period ending March 31, 2017. Candidates may find it helpful to arrange their computations on their scratch paper in an orderly manner since the computations for one question may also be utilized in answering another question.

1. The seniority score of Allen is   1.____

    A. 7 1/2%   B. 8 1/2%   C. 8%   D. 8 1/4%

2. The seniority score of Fox EXCEEDS that of Cole by   2.____

    A. 1 1/2%   B. 2%   C. 1%   D. 3/4%

3. The seniority score of Brown is   3.____

    A. *equal* to Hunt's   B. *twice* Hunt's
    C. *move* than Hunt's by 1 1/2%   D. *less* than by Hunt's by 1/2%

4. Green's efficiency score is

    .A. *twice* that of Kane
    B. *equal* to that of Kane
    C. *less* than Kane's by 1/2%
    D. *less* than Kane's by 1%

4.____

5. Of the following employees, the one who has the LOWEST efficiency score is

    A. Brown   B. Fox   C. Hunt   D. Kane

5.____

6. A comparison of Hunt's efficiency score with his seniority score reveals that his efficiency score is

    A. *less* than his seniority score by 1/2%
    B. *less* than his seniority score by 3/4%
    C. *equal* to his seniority score
    D. *greater* than his seniority score by 1/2%

6.____

7. Fox's service rating is

    A. 72 1/2%   B. 74%   C. 76 1/2%   D. 76 3/4%

7.____

8. Brown's service rating is

    A. less than 78%   B. 78%
    C. 78 1/4%   D. more than 78 1/4%

8.____

9. Cole's service rating EXCEEDS Kane's by

    A. less than 2%   B. 2%
    C. 2 1/4%   D. more than 2 1/4%

9.____

KEY (CORRECT ANSWERS)

1. A
2. C
3. B
4. C
5. B
6. D
7. D
8. B
9. A

ARITHMETICAL REASONING
EXAMINATION SECTION
TEST 1

DIRECTIONS: Each question or incomplete statement is followed by several suggested answers or completions. Select the one that BEST answers the question or completes the statement. *PRINT THE LETTER OF THE CORRECT ANSWER IN THE SPACE AT THE RIGHT.*

1. In 2015, a public agency spent $180 to buy pencils that cost three cents each. In 2017, the agency spent $420 to buy the same number of pencils that it had bought in 2015. The price per pencil that the agency paid in 2017 was _____ cents.

   A. 6 1/3   B. 2/3   C. 7   D. 7 3/4

   1._____

2. A stenographer spent her 35 hour work week on taking dictation, transcribing the dictated material, and filing.
   If she spent 20% of the work week on taking dictation and 1/2 of the remaining time on transcribing the dictated material, the number of hours of the work week that she spent on filing was

   A. 7   B. 10.5   C. 14   D. 17.5

   2._____

3. A typist typed eight pages in two hours.
   If she typed an average of 50 lines per page and an average of 12 words per line, what was her typing speed, in words per minute?

   A. 40   B. 50   C. 60   D. 80

   3._____

4. The daily compensation to be paid to each consultant hired in a certain agency is computed by dividing his professional earnings in the previous year by 250. The maximum daily compensation they can receive is $200 each. Four consultants who were hired to work on a special project had the following professional earnings in the previous year: $37,500, $144,000, $46,500, and $61,100. What will be the TOTAL daily cost to the agency for these four consultants?

   A. $932   B. $824   C. $736   D. $712

   4._____

5. In a typing and stenographic pool consisting of 30 employees, 2/5 of them are typists, 1/3 of them are senior typists and senior stenographers, and the rest are stenographers. If there are 5 more stenographers than senior stenographers, how many senior stenographers are in the typing and stenographic pool?

   A. 3   B. 5   C. 8   D. 10

   5._____

6. There are 3,330 copies of a three-page report to be collated. One clerk starts collating at 9:00 A.M. and is joined 15 minutes later by two other clerks. It takes 15 minutes for each of these clerks to collate 90 copies of the report.
   At what time should the job be completed if all three clerks continue working at the same rate without breaks?

   A. 12:00 Noon   B. 12:15 P.M.
   C. 1:00 P.M.   D. 1:15 P.M.

   6._____

7. By the end of last year, membership in the blood credit program in a certain agency had increased from the year before by 500, bringing the total to 2,500.
If the membership increased by the same percentage this year, the TOTAL number of members in the blood credit program for this agency by the end of this year should be

   A. 2,625   B. 3,000   C. 3,125   D. 3,250   7.___

8. During this year, an agency suggestion program put into practice suggestions from 24 employees, thereby saving the agency 40 times the amount of money it paid in awards. If 1/3 of the employees were awarded $50 each, 1/2 of the employees were awarded $25 each, and the rest were awarded $10 each, how much money did the agency save by using the suggestions?

   A. $18,760   B. $29,600   C. C, $32,400   D. $46,740   8.___

9. A senior stenographer earned $20,100 a year and had 4.5% state tax withheld for the year.
If she was paid every two weeks, the amount of state tax that was taken out of each of her paychecks, based on a 52-week year, was MOST NEARLY

   A. $31.38   B. $32.49   C. $34.77   D. $36.99   9.___

10. Two stenographers have been assigned to address 750 envelopes. One stenographer addresses twice as many envelopes per hour as the other stenographer.
If it takes five hours for them to complete the job, the rate of the slower stenographer is _____ envelopes per hour.

    A. 35   B. 50   C. 75   D. 100   10.___

11. Suppose that the postage rate for mailing single copies of a magazine to persons not included on a subscription list is 18 cents for the first two ounces of the single copy and 3 cents for each additional ounce.
If 19 copies of a magazine, each of which weighs eleven ounces, are mailed to 19 different people, the TOTAL postage cost of these magazines is

    A. $3.42   B. $3.99   C. $6.18   D. $8.55   11.___

12. A senior stenographer spends about 40 hours a month taking dictation. Of that time, 44% is spent taking minutes of meetings, 38% is spent taking dictation of lengthy reports, and the rest of the time is spent taking dictation of letters and memoranda.
How much MORE time is spent taking minutes of meetingsthan in taking dictation of letters and memoranda?
10 hours _____ minutes.

    A. 6   B. 16   C. 24   D. 40   12.___

13. In one week, a stenographer typed 65 letters. Forty letters had 4 copies on colored paper. The rest had 3 copies on colored paper.
If the stenographer had 500 sheets of colored paper on hand at the beginning of the week when she started typing the letters, how many sheets of colored paper did she have left at the end of the week?

    A. 190   B. 235   C. 265   D. 305   13.___

14. An agency is planning to microfilm letters and other correspondence of the last five years. The number of letter-size documents that can be photographed on a 100-foot roll of microfilm is 2,995. The agency estimates that it will need 240 feet of microfilm to do all the pages of all of the letters.
How many pages of letter-size documents can be photographed on this microfilm?

    A. 5,990   B. 6,786   C. 7,188   D. 7,985

14.____

15. In an agency, 2/3 of the total number of female stenographers and 1/2 of the total number of male stenographers attended a general staff meeting.
If there are a total of 56 stenographers in the agency and 25% of them are male, the number of female stenographers who attended the general staff meeting is

    A. 14   B. 28   C. 36   D. 42

15.____

16. A worker is currently earning $17,140 a year and pays $350 a month for rent. He expects to get a raise that will enable him to move into an apartment where his rent will be 25% of his new yearly salary.
If this new apartment is going to cost him $390 a month, what is the TOTAL amount of raise that he expects to get?

    A. $480   B. $980   C. $1,580   D. $1,840

16.____

17. The tops of five desks in an office are to be covered with a scratch-resistant material. Each desk top measures 60 inches by 36 inches.
How many square feet of material will be needed for the five desk tops?

    A. 15   B. 75   C. 96   D. 180

17.____

18. Three grades of bond paper are used in a central transcribing unit. The cost per ream of paper is $1.90 for Grade A, $1.70 for Grade B, and $1.60 for Grade C.
If the central transcribing unit used 6 reams of Grade A paper, 14 reams of Grade B paper, and 20 reams of Grade C paper, the AVERAGE cost, per ream, of the bond paper used by this unit is between

    A. $1.62 and $1.66   B. $1.66 and $1.70
    C. $1.70 and $1.74   D. $1.74 and $1.80

18.____

19. The Complaint Bureau of a city agency is composed of an investigation unit, a clerical unit, and a central transcribing unit. The sum of $264,000 has been appropriated for the operation of this bureau. Of this sum, $170,000 is to be allotted to the clerical unit.
Of this bureau's total appropriation, the percentage that is left for the central transcribing unit is MOST NEARLY ____ if $41,200 is allotted for investigations.

    A. 20%   B. 30%   C. 40%   D. 50%

19.____

20. Three typists were assigned to address a total of 2,655 postcards. Typist A addressed the postcards at the rate of 170 per hour. Typist B addressed the postcards at the rate of 150 per hour. Typist C's rate is not known. After the three typists had addressed postcards for three and a half hours, Typist C was taken off this assignment. It was necessary for Typist A and Typist B to work two and a half hours more to complete this assignment. The rate per hour at which Typist C addressed the postcards was

20.____

A. less than 150
B. between 150 and 170
C. more than 170 but less than 200
D. more than 200

21. In 2015, a city agency bought 12,000 envelopes at $4.00 per hundred. In 2016, the price of envelopes purchased was 40 percent higher than the 2010 price, but only 60 percent as many envelopes were bought.
The total cost of the envelopes purchased in 2016 was MOST NEARLY

    A. $250   B. $320   C. $400   D. $480

21.____

22. A stenographer has been assigned to place entries on 500 forms. She places entries on 25 forms by the end of half an hour, when she is joined by another stenographer. The second stenographer places entries at the rate of 45 an hour.
Assuming that both stenographers continue to work at their respective rates of speed, the TOTAL number of hours required to carry out the entire assignment is

    A. 5   B. 54   C. 64   D. 7

22.____

23. On Monday, a stenographer took dictation without interruption for 1 1/2 hours and transcribed all the dictated material in 3 1/2 hours. On Tuesday, she took dictation uninterruptedly for 1 3/4 hours and transcribed all the material in 3 3/4 hours. On Wednesday, she took dictation without interruption for 2 1/4 hours and transcribed all the material in 4 1/2 hours.
If she took dictation at the average rate of 90 words per minute during these three days, then her average transcription rate, in words per minute, for the same three days was MOST NEARLY

    A. 36   B. 41   C. 54   D. 58

23.____

24. In a division of clerks and stenographers, 15 people are currently employed, 20% of whom are stenographers.
If management plans are to maintain the current number of stenographers, but to increase the clerical staff to the point where 12% of the total staff are stenographers, what is the MAXIMUM number of additional clerks that should be hired to meet these plans?

    A. 3   B. 8   C. 10   D. 12

24.____

25. In the first quarter of the year, a certain operator sent out 230 quarterly reports. In the second quarter of that year, he sent out 310 quarterly reports.
The percent increase in the number of quarterly reports he sent out in the second quarter of the year compared to the first quarter of the year is MOST NEARLY

    A. 26%   B. 29%   C. 35%   D. 39%

25.____

KEY (CORRECT ANSWERS)

1.	C	11.	D
2.	C	12.	C
3.	A	13.	C
4.	C	14.	C
5.	A	15.	B
6.	B	16.	C
7.	C	17.	B
8.	B	18.	B
9.	C	19.	A
10.	B	20.	D

21.	C
22.	B
23.	B
24.	C
25.	C

SOLUTIONS TO PROBLEMS

1. $180 ÷ .03 = 6000 pencils bought. In 2017, the price per pencil = $420 / 6000 = .07 = 7 cents.

2. Number of hours on filing = 35 - (.20)(35) - (1/2)(28) = 14

3. Eight pages contains (8)(50)(12) = 4800 words. She thus typed 4800 words in 120 minutes = 40 words per minute.

4. $37,500 ÷ 250 = $150; $144,000 ÷ 250 = $576; $46,500 ÷ 250 = $186; $61,100 ÷ 250 = $244.40 Since $200 = maximum compensation for any single consultant, total compensation = $150 + $200 + $186 + $200 = $736

5. Number of typists = (2/5)(30) = 12, number of senior typists and senior stenographers = (1/3)(30) = 10, number of stenographers = 30 - 12 - 10 = 8. Finally, number of senior stenographers = 8-5 = 3

6. At 9:15 AM, 90 copies have been collated. The remaining 3240 copies are being collated at the rate of (3)(90) = 270 every 15 minutes = 1080 per hour. Since 3240 ÷ 1080 = 3 hours, the clerks will finish at 9:15 AM + 3 hours = 12:15 PM.

7. During last year, the membership increased from 2000 to 2500, which represents a (500/2000)(100) = 25% increase. A 25% increase during this year means the membership = (2500)(1.25) = 3125

8. Total awards = (1/3)(24)($50) + (1/2)(24)($25) + (1/6)(24)($10) = $740. Thus, the savings = (40)($740) = $29,600

9. Her pay for 2 weeks = $20,100 ÷ 26 ≈ $773.08. Thus, her state tax for 2 weeks ≈ ($773.08)(.045) ≈ $34.79. (Nearest correct answer is $34.77 in four selections.)

10. 750 ÷ 5 hours = 150 envelopes per hour for the 2 stenographers combined. Let x = number of envelopes addressed by the slower stenographer . Then, x + 2x = 150. Solving, x = 50

11. Total cost = (19)[.18+(.03)(9)] = $8.55

12. (.44)(40) - (.18)(40) = 10.4 hrs. = 10 hrs. 24 rain.

13. 500 - (40)(4) - (25)(3) = 265

14. 2995 ÷ 100 = 29.95 documents per foot of microfilm roll. Then, (29.95)(240 ft) = 7188 documents

15. There are (.75)(56) = 42 female stenographers. Then, (2/3)(42) = 28 of them attended the meeting.

16. ($390)(12) = $4680 new rent per year. Then, ($4680)(4) = $18,720 = his new yearly salary. His raise = $18,720 - $17,140 = $1580

17. Number of sq.ft. = (5)(60)(36) ÷ 144 = 75

18. Average cost per ream = [($1.90)(6) + ($1.70) (14) + ($1.60) (20)] / 40 = $1.68, which is between $1.66 and $1.70

19. $264,000 - $170,000 - $41,200 = 52,800 = 20%

20. Let x = typist C's rate. Since typists A and B each worked 6 hrs., while typist C worked only 3.5 hrs., we have (6)(170) + (6)(150) + 3.5x = 2655. Solving, x = 210, which is nore than 200.

21. In 2016, the cost per hundred envelopes was ($4.00)(1.40) = $5.60 and (.60)(12,000) = 7200 envelopes were bought. Total cost in 2016 = (72)($5.60) = $403.20, or about $400.

22. The 1st stenographer's rate is 50 forms per hour. After 1/2 hr., there are 500 - 25 = 475 forms to be done and the combined rate of the 2 stenographers is 95 forms per hr. Thus, total hrs. required = 1/2 + (475) ÷ (95) = 5 1/2

23. Total time for dictation = 1 1/4 + 1 3/4 + 2 1/4 = 5 1/4 hrs. = 315 min. The number of words = (90)(315) = 28,350. The total transcription 3 time = 3 1/4 + 3 3/4 + 44 = 11 1/2 hrs. = 690 min. Her average transcription rate = 28,350 ÷ 690 ≈ 41 words per min.

24. Currently, there are (.20)(15) = 3 stenographers, and thus 12 clerks. Let x = additional clerks. Then, $\frac{3}{3+12+x}$ = .12. This simplifies to 3 = (.12)(15+x). Solving, x = 10

25. Percent increase = $(\frac{80}{230})(100)$ ≈ 35%

TEST 2

DIRECTIONS: Each question or incomplete statement is followed by several suggested answers or completions. Select the one that BEST answers the question or completes the statement. *PRINT THE LETTER OF THE CORRECT ANSWER IN THE SPACE AT THE RIGHT.*

1. A school has 112 homeroom classes. There were 15 school days in February. The aggregate register of the school for the month of February was 52,920; the aggregate attendance was 43,860.
   The average class size, to the NEAREST tenth, is

   A. 35.3   B. 31.5   C. 29.2   D. 26.9

   1.____

2. As the school secretary in charge of supplies, you are asked to order the following items on a supplementary requisition for general supplies:
   5 gross of red pencils at $8.90 per dozen
   5,000 manila envelopes at $2.35 per C
   36 rulers at $187.20 per gross
   6 boxes of manila paper at $307.20 per carton (24 boxes to a carton)
   180 reams of composition paper at $27.80 per carton (20 reams to a carton)
   The TOTAL amount of the order is

   A. $957.20   B. $1,025.30   C. $916.80   D. $991.30

   2.____

3. In the high school to which you have been assigned as a school secretary, the annual allotment for general supplies, textbooks, repairs, etc. for the school year 2015-16 was $37,500. A special allotment of $10,000 was granted for textbooks ordered from the State Textbook List. The original requisition for general and vocational supplies amounted to $12,514.75; for science supplies, $6,287.25; for textbooks, including the special funds, $13,785.00; monies spent for equipment repairs and science perishables through December 31, 2015, $1,389.68.
   The balance in your supply allotment account on January 1, 2016 will be

   A. $14,913.00   B. $13,523.32
   C. $17,308.32   D. $3,523.32

   3.____

4. The teacher of one of the sixth term typing classes in the high school to which you are assigned as a school secretary has agreed to have her students type attendance cards for the incoming students for the new school year, commencing in September, as a work project. There are 24 students in the class; each student can complete 8 cards during a typing period. There will be 4,032 new students in September.
   The number of typing periods required to complete the task is

   A. 31   B. 21   C. 28   D. 24

   4.____

5. As a school secretary assigned to payroll duties, you are required to prepare the extra-curricular payroll report for the coaches teams in your high school. The rate of pay for these activities was increased on November 1 from $148 per session to $174.50 per session. The pay period which you are reporting is for the months of October, November, and December. Mr. Jones, the football coach, conducted 15 practice sessions in October, 20 in November, and 30 in December.
   His TOTAL gross pay on the December extra-curricular payroll report is

   5.____

A. $10,547.50
C. $10,945.00

B. $10,415.00
D. $11,342.50

6. The comparative results on a uniform examination given in your school for the last three years follow:

	2014	2015	2016
Number taking test	501	496	485
Number passing test	441	437	436

The percentage of passing, to the nearest tenth of a percent, for the year in which the HIGHEST percent of students passed is

A. 89.3%   B. 88%   C. 89.9%   D. 90.3%

7. During his first seven terms in high school, a student compiled the following averages:

Term	Numbers of Majors Completed	Average
1	4	81.25%
2	4	83.75%
3	5	86.2%
4	5	85.8%
5	5	87.0%
6	5	83.4%
7	5	82.6%

In his eighth term, the student had the following final marks in major subjects: 90%, 95%, 80%, 90%, 85%. The student's average for all eight terms of high school, correct to the nearest tenth of a percent, is

A. 84.8%   B. 84.7%   C. 84.9%   D. 85.8%

7.____

8. A secretary is asked by her employer to order an office machine which lists at a price of $360, less trade discounts of 20% and 10%, terms 2/10, n/30. There is a delivery charge of $8 and an installation charge of $12. If the machine is paid for in 10 days, the TOTAL cost of the machine will be

A. $264.80   B. $258.40   C. $266.96   D. $274.02

8.____

9. The school to which you have been assigned as school secretary has an annual allowance of 5,120 hours for all teacher aides. The principal decides to employ 5 teacher aides from 8:00 A.M. to 12:00 Noon, and 5 other teacher aides from 12:00 Noon to 4:00 P.M. daily for as many days as his allowance permits.
If a teacher aide earns $17.00 an hour, and he is present every day, his TOTAL earnings for the school year will be more than

A. $7,000 but less than $8,000
B. $8,000 but less than $9,000
C. $9,000 but less than $10,000
D. $10,000

9.____

10. During examination week in a high school to which you have been assigned as school   10.____
secretary, teachers are required to be in school at least 6 hours and 20 minutes daily
although their arrival and departure times may vary each day. A teacher's time card that
you have been asked to check shows the following entries for the week of June 17:

Date	Arrival	Departure
17	7:56 AM	2:18 PM
18	9:53 AM	4:22 PM
19	12:54 PM	7:03 PM
20	9:51 AM	4:15 PM
21	7:58 AM	2:11 PM

During the week of June 17 to June 21, the teacher was in school for AT LEAST the minimum required time on _____ days.

A. 2 of the 5   B. 3 of the 5
C. 4 of the 5   D. all 5

11. As school secretary, you are asked to find the total of the following bill received in your   11.____
school:
750 yellow envelopes at $.22 per C
2,400 white envelopes at $2.80 per M
30 rulers at $5.04 per gross
The TOTAL of the bill is

A. $69.90   B. $24.27   C. $18.87   D. $9.42

12. A department in the school to which you have been assigned as school secretary has   12.____
been given a textbook allowance of $5,500 for the school year. The department's text-
book order is:
75 books at $32.50 each
45 books at $49.50 each
25 books at $34.50 each
The TOTAL of the department's order is _____ the allowance.

A. $27.50 over   B. $27.50 under
C. $72.50 under   D. $57.50 over

13. The total receipts, including 5% city sales tax, for the G.O. store for the first week of   13.____
school amounted to $489.09.
The receipts from the G.O. store for the first week of school, excluding the 5% city
sales tax, amounted to

A. $465.80   B. $464.64   C. $464.63   D. $513.54

14. Class sizes in the school to which you have been assigned as school secretary are as   14.____
follows:

Number of Classes	Class Size
9	29 pupils
12	31 pupils
15	32 pupils
7	33 pupils
11	34 pupils

The average class size in this school, correct to the nearest tenth, is

A. 30.8   B. 31.9   C. 31.8   D. 30.9

15. In 2013, the social security tax was 4.2% for the first $6,600 earned a year. In 2014, the   15._____
social security tax was 4.4% on the first $6,600 earned a year.
For a teacher aide earning $19,200 in 2013 and $20,400 in 2014, the increase in
social security tax deduction in 2014 over 2013 was

    A. $132.00   B. $13.20   C. $19.20   D. $20.40

16. A teacher aide earning $23,900 a year will incur automatic deductions of 3.90% for social   16._____
security and .50% for medicare, based on the first $6,600 a year earnings. The TOTAL
tax deduction for these two items will be

    A. $274   B. $290.40   C. $525.80   D. $300.40

17. The school store turns in receipts totaling $131.25 to the school treasurer, including 5%   17._____
which has been collected for sales tax.
The amount of money which the treasurer MUST set aside for sales tax is

    A. $6.56   B. $6.25   C. $5.00   D. $5.25

18. One of the custodial assistants can wash all the windows in the main office in 3 hours. A   18._____
second assistant can wash the windows in the main office in 2 hours.
If the two men work together, they should complete the task in _____ hour(s) _____
minutes.

    A. 1; 0   B. 1.5; 0   C. 1; 12   D. 1; 15

19. A school secretary is requested by the principal to order an office machine which lists at   19._____
a price of $120, less discounts of 10% and 5%.
The net price of the machine to the school will be

    A. $100.50   B. $102.00   C. $102.60   D. $103.00

20. Five students are employed at school under a work-study program through which they   20._____
are paid $10.00 an hour for work in school offices, but no student may earn more than
$450 a month. Three days before the end of the month, you note that the student payroll
totals $2,062.50.
The number of hours which each of the students may work during the remainder of the
month is_____hour(s).

    A. 4   B. 2   C. 1   D. 3

21. You are asked to summarize expenditures made by the school within the budget alloca-   21._____
tion for the school year. You determine that the following expenditures have been made:
educational supplies, $2,600; postage, $650; emergency repairs, $225; textbooks,
$5,100; instructional equipment, $1,200.
Since $10,680 has been allocated to the school, the following sum still remains avail-
able for office supplies:

    A. $905   B. $1,005   C. $800   D. $755

22. In preparing the percentage of attendance for the period report, you note that the aggregate attendance is 57,585 and the aggregate register is 62,000.
The percentage of attendance, to the nearest tenth of a percent, is

    A. 91.9%   B. 93.0%   C. 92.8%   D. 92.9%

22.____

23. You borrow $1,200 from your retirement fund which you must repay over a period of three years, with interest of $144, each payment to be divided equally among 36 total payments.
The monthly deduction from your paycheck will be

    A. $37.33   B. $36.00   C. $33.00   D. $37.30

23.____

24. Tickets for a school dance are printed, starting with number 401 and ending with number 1650. They are to be sold for 750 each. The tickets remaining unsold should start with number 1569.
The amount of cash which should be collected for the sale of tickets is

    A. $876.75   B. $937.50   C. $876.00   D. $875.25

24.____

25. Stage curtains are purchased by the school and delivered on October 3 under terms of 5/10, 2/30, net/60. The curtains are paid in full by a check for $522.50 on October 12.
The invoice price was

    A. $533.16   B. $522.50   C. $540.00   D. $550.00

25.____

———————

KEY (CORRECT ANSWERS)

1.	B		11.	D
2.	B		12.	A
3.	B		13.	A
4.	B		14.	C
5.	C		15.	B
6.	C		16.	B
7.	C		17.	B
8.	D		18.	C
9.	B		19.	C
10.	B		20.	D

21.	A
22.	D
23.	A
24.	C
25.	D

SOLUTIONS TO PROBLEMS

1. Average class size = 52,920 ÷ 15 ÷ 112 = 31.5

2. Total amount = (5)(12)($8.90) + (50)($2.35) + (36) ($187.20) ÷ 144 + (6)($307.20) ÷ 24 + (9)($27.80) = $1025.30

3. Balance = $37,500 + $10,000 - $12,514.75 - $6287.25 - $13,785 - $1389.68 = $13,523.32

4. (24)(8) = 192 cards completed in one period. Then, 4032 ÷ 192 = 21 typing periods required.

5. Total pay = (15)($148.00) + (20)($174.50) + (30)($174.50) = $10,945.00

6. The passing rates for 2014, 2015, 2016 were 88.0%, 88.1%, and 89.9%, respectively. So, 89.9% was the highest.

7. His 8th term average was 88.0%. His overall average for all 8 terms = [(4)(81.25%)+(4)(83.75%)+(5)(86.2%)+(5)(85.8%)+ (5)(87.0%)+(5)(83.4%)+(5)(82.6%)+(5)(88.0%)] ÷ 38 = 84.9%

8. Total cost = ($360)(.80)(.90)(.98) + $8 + $12 ≈ $274.02 (Exact amount = $274.016)

9. 5120 ÷ 4 = 1280 teacher-days. Then, 1280 ÷ 10 = 128 days per teacher. A teacher's earnings for these 128 days = ($17.00)(4)(128)= $8704, which is more than $8000 but less than $9000.

10. The number of hours present on each of the 5 days listed was 6 hrs. 22 min., 6 hrs. 29 min., 6 hrs. 9 min., 6 hrs. 24 min., and 6 hrs. 13 min. On 3 days, he met the minimum time.

11. Total cost = (7.5)(.22) + (2.4)($2.80) + (30/144)(5.04) = $9.42

12. Textbook order = (75)($32.50) + (45)($49.50) + (25)($34.50) = $5527.50, which is $27.50 over the allowance.

13. Receipts without the tax = $489.09 ÷ 1.05 = $465.80

14. Average class size = [(9)(29)+(12)(31)+(7)(33)+(11)(34)+(15)(32)] ÷ 54 ≈ 31.8

15. ($6600)(.044-.042) = $13.20

16. ($6600)(.039+.005) = $290.40

17. $131.25 = 1.05x, x = 125, $131.25 - 125.00 = 6.25

18. Let x = hours needed working together. Then, (1/3)(x) + (1/2)(x) = 1
    Simplifying, 2x + 3x = 6. Solving, x = 1 1/5 hrs. = 1 hr. 12 min.

19. Net price = 120 - 10% (12) = 108; 108 - 5% (5.40) = 102.60

20. ($225)(5) - $1031.25 = $93.75 remaining in the month. Since the 5 students earn $25 per hour combined, $93.75 ÷ $25 = 3.75, which must be rounded down to 3 hours.

21. $10,680 - $2600 - $650 - $225 - $5100 - $1200 = $905 for office supplies.

22. 57,585 ÷ 62,000 ≈ .9288 ≈ 92.9%

23. Monthly deduction = $1344 ÷ 36 = $37.33 (Technically, 35 payments of $37.33 and 1 payment of $37.45)

24. (1569-401)(.75) = $876.00

25. The invoice price (which reflects the 5% discount) is $522.50 ÷ .95 = $550.00

TEST 3

DIRECTIONS: Each question or incomplete statement is followed by several suggested answers or completions. Select the one that BEST answers the question or completes the statement. *PRINT THE LETTER OF THE CORRECT ANSWER IN THE SPACE AT THE RIGHT.*

1. If an inch on an office layout drawing equals 4 feet of actual floor dimension, then a room which actually measures 9 feet by 14 feet is represented on the drawing by measurements equaling _____ inches x _____ inches.   1.__

    A. 2 1/4; 3 1/2   B. 2 1/2; 3 1/2   C. 2 1/4;3 1/4   D. 2 1/2;3 1/4

2. A cooperative education intern works from 1:30 P.M. to 5 P.M. on Mondays, Wednesdays, and Fridays, and from 10 A.M. to 2:30 P.M. with no lunch hour on Tuesdays and Thursdays. He earns $13.50 an hour on this job. In addition, he has a Saturday job paying $16.00 an hour at which he works from 9 A.M. to 3 P.M. with a half hour off for lunch. The gross amount that the student earns each week is MOST NEARLY   2.__

    A. $321.90   B. $355.62   C. $364.02   D. $396.30

3. Thirty-five percent of the College Discovery students who entered community college earned an associate degree. Of these students, 89% entered senior college, of which 67% went on to earn baccalaureate degrees.
   If there were 529 College Discovery students who entered community college, then the number of those who went on to finally receive a baccalaureate degree is MOST NEARLY   3.__

    A. 354   B. 315   C. 124   D. 110

4. It takes 5 office assistants two days to type 125 letters. Each of the assistants works at an equal rate of speed. How many days will it take 10 office assistants to type 200 letters?   4.__

    A. 1   B. 1 3/5   C. 2   D. 2 1/5

5. The following are the grades and credits earned by Student X during the first two years in college.   5.__

Grade	Credits	Weight	Quality Points
A	10 1/2	x4	
B	24	x3	
C	12	x2	
D	4 1/2	x1	
F, FW	5	x0	

To compute an index number:
   I.   Multiply the number of credits of each grade by the weight to get the number of *quality points*.
   II. Add the credits.
   III. Add the quality points.
   IV. Divide the total quality points by the total credits, and carry the division to two decimal places.

On the basis of the given information, the index number for Student X is

    A. 2.54   B. 2.59   C. 2.63   D. 2.68

6. Typist X can type 20 forms per hour, and Typist Y can type 30 forms per hour. If there are 30 forms to be typed and both typists are put to work on the job, how soon should they be expected to finish the work?
_____ minutes.

6._____

   A. 32   B. 34   C. 36   D. 38

7. Assume that there were 18 working days in February and that the six clerks in your unit had the following number of absences:

7._____

Clerk	Absences
F	3
G	2
H	8
I	1
J	0
K	5

The average percentage attendance for the six clerks in your unit in February was MOST NEARLY

   A. 80%   B. 82%   C. 84%   D. 86%

8. A certain employee is paid at the rate of $7.50 per hour, with time and a half for overtime. Hours in excess of 40 hours a week count as overtime. During the past week, the employee put in 48 working hours. The employee's gross wages for the week are MOST NEARLY

8._____

   A. $330   B. $350   C. $370   D. $390

9. You are making a report on the number of inside and outside calls handled by a particular switchboard. Over a 15-day period, the total number of all inside and outside calls handled by the switchboard was 5,760. The average number of inside calls per day was 234. You cannot find one day's tally of outside calls, but the total number of outside calls for the other fourteen days was 2,065. From this information, how many outside calls must have been reported on the missing tally?

9._____

   A. 175   B. 185   C. 195   D. 205

10. A floor plan has been prepared for a new building, drawn to a scale of 3/4 inch = 1 foot. A certain area is drawn 1 and 1/2 feet long and 6 inches wide on the floor plan. What are the ACTUAL dimensions of this area in the new building?
_____ feet long and _____ feet wide.

10._____

   A. 21; 8   B. 24; 8   C. 27; 9   D. 30; 9

11. You are preparing a package of six books to mail to a professor who is on sabbatical. They weigh, respectively, 1 pound 11 ounces, 1 pound 6 ounces, 2 pounds 1 ounce, 2 pounds 2 ounces, 1 pound 7 ounces, and 1 pound 8 ounces. The packaging material weighs 6 ounces.
The TOTAL weight of the package will be_____ pounds _____ ounces.

11._____

   A. 10; 3   B. 10; 9   C. 11; 5   D. 12; 5

12. Part-time students are charged $70 per credit for courses at a particular college. In addition, they must pay a $24.00 student activity fee if they take six credits or more and $14.00 lab fee for each laboratory course.
If a person takes one 3-credit course and one 4-credit course and his 4-credit course is a laboratory course, the TOTAL cost to him will be

    A. $504   B. $528   C. $542   D. $552

12._____

13. The graduating class of a certain community college consisted of 378 majors in secretarial science, 265 majors in engineering science, 57 majors in nursing, 513 majors in accounting, and 865 majors in liberal arts.
The percent of students who major in liberal arts at this college was MOST NEARLY

    A. 24.0%   B. 41.6%   C. 52.3%   D. 71.6%

13._____

14. Donald Smith earns $12.80 an hour for forty hours a week, with time and a half for all hours over forty. Last week, his total earnings amounted to $627.20.
He worked_____ hours.

    A. 46   B. 47   C. 48   D. 49

14._____

15. Mr. Jones desires to sell an article costing $28 at a gross profit of 30% of the selling price, and to allow a trade discount of 20% of the list price.
The list price of the article should be

    A. $43.68   B. $45.50   C. $48.00   D. $50.00

15._____

16. The gauge of an oil storage tank in an elementary school indicates 1/5 full. After a truck delivers 945 gallons of oil, the gauge indicates 4/5 full.
The capacity of the tank is _____ gallons.

    A. 1,260   B. 1,575   C. 1,625   D. 1,890

16._____

17. An invoice dated April 3, terms 3/10, 2/30, net/60, was paid in full with a check for $787.92 on May 1.
The amount of the invoice was

    A. $772.16   B. $787.92   C. $804.00   D. $812.29

17._____

18. Two pipes supply the water for the swimming pool at Blenheim High School. One pipe can fill the pool in 9 hours. The second pipe can fill the pool in 6 hours.
If both pipes were opened simultaneously, the pool could be filled in _____ hours minutes.

    A. 3; 36   B. 4; 30   C. 5; 15   D. 7; 30

18._____

19. John's father spent $24,000, which was one-fourth of his savings. He bought a car with three-eighths of the remainder of his savings.
His bank balance now amounts to

    A. $30,000   B. $32,000   C. $45,000   D. $50,000

19._____

20. A clock that loses 4 minutes every 24 hours was set at 6 A.M. on October 1. What time was indicated by the clock when the CORRECT time was 12:00 Noon on October 6th?
_____ A.M.

20.____

   A. 11:36   B. 11:38   C. 11:39   D. 11:40

21. Unit S's production fluctuated substantially from one year to another. In 2009, Unit S's production was 100% greater than in 2008. In 2010, production decreased by 25% from 2009. In 2011, Unit S's production was 10% greater than in 2010. On the basis of this information, it is CORRECT to conclude that Unit S's production in 2011 exceeded Unit S's production in 2008 by

21.____

   A. 65%   B. 85%   C. 95%   D. 135%

22. Agency X is moving into a new building. It has 1,500 employees presently on its staff and does not contemplate much variance from this level. The new building contains 100 available offices, each with a maximum capacity of 30 employees. It has been decided that only 2/3 of the maximum capacity of each office will be utilized. The TOTAL number of offices that will be occupied by Agency X is

22.____

   A. 30   B. 66   C. 75   D. 90

23. One typist completes a form letter every 5 minutes and another typist completes one every 6 minutes. If the two typists start together, how many minutes later will they again start typing new letters simultaneously and how many letters will they have completed by that time?
_____ minutes - _____ letters.

23.____

   A. 11; 30   B. 12; 24   C. 24; 12   D. 30; 1

24. During one week, a machine operator produces 10 fewer pages per hour of work than he usually does.
If it ordinarily takes him six hours to produce a 300-page report, how many hours LONGER will that same 300-page report take him during the week when he produces more slowly?
_____ hours longer.

24.____

   A. 1 1/2   B. 1 2/3   C. 2   D. 2 3/4

25. A study reveals that Miss Brown files N cards in M hours, and Miss Smith files the same number of cards in T hours. If the two employees work together, the number of hours it will take them to file N cards is

25.____

A. $\dfrac{N}{\dfrac{N}{M} + \dfrac{N}{N}}$ B. $\dfrac{N}{T+M} + \dfrac{2N}{MT}$

C. $N(\dfrac{M}{N} + \dfrac{N}{T})$ D. $\dfrac{N}{NT + MN}$

KEY (CORRECT ANSWERS)

1.	A		11.	B
2.	B		12.	B
3.	D		13.	B
4.	B		14.	A
5.	A		15.	D
6.	C		16.	B
7.	B		17.	C
8.	D		18.	A
9.	B		19.	C
10.	B		20.	C

21.	A
22.	C
23.	D
24.	A
25.	A

SOLUTIONS TO PROBLEMS

1. 9/4 = 2 1/4" and 14/4 = 3 1/2"

2. Gross amount = (3)($6.75)(3.5) + (2)($6.75)(4.5) + ($8.00)(5.5) = $175.625, which is closest to selection B ($177.81).

3. $(529)(.35)(.89)(.67) \approx 110$

4. 10 worker-days are needed to type 125 letters, so (200)(10) ÷ 125 = 16 worker-days are needed to type 200 letters. Finally, 16 ÷ 10 workers = 1 3/5 days.

5. Index number = [(14)(10 1/2) + (3) (24) + (2) (12) + (1)(4 1/2) +
   $(0)(5)] \div 56 \approx 2.54$

6. Typist X could do 30 forms in 30/20 = 1 1/2 hours. Let x = number of hours needed when working together with typist Y.

   Then, $(\dfrac{1}{1\frac{1}{2}})(x)+(\dfrac{1}{1})x=1$. Simplifying, $2x+3x=3$, so $x=\dfrac{3}{5}$ hr.= 36 min.

7. $(3+2+8+1+0+5) \div 6 = 3.1\overline{6}$. Then, $18 \sim 3.\overline{6} = 14.8\overline{3}$.
   Finally, $14.8\overline{3} \div 18 \approx 82\%$

8. Wages = ($7.50)(40) + ($11.25)(8) = $390

9. (234)(15) = 3510 inside calls. Then, 5760 - 3510 = 2250 outside calls. Finally, 2250 - 2065 = 185 outside calls on the missing day.

10. 18 ÷ 3/4 = 24 feet long and 6 ÷ 3/4 = 8 feet wide.

11. Total weight = 1 lb. 11 oz. + 1 lb. 6 oz. + 2 lbs. 1 oz. + 2 lbs. 2 oz + 1 lb. 7 oz. + 1 lb. 8 oz. + 6 oz. = 8 lbs. 41 oz. = 10 lbs. 9 oz.

12. Total cost = ($70)(7) + $24 + $14 = $528

13. 865 ÷ 2078 ≈ 41.6% liberal arts majors

14. ($12.80)(40)= $512, so he made $627.20 - $512 = $115.20 in overtime. His overtime rate = ($12.80)(1.5)= $19.20 per hour. Thus, he worked $115.20 ÷ $19.20 = 6 overtime hours. Total hours worked =46.

15. Let x = list price. Selling price = .80x. Then, .80x - (.30)(.80x) = $28. Simplifying, .56x = $28. Solving, x = $50.00

16. 945 gallons represents $\frac{4}{5} - \frac{1}{5} = \frac{3}{5}$ of the tank's capacity. Then, the capacity

    $= 945 \div \frac{3}{5} = 1575$ gallons

17. $787.92 \div .98 = $804.00

18. Let x = number of required hours. Then, $(1/9)(x) + (1/6)(x) = 1$ Simplifying, $2x + 3x = 18$. Solving, x = 3.6 hours = 3 hrs. 36 min.

19. Bank balance = $96,000 - $24,000 - (3/8)($72,000) = $45,000

20. From Oct. 1, 6 AM to Oct. 6, Noon = 5 1/2 days. The clock would show a loss of (4 min.)(5 1/2) = 21 min. Thus, the clock's time would (incorrectly) show 12:00 Noon - 21 min. = 11:39 AM

21. 2008 = x, 2009 = 200x, 2010 = 150x, 2011 = 165x
    65% more

22. (2/3)(30) = 20 employees in each office. Then, 1500 ÷ 20 = 75 offices

23. After 30 minutes, the typists will have finished a total of 6 + 5 = 11 letters.

24. When he works more slowly, he will only produce 300 - (6)(10) = 240 pages in 6 hrs. His new slower rate is 40 pages per hour, so he will need 60/40 = 1 1/2 more hours to do the remaining 60 pages.

25. Let x = required hours. Then, $(\frac{1}{M})(x)+(\frac{1}{T})(x)=1$. Simplifying, , x(T+M) = MT. Solving, x = MT/(T+M).
    Note: The N value is immaterial. Also, choice A reduces to MT/(T+M).

———

PRINCIPLES AND PRACTICES OF ADMINISTRATION, SUPERVISION & MANAGEMENT

TABLE OF CONTENTS

PRINCIPLES AND PRACTICES OF ADMINISTRATION, SUPERVISION & MANAGEMENT

Most people are inclined to think of administration as something that only a few persons are responsible for in a large organization. Perhaps this is true if you are thinking of Administration with a capital *A*, but administration with a lower case *a* is a responsibility of supervisors at all levels each working day.

All of us feel we are pretty good supervisors and that we do a good job of administering the workings of our agency. By and large, this is true, but every so often it is good to check up on ourselves. Checklists appear from time to time in various publications which psychologists say, tell whether or not a person will make a good wife, husband, doctor, lawyer, or supervisor.

The following questions are an excellent checklist to test yourself as a supervisor and administrator.

Remember, Administration gives direction and points the way but administration carries the ideas to fruition. Each is dependent on the other for its success. Remember, too, that no unit is too small for these departmental functions to be carried out. These statements apply equally as well to the Chief Librarian as to the Department Head with but one or two persons to supervise.

GENERAL ADMINISTRATION - General Responsibilities of Supervisors

1. Have I prepared written statements of functions, activities, and duties for my organizational unit?

2. Have I prepared procedural guides for operating activities?

3. Have I established clearly in writing, lines of authority and responsibility for my organizational unit?

4. Do I make recommendations for improvements in organization, policies, administrative and operating routines and procedures, including simplification of work and elimination of non-essential operations?

5. Have I designated and trained an understudy to function in my absence?

6. Do I supervise and train personnel within the unit to effectively perform their assignments?

7. Do I assign personnel and distribute work on such a basis as to carry out the organizational unit's assignment or mission in the most effective and efficient manner?

8. Have I established administrative controls by:

   a. Fixing responsibility and accountability on all supervisors under my direction for the proper performance of their functions and duties.

b. Preparing and submitting periodic work load and progress reports covering the operations of the unit to my immediate superior.

c. Analysis and evaluation of such reports received from subordinate units.

d. Submission of significant developments and problems arising within the organizational unit to my immediate superior.

e. Conducting conferences, inspections, etc., as to the status and efficiency of unit operations.

9. Do I maintain an adequate and competent working force?

10. Have I fostered good employee-department relations, seeing that established rules, regulations, and instructions are being carried out properly?

11. Do I collaborate and consult with other organizational units performing related functions to insure harmonious and efficient working relationships?

12. Do I maintain liaison through prescribed channels with city departments and other governmental agencies concerned with the activities of the unit?

13. Do I maintain contact with and keep abreast of the latest developments and techniques of administration (professional societies, groups, periodicals, etc.) as to their applicability to the activities of the unit?

14. Do I communicate with superiors and subordinates through prescribed organizational channels?

15. Do I notify superiors and subordinates in instances where bypassing is necessary as soon thereafter as practicable?

16. Do I keep my superior informed of significant developments and problems?

SEVEN BASIC FUNCTIONS OF THE SUPERVISOR

1. ## PLANNING
   This means working out goals and means to obtain goals. What needs to be done, who will do it, how, when, and where it is to be done.

   ## SEVEN STEPS IN PLANNING

   1. Define job or problem clearly.
   2. Consider priority of job.
   3. Consider time-limit - starting and completing.
   4. Consider minimum distraction to, or interference with, other activities.
   5. Consider and provide for contingencies - possible emergencies.
   6. Break job down into components.
   7. Consider the 5 W's and H:

WHY	...	is it necessary to do the job? (Is the purpose clearly defined?)
WHAT	...	needs to be done to accomplish the defined purpose?
	...	is needed to do the job? (money, materials, etc.)
WHO	...	is needed to do the job?
	...	will have responsibilities?
WHERE	...	is the work to be done?
WHEN	...	is the job to begin and end? (schedules, etc.)
HOW	...	is the job to be done? (methods, controls, records, etc.)

2. ORGANIZING

This means dividing up the work, establishing clear lines of responsibility and authority and coordinating efforts to get the job done.

3. STAFFING

The whole personnel function of bringing in and training staff, getting the right man and fitting him to the right job - the job to which he is best suited.
In the normal situation, the supervisor's responsibility regarding staffing normally includes providing accurate job descriptions, that is, duties of the jobs, requirements, education and experience, skills, physical, etc.; assigning the work for maximum use of skills; and proper utilization of the probationary period to weed out unsatisfactory employees.

4. DIRECTING

Providing the necessary leadership to the group supervised. Important work gets done to the supervisor's satisfaction.

5. COORDINATING

The all-important duty of inter-relating the various parts of the work.
The supervisor is also responsible for controlling the coordinated activities. This means measuring performance according to a time schedule and setting quotas to see that the goals previously set are being reached. Reports from workers should be analyzed, evaluated, and made part of all future plans.

6. REPORTING

This means proper and effective communication to your superiors, subordinates, and your peers (in definition of the job of the supervisor). Reports should be read and information contained therein should be used not be filed away and forgotten. Reports should be written in such a way that the desired action recommended by the report is forthcoming.

7. BUDGETING

This means controlling current costs and forecasting future costs. This forecast is based on past experience, future plans and programs, as well as current costs.

You will note that these seven functions can fall under three topics:

Planning	)	
Organizing	)	Make a Plan
Staffing	)	
Directing	)	Get things done
Controlling	)	

Reporting   )
Budgeting   )   Watch it work

PLANNING TO MEET MANAGEMENT GOALS

I. <u>WHAT IS PLANNING?</u>
   A. Thinking a job through before new work is done to determine the best way to do it
   B. A method of doing something
   C. Ways and means for achieving set goals
   D. A means of enabling a supervisor to deliver with a minimum of effort, all details involved in coordinating his work

II. <u>WHO SHOULD MAKE PLANS?</u>
   Everybody!
   All levels of supervision must plan work. (Top management, heads of divisions or bureaus, first line supervisors, and individual employees.) The higher the level, the more planning required.

III. <u>WHAT ARE THE RESULTS OF POOR PLANNING?</u>
   A. Failure to meet deadline
   B. Low employee morale
   C. Lack of job coordination
   D. Overtime is frequently necessary
   E. Excessive cost, waste of material and manhours

IV. <u>PRINCIPLES OF PLANNING</u>
   A. Getting a clear picture of your objectives. What exactly are you trying to accomplish?
   B. Plan the whole job, then the parts, in proper sequence.
   C. Delegate the planning of details to those responsible for executing them.
   D. Make your plan flexible.
   E. Coordinate your plan with the plans of others so that the work may be processed with a minimum of delay.
   F. Sell your plan before you execute it.
   G. Sell your plan to your superior, subordinate, in order to gain maximum participation and coordination.
   H. Your plan should take precedence. Use knowledge and skills that others have brought to a similar job.
   I. Your plan should take account of future contingencies; allow for future expansion.
   J. Plans should include minor details. Leave nothing to chance that can be anticipated.
   K. Your plan should be simple and provide standards and controls. Establish quality and quantity standards and set a standard method of doing the job. The controls will indicate whether the job is proceeding according to plan.
   L. Consider possible bottlenecks, breakdowns, or other difficulties that are likely to arise.

V. Q. WHAT ARE THE *YARDSTICKS* BY WHICH PLANNING SHOULD BE MEASURED?
   A. Any plan should:
      - Clearly state a definite course of action to be followed and goal to be achieved, with consideration for emergencies.
      - Be realistic and practical.

- State what's to be done, when it's to be done, where, how, and by whom.
- Establish the most efficient sequence of operating steps so that more is accomplished in less time, with the least effort, and with the best quality results.
- Assure meeting deliveries without delays.
- Establish the standard by which performance is to be judged.

Q. WHAT KINDS OF PLANS DOES EFFECTIVE SUPERVISION REQUIRE?
A. Plans should cover such factors as:
- Manpower - right number of properly trained employees on the job.
- Materials - adequate supply of the right materials and supplies.
- Machines - full utilization of machines and equipment, with proper maintenance.
- Methods - most efficient handling of operations.
- Deliveries - making deliveries on time.
- Tools - sufficient well-conditioned tools
- Layout - most effective use of space.
- Reports - maintaining proper records and reports.
- Supervision - planning work for employees and organizing supervisor's own time.

I. MANAGEMENT

Question: *What do we mean by management?*

Answer: *Getting work done through others.*

Management could also be defined as planning, directing, and controlling the operations of a bureau or division so that all factors will function properly and all persons cooperate efficiently for a common objective.

II. MANAGEMENT PRINCIPLES

1. There should be a hierarchy - wherein authority and responsibility run upward and downward through several levels - with a broad base at the bottom and a single head at the top.

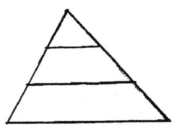

2. Each and every unit or person in the organization should be answerable ultimately to the manager at the apex. In other words, *The buck stops here!*

3. Every necessary function involved in the bureau's objectives is assigned to a unit in that bureau.

4. Responsibilities assigned to a unit are specifically clear-cut and understood.

5. Consistent methods of organizational structure should be applied at each level of the organization.

6. Each member of the bureau from top to bottom knows:
      to whom he reports
      who reports to him.

7. No member of one bureau reports to more than one supervisor.
      No dual functions

8. Responsibility for a function is matched by authority necessary to perform that function.
      Weight of authority

9. Individuals or units reporting to a supervisor do not exceed the number which can be feasibly and effectively coordinated and directed.
      Concept of *span of control*

10. Channels of command (management) are not violated by staff units, although there should be staff services to facilitate and coordinate management functions.

11. Authority and responsibility should be decentralized to units and individuals who are responsible for the actual performance of operations.
      Welfare - down to Welfare Centers
      Hospitals - down to local hospitals

12. Management should exercise control through attention to policy problems of exceptional importance, rather than through review of routine actions of subordinates.

13. Organizations should never be permitted to grow so elaborate as to hinder work accomplishments.
      Empire building

II. ORGANIZATION STRUCTURE
Types of Organizations.
The purest form is a leader and a few followers, such as:

```
                        ┌─────────────┐
                        │  Supervisor │
                        └─────────────┘
 ┌──────────┐    ┌──────────┐    ┌──────────┐    ┌──────────┐
 │  Worker  │    │  Worker  │    │  Worker  │    │  Worker  │
 └──────────┘    └──────────┘    └──────────┘    └──────────┘
```

(Refer to organization chart) from supervisor to workers.

The line of authority is direct,
The workers know exactly where they stand in relation to their boss, to whom they report for instructions and direction.

Unfortunately, in our present complex society, few organizations are similar to this example of a pure line organization. In this era of specialization, other people are often needed in the simplest of organizations. These specialists are known as staff. The sole purpose for their existence (staff) is to assist, advise, suggest, help or counsel line organizations. Staff has no authority to direct line people - nor do they give them direct instructions.

```
                          ┌──────────────┐
                          │  SUPERVISOR  │
                          └──────┬───────┘
    ──────────────────────────────────────────────────────────
 ┌─────────────┐  ┌──────────────┐  ┌──────────────┐  ┌──────────┐
 │  Personnel  │  │  Accounting  │  │  Inspection  │  │  Legal   │
 └─────────────┘  └──────────────┘  └──────────────┘  └──────────┘
   ┌──────────┐     ┌──────────┐      ┌──────────┐     ┌──────────┐
   │  Worker  │     │  Worker  │      │  Worker  │     │  Worker  │
   └──────────┘     └──────────┘      └──────────┘     └──────────┘
```

Line Functions

1. Directs

2. Orders

3. Responsibility for carrying out activities from beginning to end

4. Follows chain of command

5. Is identified with what it does

6. Decides when and how to use staff advice

7. Line executes

Staff Functions

1. Advises

2. Persuades and sells

3. Staff studies, reports, recommends but does not carry out

4. May advise across department lines

5. May find its ideas identified with others

6. Has to persuade line to want its advice

7. Staff - Conducts studies and research. Provides advice and instructions in technical matters. Serves as technical specialist to render specific services

Types and Functions of Organization Charts.
An organization chart is a picture of the arrangement and inter-relationship of the subdivisions of an organization.

1. Types of Charts:
   a. Structural - basic relationships only
   b. Functional - includes functions or duties
   c. Personnel - positions, salaries, status, etc.
   d. Process Chart - work performed
   e. Gantt Chart - actual performance against planned
   f. Flow Chart - flow and distribution of work

2. Functions of Charts:
   a. Assist in management planning and control
   b. Indicate duplication of functions
   c. Indicate incorrect stressing of functions
   d. Indicate neglect of important functions
   e. Correct unclear authority
   f. Establish proper span of control

3. Limitations of Charts:
   a. Seldom maintained on current basis

b. Chart is oversimplified
c. Human factors cannot adequately be charted

4. Organization Charts should be:
   a. Simple
   b. Symmetrical
   c. Indicate authority
   d. Line and staff relationship differentiated
   e. Chart should be dated and bear signature of approving officer
   f. Chart should be displayed, not hidden

ORGANIZATION

There are four basic principles of organization:

1. Unity of command
2. Span of control
3. Uniformity of assignment
4. Assignment of responsibility and delegation of authority

Unity of Command

Unity of command means that each person in the organization should receive orders from one, and only one, supervisor. When a person has to take orders from two or more people, (a) the orders may be in conflict and the employee is upset because he does not know which he should obey, or, (b) different orders may reach him at the same time and he does not know which he should carry out first.

Equally as bad as having two bosses is the situation where the supervisor is by-passed. Let us suppose you are a supervisor whose boss by-passes you (deals directly with people reporting to you). To the worker, it is the same as having two bosses; but to you, the supervisor, it is equally serious. By-passing on the part of your boss will undermine your authority, and the people under you will begin looking to your boss for decisions and even for routine orders.

You can prevent by-passing by telling the people you supervise that if anyone tries to give them orders, they should direct that person to you.

Span of Control

Span of control on a given level involves:

a. The number of people being supervised
b. The distance
c. The time involved in supervising the people. (One supervisor cannot supervise too many workers effectively.)

Span of control means that a supervisor has the right number (not too many and not too few) of subordinates that he can supervise well.

Uniformity of Assignment

In assigning work, you as the supervisor should assign to each person jobs that are similar in nature. An employee who is assigned too many different types of jobs will waste time in going from one kind of work to another. It takes time for him to get to top production in one kind of task and, before he does so, he has to start on another.

When you assign work to people, remember that:

a. Job duties should be definite. Make it clear from the beginning <u>what</u> they are to do, <u>how</u> they are to do it, and <u>why</u> they are to do it. Let them know how much they are expected to do and how well they are expected to do it.

b. Check your assignments to be certain that there are no workers with too many unrelated duties, and that no two people have been given overlapping responsibilities. Your aim should be to have every task assigned to a specific person with the work fairly distributed and with each person doing his part.

Assignment of Responsibility and Delegation of Authority

A supervisor cannot delegate his final responsibility for the work of his department. The experienced supervisor knows that he gets his work done through people. He can't do it all himself. So he must assign the work and the responsibility for the work to his employees. Then they must be given the authority to carry out their responsibilities.

By assigning responsibility and delegating authority to carry out the responsibility, the supervisor builds in his workers initiative, resourcefulness, enthusiasm, and interest in their work. He is treating them as responsible adults. They can find satisfaction in their work, and they will respect the supervisor and be loyal to the supervisor.

PRINCIPLES OF ORGANIZATION

1. Definition
   Organization is the method of dividing up the work to provide the best channels for coordinated effort to get the agency's mission accomplished.

2. Purpose of Organization
   a. To enable each employee within the organization to clearly know his responsibilities and relationships to his fellow employees and to organizational units.
   b. To avoid conflicts of authority and overlapping of jurisdiction.
   c. To ensure teamwork.

3. Basic Considerations in Organizational Planning
   a. The basic plans and objectives of the agency should be determined, and the organizational structure should be adapted to carry out effectively such plans and objectives.
   b. The organization should be built around the major functions of the agency and not individuals or groups of individuals.
   c. The organization should be sufficiently flexible to meet new and changing conditions which may be brought about from within or outside the department.
   d. The organizational structure should be as simple as possible and the number of organizational units kept at a minimum.
   e. The number of levels of authority should be kept at a minimum. Each additional management level lengthens the chain of authority and responsibility and increases the time for instructions to be distributed to operating levels and for decisions to be obtained from higher authority.

    f. The form of organization should permit each executive to exercise maximum initiative within the limits of delegated authority.

4. Bases for Organization
   a. Purpose (Examples: education, police, sanitation)
   b. Process (Examples: accounting, legal, purchasing)
   c. Clientele (Examples: welfare, parks, veteran)
   d. Geographic (Examples: borough offices, precincts, libraries)

5. Assignments of Functions
   a. Every function of the agency should be assigned to a specific organizational unit. Under normal circumstances, no single function should be assigned to more than one organizational unit.
   b. There should be no overlapping, duplication, or conflict between organizational elements.
   c. Line functions should be separated from staff functions, and proper emphasis should be placed on staff activities.
   d. Functions which are closely related or similar should normally be assigned to a single organizational unit.
   e. Functions should be properly distributed to promote balance, and to avoid overemphasis of less important functions and underemphasis of more essential functions.

6. Delegation of Authority and Responsibility
   a. Responsibilities assigned to a specific individual or organizational unit should carry corresponding authority, and all statements of authority or limitations thereof should be as specific as possible.
   b. Authority and responsibility for action should be decentralized to organizational units and individuals responsible for actual performance to the greatest extent possible, without relaxing necessary control over policy or the standardization of procedures. Delegation of authority will be consistent with decentralization of responsibility but such delegation will not divest an executive in higher authority of his overall responsibility.
   c. The heads of organizational units should concern themselves with important matters and should delegate to the maximum extent details and routines performed in the ordinary course of business.
   d. All responsibilities, authorities, and relationships should be stated in simple language to avoid misinterpretation.
   e. Each individual or organizational unit charged with a specific responsibility will be held responsible for results.

7. Employee Relationships
   a. The employees reporting to one executive should not exceed the number which can be effectively directed and coordinated. The number will depend largely upon the scope and extent of the responsibilities of the subordinates.
   b. No person should report to more than one supervisor. Every supervisor should know who reports to him, and every employee should know to whom he reports. Channels of authority and responsibility should not be violated by staff units.
   c. Relationships between organizational units within the agency and with outside organizations and associations should be clearly stated and thoroughly understood to avoid misunderstanding.

DELEGATING

1. <u>What is Delegating</u>?
Delegating is assigning a job to an employee, giving him the authority to get that job done, and giving him the responsibility for seeing to it that the job is done.

   a. <u>What to Delegate</u>
      (1) Routine details
      (2) Jobs which may be necessary and take a lot of time, but do not have to be done by the supervisor personally (preparing reports, attending meetings, etc.)
      (3) Routine decision-making (making decisions which do not require the supervisor's personal attention)

   b. <u>What Not to Delegate</u>
      (1) Job details which are *executive functions* (setting goals, organizing employees into a good team, analyzing results so as to plan for the future)
      (2) Disciplinary power (handling grievances, preparing service ratings, reprimands, etc.)
      (3) Decision-making which involves large numbers of employees or other bureaus and departments
      (4) Final and complete responsibility for the job done by the unit being supervised

   c. <u>Why Delegate</u>?
      (1) To strengthen the organization by developing a greater number of skilled employees
      (2) To improve the employee's performance by giving him the chance to learn more about the job, handle some responsibility, and become more interested in getting the job done
      (3) To improve a supervisor's performance by relieving him of routine jobs and giving him more time for *executive functions* (planning, organizing, controlling, etc.) which cannot be delegated

2. <u>To Whom to Delegate</u>
People with abilities not being used. Selection should be based on ability, not on favoritism.

REPORTS

<u>Definition</u>
A report is an orderly presentation of factual information directed to a specific reader for a specific purpose.

<u>Purpose</u>
The general purpose of a report is to bring to the reader useful and factual information about a condition or a problem. Some specific purposes of a report may be:

1. To enable the reader to appraise the efficiency or effectiveness of a person or an operation
2. To provide a basis for establishing standards
3. To reflect the results of expenditures of time, effort, and money
4. To provide a basis for developing or altering programs

Types

1. Information Report - Contains facts arranged in sequence
2. Summary (Examination) Report - Contains facts plus an analysis or discussion of the significance of the facts. Analysis may give advantages and disadvantages or give qualitative and quantitative comparisons
3. Recommendation Report - Contains facts, analysis, and conclusion logically drawn from the facts and analysis, plus a recommendation based upon the facts, analysis, and conclusions

Factors to Consider Before Writing Report

1. Why write the report - The purpose of the report should be clearly defined.
2. Who will read the report - What level of language should be used? Will the reader understand professional or technical language?
3. What should be said - What does the reader need or want to know about the subject?
4. How should it be said - Should the subject be presented tactfully? Convincingly? In a stimulating manner?

Preparatory Steps

1. Assemble the facts - Find out who, why, what, where, when, and how.
2. Organize the facts - Eliminate unnecessary information.
3. Prepare an outline - Check for orderliness, logical sequence.
4. Prepare a draft - Check for correctness, clearness, completeness, conciseness, and tone.
5. Prepare it in final form - Check for grammar, punctuation, appearance.

Outline For a Recommendation Report

Is the report:

1. Correct in information, grammar, and tone?
2. Clear?
3. Complete?
4. Concise?
5. Timely?
6. Worth its cost?

Will the report accomplish its purpose?

MANAGEMENT CONTROLS

1. Control
   What is control? What is controlled? Who controls?

The essence of control is action which adjusts operations to predetermined standards, and its basis is information in the hands of managers. Control is checking to determine whether plans are being observed and suitable progress toward stated objectives is being made, and action is taken, if necessary, to correct deviations.

We have a ready-made model for this concept of control in the automatic systems which are widely used for process control in the chemical and petroleum industries. A process control system works this way. Suppose, for example, it is desired to maintain a constant rate of flow of oil through a pipe at a predetermined or set-point value. A signal, whose strength represents the rate of flow, can be produced in a measuring device and transmitted to a control mechanism. The control mechanism, when it detects any deviation of the actual from the set-point signal, will reposition the value regulating flow rate.

2. Basis For Control

A process control mechanism thus acts to adjust operations to predetermined standards and does so on the basis of information it receives. In a parallel way, information reaching a manager gives him the opportunity for corrective action and is his basis for control. He cannot exercise control without such information, and he cannot do a complete job of managing without controlling.

3. Policy

What is policy?

Policy is simply a statement of an organization's intention to act in certain ways when specified types of circumstances arise. It represents a general decision, predetermined and expressed as a principle or rule, establishing a normal pattern of conduct for dealing with given types of business events - usually recurrent. A statement is therefore useful in economizing the time of managers and in assisting them to discharge their responsibilities equitably and consistently.

Policy is not a means of control, but policy does generate the need for control.

Adherence to policies is not guaranteed nor can it be taken on faith. It has to be verified. Without verification, there is no basis for control. Policy and procedures, although closely related and interdependent to a certain extent, are not synonymous. A policy may be adopted, for example, to maintain a materials inventory not to exceed one million dollars. A procedure for inventory control would interpret that policy and convert it into methods for keeping within that limit, with consideration, too, of possible but foreseeable expedient deviation.

4. Procedure

What is procedure?

A procedure specifically prescribes:

    a. What work is to be performed by the various participants
    b. Who are the respective participants
    c. When and where the various steps in the different processes are to be performed
    d. The sequence of operations that will insure uniform handling of recurring transactions
    e. The *paper* that is involved, its origin, transition, and disposition

Necessary appurtenances to a procedure are:

    a. Detailed organizational chart

    b.   Flow charts
    c.   Exhibits of forms, all presented in close proximity to the text of the procedure

5.   <u>Basis of Control - Information in the Hands of Managers</u>
If the basis of control is information in the hands of managers, then <u>reporting</u> is elevated to a level of very considerable importance.

Types of reporting may include:

    a.   Special reports and routine reports
    b.   Written, oral, and graphic reports
    c.   Staff meetings
    d.   Conferences
    e.   Television screens
    f.   Non-receipt of information, as where management is by exception
    g.   Any other means whereby information is transmitted to a manager as a basis for control action

FRAMEWORK OF MANAGEMENT

<u>Elements</u>
1.   <u>Policy</u> - It has to be verified, controlled.

2.   <u>Organization</u> - is part of the giving of an assignment. The organizational chart gives to each individual in his title, a first approximation of the nature of his assignment and orients him as being accountable to a certain individual. Organization is not in a true sense a means of control. Control is checking to ascertain whether the assignment is executed as intended and acting on the basis of that information.

3.   <u>Budgets</u> - perform three functions:

    a.   They present the objectives, plans, and programs of the organization in financial terms.
    b.   They report the progress of actual performance against these predetermined objectives, plans, and programs.
    c.   Like organizational charts, delegations of authority, procedures and job descriptions, they define the assignments which have flowed from the Chief Executive. Budgets are a means of control in the respect that they report progress of actual performance against the program. They provide information which enables managers to take action directed toward bringing actual results into conformity with the program.

4.   <u>Internal Check</u> - provides in practice for the principle that the same person should not have responsibility for all phases of a transaction. This makes it clearly an aspect of organization rather than of control. Internal Check is static, or built-in.

5.   <u>Plans, Programs, Objectives</u>
People must know what they are trying to do. <u>Objectives</u> fulfill this need. Without them, people may work industriously and yet, working aimlessly, accomplish little.

Plans and Programs complement Objectives, since they propose how and according to what time schedule the objectives are to be reached.

6. Delegations of Authority

Among the ways we have for supplementing the titles and lines of authority of an organizational chart are delegations of authority. Delegations of authority clarify the extent of authority of individuals and in that way serve to define assignments. That they are not means of control is apparent from the very fact that wherever there has been a delegation of authority, the need for control increases. This could hardly be expected to happen if delegations of authority were themselves means of control.

Manager's Responsibility

Control becomes necessary whenever a manager delegates authority to a subordinate because he cannot delegate and then simply sit back and forget all about it. A manager's accountability to his own superior has not diminished one whit as a result of delegating part of his authority to a subordinate. The manager must exercise control over actions taken under the authority so delegated. That means checking serves as a basis for possible corrective action.

Objectives, plans, programs, organizational charts, and other elements of the managerial system are not fruitfully regarded as either controls or means of control. They are pre-established standards or models of performance to which operations are adjusted by the exercise of management control. These standards or models of performance are dynamic in character for they are constantly altered, modified, or revised. Policies, organizational set-up, procedures, delegations, etc. are constantly altered but, like objectives and plans, they remain in force until they are either abandoned or revised. All of the elements (or standards or models of performance), objectives, plans and prpgrams, policies, organization, etc. can be regarded as a *framework of management*.

Control Techniques

Examples of control techniques:
1. Compare against established standards
2. Compare with a similar operation
3. Compare with past operations
4. Compare with predictions of accomplishment

Where Forecasts Fit

Control is after-the-fact while forecasts are before. Forecasts and projections are important for setting objectives and formulating plans.

Information for aiming and planning does not have to before-the-fact. It may be an after-the-fact analysis proving that a certain policy has been impolitic in its effect on the relation of the company or department with customer, employee, taxpayer, or stockholder; or that a certain plan is no longer practical, or that a certain procedure is unworkable.

The prescription here certainly would not be in control (in these cases, control would simply bring operations into conformity with obsolete standards) but the establishment of new standards, a new policy, a new plan, and a new procedure to be controlled too.

Information is, of course, the basis for all communication in addition to furnishing evidence to management of the need for reconstructing the framework of management.

PROBLEM SOLVING

The accepted concept in modern management for problem solving is the utilization of the following steps:

1. Identify the problem
2. Gather data
3. List possible solutions
4. Test possible solutions
5. Select the best solution
6. Put the solution into actual practice

Occasions might arise where you would have to apply the second step of gathering data before completing the first step.

You might also find that it will be necessary to work on several steps at the same time.

1. Identify the Problem

Your first step is to define as precisely as possible the problem to be solved. While this may sound easy, it is often the most difficult part of the process.

It has been said of problem solving that you are halfway to the solution when you can write out a clear statement of the problem itself.

Our job now is to get below the surface manifestations of the trouble and pinpoint the problem. This is usually accomplished by a logical analysis, by going from the general to the particular; from the obvious to the not-so-obvious cause.
Let us say that production is behind schedule. WHY? Absenteeism is high. Now, is absenteeism the basic problem to be tackled, or is it merely a symptom of low morale among the workforce? Under these circumstances, you may decide that production is not the problem; the problem is *employee morale*.

In trying to define the problem, remember there is seldom one simple reason why production is lagging, or reports are late, etc.

Analysis usually leads to the discovery that an apparent problem is really made up of several subproblems which must be attacked separately.

Another way is to limit the problem, and thereby ease the task of finding a solution, and concentrate on the elements which are within the scope of your control.

When you have gone this far, write out a tentative statement of the problem to be solved.

2. Gather Data

In the second step, you must set out to collect all the information that might have a bearing on the problem. Do not settle for an assumption when reasonable fact and figures are available.

If you merely go through the motions of problem-solving, you will probably shortcut the information-gathering step. Therefore, do not stack the evidence by confining your research to your own preconceived ideas.

As you collect facts, organize them in some form that helps you make sense of them and spot possible relationships between them. For example: Plotting cost per unit figures on a graph can be more meaningful than a long column of figures.

Evaluate each item as you go along. Is the source material: absolutely reliable, probably reliable, or not to be trusted.

One of the best methods for gathering data is to go out and look the situation over carefully. Talk to the people on the job who are most affected by this problem.

Always keep in mind that a primary source is usually better than a secondary source of information.

3. List Possible Solutions

This is the creative thinking step of problem solving. This is a good time to bring into play whatever techniques of group dynamics the agency or bureau might have developed for a joint attack on problems.

Now the important thing for you to do is: Keep an open mind. Let your imagination roam freely over the facts you have collected. Jot down every possible solution that occurs to you. Resist the temptation to evaluate various proposals as you go along. List seemingly absurd ideas along with more plausible ones. The more possibilities you list during this step, the less risk you will run of settling for merely a workable, rather than the best, solution.

Keep studying the data as long as there seems to be any chance of deriving additional - ideas, solutions, explanations, or patterns from it.

4. Test Possible Solutions

Now you begin to evaluate the possible solutions. Take pains to be objective. Up to this point, you have suspended judgment but you might be tempted to select a solution you secretly favored all along and proclaim it as the best of the lot.

The secret of objectivity in this phase is to test the possible solutions separately, measuring each against a common yardstick. To make this yardstick try to enumerate as many specific criteria as you can think of. Criteria are best phrased as questions which you ask of each possible solution. They can be drawn from these general categories:

Suitability - Will this solution do the job?
Will it solve the problem completely or partially?

Is it a permanent or a stopgap solution?

Feasibility - Will this plan work in actual practice?
Can we afford this approach?
How much will it cost?

Acceptability - Will the boss go along with the changes required in the plan?
Are we trying to drive a tack with a sledge hammer?

5. Select the Best Solution

This is the area of executive decision.

Occasionally, one clearly superior solution will stand out at the conclusion of the testing process. But often it is not that simple. You may find that no one solution has come through all the tests with flying colors.

You may also find that a proposal, which flunked miserably on one of the essential tests, racked up a very high score on others.

The best solution frequently will turn out to be a combination.

Try to arrange a marriage that will bring together the strong points of one possible solution with the particular virtues of another. The more skill and imagination that you apply, the greater is the likelihood that you will come out with a solution that is not merely adequate and workable, but is the best possible under the circumstances.

6. Put the Solution Into Actual Practice
As every executive knows, a plan which works perfectly on paper may develop all sorts of bugs when put into actual practice.

Problem-solving does not stop with selecting the solution which looks best in theory. The next step is to put the chosen solution into action and watch the results. The results may point towards modifications.

If the problem disappears when you put your solution into effect, you know you have the right solution.

If it does not disappear, even after you have adjusted your plan to cover unforeseen difficulties that turned up in practice, work your way back through the problem-solving solutions.

Would one of them have worked better?
Did you overlook some vital piece of data which would have given you a different slant on the whole situation? Did you apply all necessary criteria in testing solutions? If no light dawns after this much rechecking, it is a pretty good bet that you defined the problem incorrectly in the first place.

You came up with the wrong solution because you tackled the wrong problem.

Thus, step six may become step one of a new problem-solving cycle.

COMMUNICATION

1. <u>What is Communication</u>?
    We communicate through writing, speaking, action or inaction. In speaking to people face-to-face, there is opportunity to judge reactions and to adjust the message. This makes the supervisory chain one of the most, and in many instances the most, important channels of communication.

    In an organization, communication means keeping employees informed about the organization's objectives, policies, problems, and progress. Communication is the free interchange of information, ideas, and desirable attitudes between and among employees and between employees and management.

2. <u>Why is Communication Needed</u>?
    a. People have certain social needs
    b. Good communication is essential in meeting those social needs
    c. While people have similar basic needs, at the same time they differ from each other
    d. Communication must be adapted to these individual differences

    An employee cannot do his best work unless he knows why he is doing it. If he has the feeling that he is being kept in the dark about what is going on, his enthusiasm and productivity suffer.

    Effective communication is needed in an organization so that employees will understand what the organization is trying to accomplish; and how the work of one unit contributes to or affects the work of other units in the organization and other organizations.

3. <u>How is Communication Achieved?</u>
    Communication flows downward, upward, sideways.

    a. Communication may come from top management down to employees. This is <u>downward communication</u>.

        Some means of downward communication are:
        (1) Training (orientation, job instruction, supervision, public relations, etc.)
        (2) Conferences
        (3) Staff meetings
        (4) Policy statements
        (5) Bulletins
        (6) Newsletters
        (7) Memoranda
        (8) Circulation of important letters

        In downward communication, it is important that employees be informed in advance of changes that will affect them.

    b. Communications should also be developed so that the ideas, suggestions, and knowledge of employees will flow <u>upward</u> to top management.

Some means of upward communication are:
(1) Personal discussion conferences
(2) Committees
(3) Memoranda
(4) Employees suggestion program
(5) Questionnaires to be filled in giving comments and suggestions about proposed actions that will affect field operations

Upward communication requires that management be willing to listen, to accept, and to make changes when good ideas are present. Upward communication succeeds when there is no fear of punishment for speaking out or lack of interest at the top. Employees will share their knowledge and ideas with management when interest is shown and recognition is given.

c. The *advantages* of downward communication:
   (1) It enables the passing down of orders, policies, and plans necessary to the continued operation of the station.
   (2) By making information available, it diminishes the fears and suspicions which result from misinformation and misunderstanding.
   (3) It fosters the pride people want to have in their work when they are told of good work.
   (4) It improves the morale and stature of the individual to be *in the know.*
   (5) It helps employees to understand, accept, and cooperate with changes when they know about them in advance.

d. The *advantages* of upward communication:
   (1) It enables the passing upward of information, attitudes, and feelings.
   (2) It makes it easier to find out how ready people are to receive downward communication.
   (3) It reveals the degree to which the downward communication is understood and accepted.
   (4) It helps to satisfy the basic *social* needs.
   (5) It stimulates employees to participate in the operation of their organization.
   (6) It encourages employees to contribute ideas for improving the efficiency and economy of operations.
   (7) It helps to solve problem situations before they reach the explosion point.

4. <u>Why Does Communication Fail</u>?
   a. The technical difficulties of conveying information clearly
   b. The emotional content of communication which prevents complete transmission
   c. The fact that there is a difference between what management needs to say, what it wants to say, and what it does say
   d. The fact that there is a difference between what employees would like to say, what they think is profitable or safe to say, and what they do say

5. <u>How to Improve Communication.</u>
   As a supervisor, you are a key figure in communication. To improve as a communicator, you should:
   a. <u>Know</u> - Knowing your subordinates will help you to recognize and work with individual differences.

b. <u>Like</u> - If you like those who work for you and those for whom you work, this will foster the kind of friendly, warm, work atmosphere that will facilitate communication.

c. <u>Trust</u> - Showing a sincere desire to communicate will help to develop the mutual trust and confidence which are essential to the free flow of communication.

d. <u>Tell</u> - Tell your subordinates and superiors *what's doing*. Tell your subordinates *why* as well as *how*.

e. <u>Listen</u> - By listening, you help others to talk and you create good listeners. Don't forget that listening implies action.

f. <u>Stimulate</u> - Communication has to be stimulated and encouraged. Be receptive to ideas and suggestions and motivate your people so that each member of the team identifies himself with the job at hand.

g. <u>Consult</u> - The most effective way of consulting is to let your people participate, insofar as possible, in developing determinations which affect them or their work.

6. <u>How to Determine Whether You are Getting Across</u>.
   a. Check to see that communication is received and understood
   b. Judge this understanding by actions rather than words
   c. Adapt or vary communication, when necessary
   d. Remember that good communication cannot cure all problems

7. <u>The Key Attitude</u>.
   Try to see things from the other person's point of view. By doing this, you help to develop the permissive atmosphere and the shared confidence and understanding which are essential to effective two-way communication.

   Communication is a two-way process.
   a. The basic purpose of any communication is to get action.
   b. The only way to get action is through acceptance.
   c. In order to get acceptance, communication must be humanly satisfying as well as technically efficient.

HOW ORDERS AND INSTRUCTIONS SHOULD BE GIVEN

<u>Characteristics of Good Orders and Instructions</u>

1. <u>Clear</u>
   Orders should be definite as to
   - <u>What</u> is to be done
   - <u>Who</u> is to do it
   - <u>When</u> it is to be done
   - <u>Where</u> it is to be done
   - <u>How</u> it is to be done

2. <u>Concise</u>
   Avoid wordiness. Orders should be brief and to the point.

3. <u>Timely</u>
   Instructions and orders should be sent out at the proper time and not too long in advance of expected performance.

4. <u>Possibility of Performance</u>
Orders should be feasible:
   a. Investigate before giving orders
   b. Consult those who are to carry out instructions before formulating and issuing them

5. <u>Properly Directed</u>
Give the orders to the people concerned. Do not send orders to people who are not concerned. People who continually receive instructions that are not applicable to them get in the habit of neglecting instructions generally.

6. <u>Reviewed Before Issuance</u>
Orders should be reviewed before issuance:
   a. Test them by putting yourself in the position of the recipient
   b. If they involve new procedures, have the persons who are to do the work review them for suggestions

7. <u>Reviewed After Issuance</u>
Persons who receive orders should be allowed to raise questions and to point out unforeseen consequences of orders.

8. <u>Coordinated</u>
Orders should be coordinated so that work runs smoothly.

9. <u>Courteous</u>
Make a request rather than a demand. There is no need to continually call attention to the fact that you are the boss.

10. <u>Recognizable as an Order</u>
Be sure that the order is recognizable as such.

11. <u>Complete</u>
Be sure recipient has knowledge and experience sufficient to carry out order. Give illustrations and examples.

A DEPARTMENTAL PERSONNEL OFFICE IS RESPONSIBLE <u>FOR THE FOLLOWING FUNCTIONS</u>

1. Policy
2. Personnel Programs
3. Recruitment and Placement
4. Position Classification
5. Salary and Wage Administration
6. Employee Performance Standards and Evaluation
7. Employee Relations
8. Disciplinary Actions and Separations
9. Health and Safety
10. Staff Training and Development
11. Personnel Records, Procedures, and Reports
12. Employee Services
13. Personnel Research

SUPERVISION

<u>Leadership</u>

All leadership is based essentially on authority. This comes from two sources: it is received from higher management or it is earned by the supervisor through his methods of supervision. Although effective leadership has always depended upon the leader's using his authority in such a way as to appeal successfully to the motives of the people supervised, the conditions for making this appeal are continually changing. The key to today's problem of leadership is flexibility and resourcefulness on the part of the leader in meeting changes in conditions as they occur.

Three basic approaches to leadership are generally recognized:

1. <u>The Authoritarian Approach</u>
    a. The methods and techniques used in this approach emphasize the *I* in leadership and depend primarily on the formal authority of the leader. This authority is sometimes exercised in a hardboiled manner and sometimes in a benevolent manner, but in either case the dominating role of the leader is reflected in the thinking, planning, and decisions of the group.
    b. Group results are to a large degree dependent on close supervision by the leader. Usually, the individuals in the group will not show a high degree of initiative or acceptance of responsibility and their capacity to grow and develop probably will not be fully utilized. The group may react with resentment or submission, depending upon the manner and skill of the leader in using his authority
    c. This approach develops as a natural outgrowth of the authority that goes with the leader's job and his feeling of sole responsibility for getting the job done. It is relatively easy to use and does not require much resourcefulness.
    d. The use of this approach is effective in times of emergencies, in meeting close deadlines as a final resort, in settling some issues, in disciplinary matters, and with dependent individuals and groups.

2. <u>The Laissez-Faire or *Let 'em Alone* Approach</u>
    a. This approach generally is characterized by an avoidance of leadership responsibility by the leader. The activities of the group depend largely on the choice of its members rather than the leader.
    b. Group results probably will be poor. Generally, there will be disagreements over petty things, bickering, and confusion. Except for a few aggressive people, individuals will not show much initiative and growth and development will be retarded. There may be a tendency for informal leaders to take over leadership of the group.
    c. This approach frequently results from the leader's dislike of responsibility, from his lack of confidence, from failure of other methods to work, from disappointment or criticism. It is usually the easiest of the three to use and requires both understanding and resourcefulness on the part of the leader.
    d. This approach is occasionally useful and effective, particularly in forcing dependent individuals or groups to rely on themselves, to give someone a chance to save face by clearing his own difficulties, or when action should be delayed temporarily for good cause.

3. <u>The Democratic Approach</u>
    a. The methods and techniques used in this approach emphasize the *we* in leadership and build up the responsibility of the group to attain its objectives. Reliance is placed largely on the earned authority of the leader.
    b. Group results are likely to be good because most of the job motives of the people will be satisfied. Cooperation and teamwork, initiative, acceptance of responsibility, and the individual's capacity for growth probably will show a high degree of development.
    c. This approach grows out of a desire or necessity of the leader to find ways to appeal effectively to the motivation of his group. It is the best approach to build up inside the person a strong desire to cooperate and apply himself to the job.
        It is the most difficult to develop, and requires both understanding and resourcefulness on the part of the leader.
    d. The value of this approach increases over a long period where sustained efficiency and development of people are important. It may not be fully effective in all situations, however, particularly when there is not sufficient time to use it properly or where quick decisions must be made.

All three approaches are used by most leaders and have a place in supervising people. The extent of their use varies with individual leaders, with some using one approach predominantly. The leader who uses these three approaches, and varies their use with time and circumstance, is probably the most effective. Leadership which is used predominantly with a democratic approach requires more resourcefulness on the part of the leader but offers the greatest possibilities in terms of teamwork and cooperation.

The one best way of developing democratic leadership is to provide a real sense of participation on the part of the group, since this satisfies most of the chief job motives. Although there are many ways of providing participation, consulting as frequently as possible with individuals and groups on things that affect them seems to offer the most in building cooperation and responsibility. Consultation takes different forms, but it is most constructive when people feel they are actually helping in finding the answers to the problems on the job.

There are some requirements of leaders in respect to human relations which should be considered in their selection and development. Generally, the leader should be interested in working with other people, emotionally stable, self-confident, and sensitive to the reactions of others. In addition, his viewpoint should be one of getting the job done through people who work cooperatively in response to his leadership. He should have a knowledge of individual and group behavior, but, most important of all, he should work to combine all of these requirements into a definite, practical skill in leadership.

<u>Nine Points of Contrast Between *Boss* and *Leader*</u>

1. The boss drives his men; the leader coaches them.
2. The boss depends on authority; the leader on good will.
3. The boss inspires fear; the leader inspires enthusiasm.
4. The boss says J; the leader says *We*.
5. The boss says *Get here on time;* the leader gets there ahead of time.
6. The boss fixes the blame for the breakdown; the leader fixes the breakdown.
7. The boss knows how it is done; the leader shows how.
8. The boss makes work a drudgery; the leader makes work a game.
9. The boss says *Go*; the leader says *Let's go.*

EMPLOYEE MORALE

Employee morale is the way employees feel about each other, the organization or unit in which they work, and the work they perform.

Some Ways to Develop and Maintain Good Employee Morale

1. Give adequate credit and praise when due.
2. Recognize importance of all jobs and equalize load with proper assignments, always giving consideration to personality differences and abilities.
3. Welcome suggestions and do not have an *all-wise* attitude. Request employees' assistance in solving problems and use assistants when conducting group meetings on certain subjects.
4. Properly assign responsibilities and give adequate authority for fulfillment of such assignments.
5. Keep employees informed about matters that affect them.
6. Criticize and reprimand employees privately.
7. Be accessible and willing to listen.
8. Be fair.
9. Be alert to detect training possibilities so that you will not miss an opportunity to help each employee do a better job, and if possible with less effort on his part.
10. Set a good example.
11. Apply the golden rule.

Some Indicators of Good Morale
1. Good quality of work
2. Good quantity
3. Good attitude of employees
4. Good discipline
5. Teamwork
6. Good attendance
7. Employee participation

MOTIVATION

Drives

A *drive,* stated simply, is a desire or force which causes a person to do or say certain things. These are some of the most usual drives and some of their identifying characteristics recognizable in people motivated by such drives:

1. Security (desire to provide for the future)
   Always on time for work
   Works for the same employer for many years
   Never takes unnecessary chances Seldom resists doing what he is told

2. Recognition (desire to be rewarded for accomplishment)
   Likes to be asked for his opinion
   Becomes very disturbed when he makes a mistake
   Does things to attract attention

Likes to see his name in print

3. Position (desire to hold certain status in relation to others)
Boasts about important people he knows
Wants to be known as a key man
Likes titles
Demands respect
Belongs to clubs, for prestige

4. Accomplishment (desire to get things done)
Complains when things are held up
Likes to do things that have tangible results
Never lies down on the job
Is proud of turning out good work

5. Companionship (desire to associate with other people)
Likes to work with others
Tells stories and jokes
Indulges in horseplay
Finds excuses to talk to others on the job

6. Possession (desire to collect and hoard objects)
Likes to collect things
Puts his name on things belonging to him
Insists on the same work location

Supervisors may find that identifying the drives of employees is a helpful step toward motivating them to self-improvement and better job performance. For example: An employee's job performance is below average. His supervisor, having previously determined that the employee is motivated by a drive for security, suggests that taking training courses will help the employee to improve, advance, and earn more money. Since earning more money can be a step toward greater security, the employee's drive for security would motivate him to take the training suggested by the supervisor. In essence, this is the process of charting an employee's future course by using his motivating drives to positive advantage.

EMPLOYEE PARTICIPATION

What is Participation?

Employee participation is the employee's giving freely of his time, skill and knowledge to an extent which cannot be obtained by demand.

Why is it Important?

The supervisor's responsibility is to get the job done through people. A good supervisor gets the job done through people who work willingly and well. The participation of employees is important because:

1. Employees develop a greater sense of responsibility when they share in working out operating plans and goals.
2. Participation provides greater opportunity and stimulation for employees to learn, and to develop their ability.

3. Participation sometimes provides better solutions to problems because such solutions may combine the experience and knowledge of interested employees who want the solutions to work.
4. An employee or group may offer a solution which the supervisor might hesitate to make for fear of demanding too much.
5. Since the group wants to make the solution work, they exert *pressure* in a constructive way on each other.
6. Participation usually results in reducing the need for close supervision.

How May Supervisors Obtain It?

Participation is encouraged when employees feel that they share some responsibility for the work and that their ideas are sincerely wanted and valued. Some ways of obtaining employee participation are:

1. Conduct orientation programs for new employees to inform them about the organization and their rights and responsibilities as employees.
2. Explain the aims and objectives of the agency. On a continuing basis, be sure that the employees know what these aims and objectives are.
3. Share job successes and responsibilities and give credit for success.
4. Consult with employees, both as individuals and in groups, about things that affect them.
5. Encourage suggestions for job improvements. Help employees to develop good suggestions. The suggestions can bring them recognition. The city's suggestion program offers additional encouragement through cash awards.

The supervisor who encourages employee participation is not surrendering his authority. He must still make decisions and initiate action, and he must continue to be ultimately responsible for the work of those he supervises. But, through employee participation, he is helping his group to develop greater ability and a sense of responsibility while getting the job done faster and better.

STEPS IN HANDLING A GRIEVANCE

1. Get the facts
   a. Listen sympathetically.
   b. Let him talk himself out.
   c. Get his story straight.
   d. Get his point of view.
   e. Don't argue with him.
   f. Give him plenty of time.
   g. Conduct the interview privately.
   h. Don't try to shift the blame or pass the buck.

2. Consider the facts
   a. Consider the employee's viewpoint.
   b. How will the decision affect similar cases.
   c. Consider each decision as a possible precedent.
   d. Avoid snap judgments - don't jump to conclusions.

3. <u>Make or get a decision</u>
    a. Frame an effective counter-proposal.
    b. Make sure it is fair to all.
    c. Have confidence in your judgment.
    d. Be sure you can substantiate your decision.

4. <u>Notify the employee of your decision</u>
Be sure he is told; try to convince him that the decision is fair and just.

5. <u>Take action when needed and if within your authority</u>
Otherwise, tell employee that the matter will be called to the attention of the proper person or that nothing can be done, and why it cannot.

6. <u>Follow through</u> to see that the desired result is achieved.

7. <u>Record key facts</u> concerning the complaint and the action taken.

8. <u>Leave the way open to him to appeal your decision</u> to a higher authority.

9. <u>Report all grievances to your superior</u>, whether they are appealed or not.

DISCIPLINE

Discipline is training that develops self-control, orderly conduct, and efficiency.

To discipline does not necessarily mean to punish.

To discipline does mean to train, to regulate, and to govern conduct.

<u>The Disciplinary Interview</u>

Most employees sincerely want to do what is expected of them. In other words, they are self-disciplined. Some employees, however, fail to observe established rules and standards, and disciplinary action by the supervisor is required.

The primary purpose of disciplinary action is to improve conduct without creating dissatisfaction, bitterness, or resentment in the process.

Constructive disciplinary action is more concerned with causes and explanations of breaches of conduct than with punishment. The disciplinary interview is held to get at the causes of apparent misbehavior and to motivate better performance in the future.

It is important that the interview be kept on as impersonal a basis as possible. If the supervisor lets the interview descend to the plane of an argument, it loses its effectiveness.

<u>Planning the Interview</u>

Get all pertinent facts concerning the situation so that you can talk in specific terms to the employee.

Review the employee's record, appraisal ratings, etc.

Consider what you know about the temperament of the employee. Consider your attitude toward the employee. Remember that the primary requisite of disciplinary action is fairness.

Don't enter upon the interview when angry.

Schedule the interview for a place which is private and out of hearing of others.

<u>Conducting the Interview</u>

1. Make an effort to establish accord.

2. Question the employee about the apparent breach of discipline. Be sure that the question is not so worded as to be itself an accusation.

3. Give the employee a chance to tell his side of the story. Give him ample opportunity to talk.

4. Use understanding-listening except where it is necessary to ask a question or to point out some details of which the employee may not be aware. If the employee misrepresents facts, make a plain, accurate statement of the facts, but don't argue and don't engage in personal controversy.

5. Listen and try to understand the reasons for the employee's (mis)conduct. First of all, don't assume that there has been a breach of discipline. Evaluate the employee's reasons for his conduct in the light of his opinions and feelings concerning the consistency and reasonableness of the standards which he was expected to follow. Has the supervisor done his part in explaining the reasons for the rules? Was the employee's behavior unintentional or deliberate? Does he think he had real reasons for his actions? What new facts is he telling? Do the facts justify his actions? What causes, other than those mentioned, could have stimulated the behavior?

6. After listening to the employee's version of the situation, and if censure of his actions is warranted, the supervisor should proceed with whatever criticism is justified. Emphasis should be placed on future improvement rather than exclusively on the employee's failure to measure up to expected standards of job conduct.

7. Fit the criticism to the individual. With one employee, a word of correction may be all that is required.

8. Attempt to distinguish between unintentional error and deliberate misbehavior. An error due to ignorance requires training and not censure.

9. Administer criticism in a controlled, even tone of voice, never in anger. Make it clear that you are acting as an agent of the department. In general, criticism should refer to the job or the employee's actions and not to the person. Criticism of the employee's work is not an attack on the individual.

10. Be sure the interview does not destroy the employee's self-confidence. Mention his good qualities and assure him that you feel confident that he can improve his performance.

11. Wherever possible, before the employee leaves the interview, satisfy him that the incident is closed, that nothing more will be said on the subject unless the offense is repeated.

———